DUBROVNIK · THE CITY OF CULTURE AND ART

DUBROVNIK
THE CITY OF CULTURE AND ART

Written, edited and designed by
ANTUN TRAVIRKA

Photographs by
MLADEN RADOLOVIĆ
ANDRIJA CARLI
ŽIVKO ŠOKOTA
KREŠIMIR TADIĆ

Editor-in-Chief and Responsible Editor
ĐURĐICA ŠOKOTA

For the Publishers
ŽIVKO ŠOKOTA

Translated by
VJEKOSLAV SUZANIĆ

Set and printed by
GORENJSKI TISK, KRANJ, SLOVENIA, 2006.

© FORUM - ZADAR, 2006.

CIP - Katalogizacija v knjigi
Znanstvena knjižnica v Zadru
UDK 914.975(036) Dubrovnik

TRAVIRKA, Antun
    Dubrovnik : the city of culture and art / Antun
Travirka ; [photographs by Mladen Radolović... et
al. ; translated by Vjekoslav Suzanić]. - Zadar : Forum,
2006. - 96 str. : ilustr. ; 22 cm + [1] list s planom grada
slobodno priložen

ISBN 953-179-505-3

DUBROVNIK

THE CITY OF CULTURE AND ART

ANTUN TRAVIRKA

FORUM

Dubrovnik is a city and port on the Croatian coast of the Adriatic Sea. The city has 49,728 inhabitants (1991) and is the economic, cultural and educational centre of southern Dalmatia and the seat of the administration of the County Dubrovnik-Neretva. Besides the area around the mouth of the river Neretva, the county comprises the narrow coast belt which is separated from the interior by the Dinaric mountain range. This range runs in three parallel chains and its height rises towards the interior. The peaks of

this range form the natural boundary between the seaboard and Herze-
govina, as well as the climatic and anthropogeographical boundary
between Dubrovnik and its hinterland.

In the north-western part of the region, the coast belt comprises the
Pelješac peninsula, the isthmus of Ston, and the very narrow Dubrovnik
seaboard as far as Rijeka Dubrovačka. To the east of the city of Dubrovnik
is the coast belt of Župa Dubrovačka along the Gulf of Župa, and to the

Palms, blue sea, walls

south-east of the township of Cavtat, the somewhat wider coast belt of Konavle. The Prevlaka peninsula and Point Oštro at the entrance to the gulf of Boka is the southernmost land point of the Dubrovnik region and of the Croatian coast. A number of islands lie along the coast of the county, from Korčula, Lastovo, and Mljet in the west, continuing with the Elaphite group of inshore islands - the islands of Olipa, Jakljan, Šipan, Lopud, Koločep and Daksa. The chain ends with Lokrum, which is immediate vicinity - to the south-east right in front of the old city port.

The city of Dubrovnik is situated in 42°40' N and 18°5'E, and is the most southerly Croatian town. Its climate is Mediterranean. Therefore the average yearly temperature is 17°C, characterised by very mild winters and very dry, sunny summer. The average temperature is about 10°C in winter, and about 26°C in the summer. The city is protected from the cold northerly *bura* by mount Srđ, and from the damp southerly *jugo* by the island of Lokrum. Like the rest of the Croatian coast Dubrovnik is refreshed in the summer by the north-westerly breeze *maestral*. Rains fall mostly in winter, and the snow is seldom recorded. The average summer temperature of the sea is over 21°C.

All these features of climate have resulted in typical Mediterranean vegetation, lush and varied in the coastal belt. It is the result of the action of man who has cultivated this land, reforested it and worked it. It is precisely this combination of natural exuberance and centuries-long activity of the population that have made this region exceptionally beautiful and rich in vegetation. In addition to the native Mediterranean plants the region abounds in specimens of subtropical and continental plants cultivated in numerous gardens and arboretums of the villas scattered all over the coast and the islands. The environs of Dubrovnik get their particular charm from numerous orange and lemon groves, palms and agaves. Many tropical and sub-tropical plants and trees have been brought by seamen from their distant voyages. Close to the city, in the residential areas which cluster round the old historic city, but also in other areas in the vicinity (Trsteno, Lopud, Lapad, Lokrum, Cavtat), flowers are cultivated in private gardens and other horticultural areas, giving these areas a special atmosphere from early spring until late autumn.

The varied geomorphology of the region - steep rocky coast, deep coves, sandy beaches, small fields, high mountains which in places come right to the sea, numerous islands and rocks, together with the rich vegetation and exceptionally clear sea - all this makes the region very attractive. Man has been civilizing the environment for centuries. Man and nature have worked together, combining natural beauty, architecture and horticulture. The result of this happy connection is one of the most beautiful and impressive regions, not only on the Croatian coast and the whole of the Adriatic area but also one of the best cultivated oases of the Mediterranean.

With the exception of the area of the Neretva estuary and the island of Korčula, the territory of the present-day county is the same as the territory of the former Republic of Dubrovnik. With an area of 1375 sq. km it was among the smallest but very important merchant republics of the Mediterranean. Its role of linking the commercial routes between eastern and western Adriatic areas, and between the eastern and western parts of the Mediterranean was of great importance, particularly from the 14th to the 17th century. The centre of this republic, a city-state, was Dubrovnik.

Dubrovnik arose in a very significant place. Close to the shore and right in front of the city is the island of Lokrum, the last in the series of many islands of the east Adriatic. To the south-east spreads the wide open sea, leading on to the Strait of Otranto and to the vast area of the Mediterranean sea. Towards the north-east, near the coast, island groups form protected channels, suitable for navigation of ships. In immediate vicinity of Dubrovnik, the Dinaric range becomes lower, allowing mountain passes over which caravan roads towards the interior could be organised. A city in such a position had to be predestined for navigation and sea trade, and natural barriers separated and protected it from the neighbouring geographic and geopolitical units.

The beginnings of Dubrovnik fall in the relatively distant past and - like many old Mediterranean cities - are veiled in legend. Among several legends about its origin, historically the most credible is the one linking the foundation of the new city with the destruction and fall of the Roman city of Epidaurum (at the site of present-day Cavtat) in the 7th century. Epidaurum was a very old settlement. It was very probably founded as a Greek colony, although there are no certain finds. In Roman times it was a developed town and an important sea-trading emporium. It is presumed that it suffered heavily from an earthquake in the 4th century, when parts of the city fell into the sea, but it continued its existence as an important centre. It was also mentioned as the seat of a bishop. In 614 Epidaurum was captured and destroyed by the Avars and Slavs, and the survivors fled to the nearby woods and to a small rocky islet named *Laus*. *Laus* or *Lave* is 'rock' in Greek, *labes* is 'sheer slope' or 'chasm' in Latin, which describes a locality which obviously had a steep coast, a cliff. The islet was separated from dry land by a narrow channel so that the settlement on it was protected from both sea and land. The rock was probably inhabited even before the arrival of refugees from Epidaurum, and the newcomers only increased the number of inhabitants. The latest archaeological excavations, particularly the discovery of the first cathedral from the 7th century, seem to corroborate this fact. The fate of Epidaurum and the origins of Dubrovnik show historical similarity to the origins of Venice and Split. Venice came into being because the refugees from Aquileia fled to the marshlands of the lagoon before Attila's Huns in the 5th century, and Split began in the 7th century after the destruction of Salona by the Avars and Slavs when the refugees found shelter in the fortified palace of the Roman Emperor Diocletian. The city which rose on Lausa took its name from it: *Rausa*, *Ragusa* and *Ragusium*. It is obvious that in the 9th century Dubrovnik was a highly organised municipal unit with a system of protective ramparts because it successfully resisted a 15-month siege of the Saracens. The city was aided in defence by the Byzantine fleet.

From the 7th to the 12th century the city grew under the domination of Byzantium. As with many other seaside communes ruled by Byzantium, aspirations towards autonomy gradually grew stronger, leading to the development of commerce and related activities. In the meantime, a Croatian settlement developed on the mainland opposite Ragusa, which was named Dubrovnik, probably after the groves of holm-oak (*dubrava* in Croatian). Links between the two settlement became stronger with time, which resulted in a mixed Croatian and Latin population. The channel

*Splendid view of the island of Lokrum
and Župa Dubrovačka bay from the walls*

between the islet and the mainland had become silted in the course of the 10th and 11th centuries, and was filled with carted material at the close of the 11th century. The widest and most famous street in the city - Placa (Stradun) - runs today in the place where the islet was joined to firm land. Both parts were finally integrated in the 12th century: they were protected by a system of defence walls. The northern suburb was also included in the 13th century, the streets were regulated, and Dubrovnik acquired its present shape. The first records of Dubrovnik's name occur in the documents issued by the Bosnian ruler Kulin in 1189. He gave preferential treatment to the merchants of Dubrovnik. The same name is recorded in the chronicle written by the so-called Priest of Dioclea (Pop Dukljanin) in the 12th century. The fact that the Latin speaking people on the islet of Lausa were isolated among the Croatian majority is proof of a relatively speedy assimilation and the domination of the Croatian element, much sooner and to a higher degree than in other Dalmatian cities which were part of the Byzantine Theme. By the 14th city was Croatized completely. This fact will be crucial for the flowering of Croatian literature in the city of Dubrovnik.

In 1032 the ships of Dubrovnik joined the fleet of Byzantium in the war against the Arabs. In 1153 the Arabian author Al-Idrisi describes Dubrovnik as the southernmost city in Croatia, a city owning many ships which sail on distant voyages. Dubrovnik and Pisa signed a contract in 1169 regulating sea trade in the Mediterranean sea from Pisa to Constaninople. By the end of the 12th century Dubrovnik negotiated contracts with many Adriatic cities: Molfetta, Ravenna, Fano, Ancona, Monopoli, Bari, Tremoli and with Rovinj and Kotor. Dubrovnik made very important commercial arrangements with its land neighbours, Bosnia and Serbia, ensuring for itself in this way the status of the principal commercial emporium for these Balkan countries.

In the 12th century Dubrovnik was ruled by a rector elected by the citizens. His decisions were crucial for functioning and development of the city. This period saw changes in the structure of Dubrovnik, and a class of noblemen landowners was established. They gradually assumed all administrative functions in the city, which now developed as a typical Mediterranean aristocratic republic. With its successfully organized sea trade Dubrovnik now competed with Venice, which used all methods to check her rising rival. In 1205 Dubrovnik came under Venetian authority. Venice ruled Dubrovnik for the next 150 years, which left a fairly strong imprint on the social structure of the city. Dubrovnik was forced to accept the rector and the bishop from Venice. She also nominated the members of the Major Council, and made every effort to acquire full power in the city. In the 13th century Dubrovnik attempted to defect on several occasions. Although the development of the city was slowed, Venice could never acquire complete control over its trade. In the same century, in addition to numerous agreements with Italian and Croatian coastal cities, Dubrovnik established commercial relations with Epirus and Albania, and also extended its trade to Syria and northern Africa.

Trade brought many foreigners and foreign ships to Dubrovnik, and Dubrovnik was compelled to hire foreign ships for its ever-growing business. Yet with all this large volume of sea trade in the period of Venetian domination, connections with the interior of the Balkans were much more important. Dubrovnik acquired the Island of Lastovo in 1252, the Pelješac Peninsula in 1333, and the Island of Mljet in 1345.

With the peace treaty of Zadar in 1358, Dubrovnik was freed of the Venetian supremacy for she was forced to renounce her possession on the east coast of the Adriatic. From then Dubrovnik acknowledged the supreme authority of the Hungaro-Croatian kings. This would influence the future development of the city. These kings never interfered in the administration of the city, its commercial and sea affairs, which resulted in full autonomy of the free and sovereign aristocratic republic. Thus the earlier title of COMMUNITAS RAGUSINA (The Municipality of Dubrovnik) was replaced by RESPUBLICA RAGUSINA (The Republic of Dubrovnik). In 1399 the Republic gained the coastal belt from Ston to

Orašac, and in 1419 and 1427 it reached its final size - when it acquired Konavle and Cavtat. Growing unrest and disorder in the Balkans forced Dubrovnik to turn to sea trade.

Withdrawal of Venetian ships from joint ventures gave impetus to shipbuilding and almost complete dependence on own ships. In the 14th and the 15th century the trade of Dubrovnik spread to Egypt, Syria and Sicily, but also to the ports of Aragon in Spain and to France. In the 15th century, Turkey rose as a naval power in the Mediterranean, and

Dubrovnik established exceptional commercial relations with Turkey, at the same time paying Turkey tribute for trading privileges.

In 1526, after the battle of Mohács, when the Turks defeated the Hungaro-Croatian army, Dubrovnik stopped paying tribute to the Hungaro-Croatian kings, and their authority over Dubrovnik was over. Dubrovnik maintained particularly careful relations with Turkey, paying them tribute. The Turks did not interfere in the internal affairs of Dubrovnik, but - in addition to regular tribute - they exacted various gifts and bribes.

In the centuries of its greatest power, Dubrovnik was a typical aristocratic republic. All power was in the hands of the patricians. They had become a closed social class in the first half of the 14th century. The urban society was divided into three classes: the patricians, the "good citizens", and the commoners. The patricians had exclusive right to political power, and because of power they acquired all the land. Their multiplied continuously, and in mid 16th century their number rose almost to 1500 members. The most prestigious families formed an oligarchy which played crucial role in politics and state business. The so-called "good citizens" were a thin layer of the richest merchants, who were financially equal to the patricians but did not share political power with them. Small merchants, craftsmen, workshop labourers, boys and sailors formed the general layer of the population. In mid 16th century Dubrovnik had 4000 sailors. The Republic had

Semi-capital in relief from Rector's palace

Rijeka Dubrovačka, Villa Sorkočević

passed laws forbidding sailors to sign on foreign ships. Social stratification of the rural areas varied from bondsmen to share-croppers to yeomen on the island of Lastovo. Irrespective of the great need for sailors, the Republic did not allow villagers to sign on ships lest the drain of manpower should result in neglect of agriculture. The Jewish community enjoyed special status. They were active in finance and trade, but they were also physicians. The Jewish community lived in the ghetto, but fairly free. They worshipped in the synagogue which was the only non-Catholic temple in the Republic. As Dubrovnik was a developing society, living in relative comfort, the patricians ruled without oppression.

The Republic was ruled by three councils headed by the rector whose term of office was one month only, and who had the same rights as all other members. The Major Council was composed of all adult patrician males. They elected the Senate and the Minor Council. Real power was held by the Senate. Until 1491 it had 51 members, later 61. The Minor Council was in fact the executive authority, being an organ of the Senate and the Major Council. The term of office of all the organs of the Republic was one year. The judiciary was controlled by the Senate and the Minor Council. All major posts in the government and in the administration of justice were held by the patricians; ordinary citizens and commoners filled insignificant offices only. Occasional exceptions can be met in the diplomacy and consular functions. The territory of the Republic was divided in 12 administrative units.

In the golden age of the Republic its material riches were based on widespread production and transfer of silver and lead from Bosnian and Serbian mines to the developed areas of Europe where demand for these metals was enormous. The merchants of Dubrovnik had indeed concentrated considerable trade with these mineral products in their hands. They leased and even owned some mines, they organised production and transport of metals to the port of Dubrovnik and then re-exported it to Florence, Venice, Spain and France. In order to promote functioning of these important activities, the businessmen of Dubrovnik organised a number of colonies at key points of the caravan trails. This important activity had ceased completely after the Turkish conquest of Serbia and Bosnia. The same happened to the production of textile. The trade in silver had enabled the purchase of high quality wool from Catalonia, which was used to manufacture and dye cloth of high quality in the workshops in Pile, Rijeka Dubrovačka and Župa Dubrovačka. The textiles manufactured in these workshops were competitive on foreign markets. However, Turkish conquests stopped purchases of raw materials, and because of immediate Turkish danger, the Republic decided in 1463 to pull down all the workshops outside the city, so that this production came to a standstill. Dubrovnik maintained its salt monopoly in the area between the Neretva and the Drin rivers, which made the Balkan countries dependent. The craftsmen of Dubrovnik now turned to supplying local markets, but a modest trade in leather goods and gold was somehow maintained. Commerce, sea-trade and shipbuilding became the most important activities after the Turkish conquests of the Balkans. The shipbuilders of Dubrovnik were far known, so ships built "in the manner of Dubrovnik" meant durable, strong and simple construction. In mid 16th century Dubrovnik owned over 180 large ships with total burden of 36 000 "kola". This fleet was valued at about 700,000 ducats. Credit transactions and naval insurance brought great profits. Dubrovnik passed law on naval insurance as early as 1568. Its ships sailed as far as England, but the discovery of new naval routes to India round Africa severed the trade in spices in the Levant. Like other Mediterranean trading republics, Dubrovnik was hit by ever-growing recession caused by the discovery of America and new sea routes to Asia. But the merchants of Dubrovnik found ways to master these problems. Thus Vice

Neptune's fountain in the garden of Villa Gučetić at Trsteno

Bune, master mariner of Dubrovnik, entered Spanish service and in the late 16th century, sailed to East India and invested his money in the port of Goa. That Dubrovnik trade was extensive in spite of recession at the close of the 18th century can be seen from the fact that Dubrovnik had consulates in over 80 cities, among them Lisbon, Madrid, Gibraltar, Malaga, Tangier, Barcelona, Marseilles, Nice, Mayorca, Tunis, Tripoli, Genoa, Leghorn, Venice, Pesaro, Ancona, Naples, Palermo, Malta, Alger, Brindisi, Taranto, Triest, Rijeka, Shkodra, Durrës, Vlorë, Corfu, Thessaloniki, Varna, Constantinople, Smyrna, Latakia, Rhodos, Alexandria, Cyprus etc. The

Dominican monastery, Nikola Božidarević, Dubrovnik,
detail of triptych, 16th century

fleet, including the fishing boats, totalled 673 sailing ships, of which 255
larger ships sailed to foreign waters, and 230 were ocean ships. These data
show clearly the size and strength of Dubrovnik's commerce and navigation, even in the period of decline. In its most glorious days the fleet of
Dubrovnik was equal to that of Venice, but incomparably weaker than the
fleet of the Netherlands.

Political activities of all men who filled offices in the Republic and all
their private interests and ethical norms were subordinated to the welfare
of the state. Because of its size and delicate strategic position, the Repub-

lic relied most heavily on the diplomatic ability of its representatives and ambassadors. Centuries of diplomatic experience in extremely complex political conditions had created in Dubrovnik one of the most subtle schools of diplomatic business in the world. The ability of its ambassadors is even now the subject of scholarly and practical research. The fact that Dubrovnik had never fought a war of aggression but had acquired new territory, that it maintained trade relationships with the Levant - with Pope's permission - in the times of most violent wars between Christians and Moslems, that it never took part in any action of the allies against the Turks, that it maintained trade relations with Turkey throughout its existence, that in spite of direct military threats from the Balkan countries and the Turkish empire, and in permanent danger from Venice, it never fought war after early 15th century - all this is the best proof of the skill of its diplomacy. Even when completely destroyed by earthquake, Dubrovnik successfully averted the immediate danger from the Turks and Venice because of the ability and courage of its diplomats. There are many examples, in the history of diplomacy, of ability, of courage, and of sacrifice for the welfare

Lovro Dobričević, St. Julian, detail of polyptych The Virgin with Child, church of St. Mary at Danče, 1465

of the Republic. It may be of interest to know that the Republic was among the first countries of Europe to recognize the United States officially.

Long peaceful periods in the history of Dubrovnik and the relative bounty in which the city lived made it possible for science and art to flourish. Renaissance was especially fruitful in literature. The first 15th century poets to distinguish themselves writing in Latin were Karlo Pucić, Jakov Bunić and the famous poet laureate Ilija Crijević who was crowned with laurel in Rome in 1485. But early 15th century also saw first attempts to write verse in Croatian. Đono Kalić wrote some Croatian verse in 1421, but it was only the Petrarchan tradition that created lyric poetry in the Croatian language. The early Renaissance poetry by Džore Držić and Šiško Menčetić deserves especial note. The first stage attempts were made by Mavro Vetranović, followed by the comedies of Nikola Nalješković, and in mid 16th century came the dramatic work of Marin Držić, which has almost no contemporary match in Europe for its scope, imaginativeness and poetic quality. The same could be said of the famous Baroque poet Ivan Gundulić, the author of the splendid epic "Osman" and of the most beautiful verse on freedom ever written. Many scientists and scholars lived in Dubrovnik - the historian Ludovik Crijević Tuberon, Benko Kotruljić, who wrote a book on commerce in 1573, Nikola Sagrojević, who studied the phenomena of the tides, the mathematician, physicist and opticians Marin Getaldić and the greatest of them all: physicist, mathematician and philosopher Ruđer Bošković, one of the greatest minds of the Baroque period, whose works presents some ideas that are current even today.

Dubrovnik had outstanding painters in the 15th and 16th centuries. Numerous painters' workshops flourished in those times. Unfortunately, first the earthquake and then the fires have destroyed most of the production. Few unharmed paintings survived to the present day, and they testify to a production of high quality, which shifted from international Gothic

Dominican monastery, Nikola Božidarević, The Annunciation, 1513

towards Renaissance. Worth mentioning are the paintings by Lovro Dobričević, by his son Vicko Dobričević, by Mihajlo Hamzić, and by the brilliant Renaissance painter Nikola Božidarević whose four polyptychs represent the peak of the Renaissance painting school in Dubrovnik.

The most tragic event which occurred in Dubrovnik in its whole history was a devastating earthquake on April 6, 1667. More than 5000 citizens died under the ruins of their city. One of the most beautiful and harmonious cities of the Mediterranean vanished in ruins and fires which ravaged what was left of the city for days. The whole historic centre, its beautiful Romanesque cathedral and the representative Gothic and Renaissance

palaces, churches and monasteries were turned into an irreparable pile of debris. There were losses even among the ships in the port. Dubrovnik recovered slowly and with difficulty.

The city changed completely. Instead of the characteristic Gothic and Renaissance house fronts and the architectural vividness which occurs when a city grows and develops in centuries of peace and prosperity, Dubrovnik was now rebuilt in stern and modest Baroque houses of the same appearance and design, with compulsory shops on the ground-floor. All the representative sacral buildings that had been destroyed were now renewed in the Roman Baroque style. The Sponza Palace alone has preserved its original shape, and partly the front of the Rector's Palace. Fortunately, most of the fortifications had withstood the devastating force of the earthquake, except for minor damage. But even with such changes in its outlook, Dubrovnik has remained one of the most beautiful and architecturally most precious urban units in the Mediterranean.

The Republic did not die because of historical wear: it was abolished in 1808 as an act of Napoleon's occupying power. After the fall of Napoleon hopes were nurtured that the Congress of Vienna would renew the Republic, but the Austrian imperial authorities opposed it because of their pretensions to extend their rule to the whole eastern Adriatic territory. Within the Austrian empire Dubrovnik led an empty existence as a provincial town of Dalmatia, only its shipping remained important. Social disintegration brought decay and total collapse of the gentry. This decay described by Ivo Vojnović, the great writer and playwright from Dubrovnik. Between the two wars, Dubrovnik lived mostly from its shipping, but also from tourism which developed systematically.

After 1950, Dubrovnik experienced sudden increase of the tourist industry. Many new hotels were built, to be followed by entire tourist villages in the immediate vicinity. The new airport at Čilipi (Konavle) has considerably advanced and accelerated the development of tourism. In the late nineteen-eighties Dubrovnik was one of the most prized tourist destinations in Europe. The ideal combination of natural beauty, cultural heritage and entertainment was attracting thousands of tourists.

Since the free elections of 1990 Dubrovnik has been one of the most important cities of the independent Croatia. But before it had achieved full freedom it had to go through the most difficult temptations. In the autumn of 1991, the Yugoslav People's Army launched a most brutal and criminal attack against the city and the unarmed civilians. For months, they ravaged, looted, burned and thoroughly destroyed what man had created in the area. Having devastated Konavle, the coastal belt and Župa Dubrovačka, the enemy attacked the city and its cultural and art heritage. The bestial shelling of the city, recorded by TV cameras and broadcast to the world, warned the world about the horrible war in the very heart of Europe. Having withstood the siege, Dubrovnik survived the terror. Wounded but proud, Dubrovnik is recovering in free Croatia, and tourists are coming again to see its walls and palaces. Dubrovnik is now the pride of Croatia and a true jewel of Europe.

The City Walls

The most recognizable feature which defines the physiognomy of the historic city of Dubrovnik and gives it its characteristic appearance, famous all over the world, are its intact city walls, which run uninterrupted for 1940 metres encircling the city. This complex structure, one of the most beautiful and strongest fort systems in the Mediterranean, consists of a series of forts, bastions, casemates, towers and detached forts. The walls were built systematically in the difficult times of permanent danger to the City and

the Republic, and they have been preserved to the present day and are still functional, not only because of the proficiency of their skillful builders, diligence and care of the citizens of Dubrovnik who maintained them and added to them as necessary, but also because of the splendid ability of the famous diplomats who knew how to obviate and avert the dangerous intents of the enemies and rivals of the Republic. The city of Dubrovnik is completely surrounded with walls and forts, including the Old Port. The

A view of the fortifications from the sea

history of the fortifications goes back to the early Middle Ages. No doubt the earliest urban settlement upon the islet of Laus was protected by walls. The fact that the city was able to resist the Saracens who besieged the city for fifteen months in the 9th century means that it was fortified well. The city first spread towards the uninhabited eastern part of the islet. The present name Pustijerna for the south-eastern end of the city close to the Fortress of St. John, derives from the Latin expression *post terra* which could be freely translated as "outskirts". This eastern section was included within the defence walls in the 9th and 10th century. When the sea channel which separated the city from firm land was filled with earth in the 11th century, the city merged with the settlement on land and soon a single wall was built around the area of the present-day city core. The whole city was enclosed by walls in the 13th century, except for the Dominican monastery, which came under their protection only in the 14th century. The average thickness of the wall was 1.5 metres, and it was built of stone and lime. To increase the strength of the wall and ensure better defence, 15 square forts were built in the 14th century. Extensive work was done on the walls towards the close of the 14th century, at the time of the final liberation

from the Venetian supremacy. The sudden danger from the attacks of the Turks after the fall of Constantinople in 1453, coupled with the simultaneous latent threat from Venice gave the greatest stimulus to further reconstruction and urgent repair of the fortifications. Owing to the enormous efforts of the citizens and noblemen, as well as the skill of many urgently hired fort builders, most of the forts were strengthened, especially the ones towards the mainland, and new forts and semicircular bastions before the walls were completed in less than three years. The system was extended and modernized during the 16th century, even later. The design of the walls derives from the 14th century, while the definite shape was fixed in the period which is, not without reason, referred to as the Golden Age of Dubrovnik, i.e. from the fall of Constantinople in 1453 until the devastating earthquake of 1667. The main wall on the land side is 4 to 6 metres thick, but narrower on the side facing the sea - 1.5 to 3 metres thick. Its height reaches 25 metres in some places. The wall on the land side is protected by an additional scarp wall as

Strong land walls dominated by the tower Minčeta

defence against artillery fire. The irregular quadrilateral formed by the walls is protected at four prominent points by strong forts. The strong round Tower Minčeta is to the north, the port is protected by the detached Fortress Revelin in the east and by the big complex of the Fortress of Saint John in the south-east. The western entrance to the city is protected by the strong and beautiful tower Bokar. The western end of the city is also protected from danger from the sea and land by the powerful detached Fortress Lovrijenac. In addition to these strong and most prominent forti-

fications, the city walls are protected additionally by two round towers, 12 quadrilateral forts, 5 bastions and two corner towers, while the scarp wall is flanked by one large and 9 small semi-circular bastions. Along the part of the wall facing inland a deep ditch was dug as additional protection. The whole system was furnished with a large number of guns. They were mostly cast in local workshops, which were famous in these parts. The most prominent 16th century cannon designer and producer in Dubrovnik was Ivan of Rab. In times of full alert Dubrovnik was defended by over 120 artillery pieces. The city maintained communication with the outer world by means of two well protected gates, situated east and west. Entry from the west was through the fortified and well protected Pile Gate (Vrata od Pila), while the eastern Ploče Gate (Vrata od Ploča) was additionally protected by the detached fortress Revelin. Both entrances were constructed in such a way that communication with the city was not direct, but anyone entering the city was forced to pass through several gates and winding lanes, which testifies to cautionary measures against sudden raids or entry of undesirable visitors. Entry to the port, a most important area of this commercial and maritime city, was through two gates: the Port Gate (Vrata od Ponte) and the Fish Market Gate. The port was protected from the force of the waves or sudden attack from the sea by the breakwater named Kaše. The whole network of streets was subordinated to quick and purposeful communication with the forts. Nowadays, a walk upon the city walls is an attraction for tourists. Such a walk can best reveal the fabric of old Dubrovnik, because different points offer new vistas. It is particularly the higher parts that reveal many picturesque details, as well as the general lay of the city and its streets, squares and widenings, which cannot be visualised during a walk along the streets. In addition to unforgettable views of the city, such a walk will offer a magnificent view of the open sea before Dubrovnik and of the immediate surroundings. A walk along the city walls can start from two points. In the east the entry is near the Bell tower, and in the west near the Church of the Saviour, at the Pile Gate.

The Tower Minčeta

The most prominent point in the defence system toward the land is the round tower Minčeta. The name derives from the name of the Menčetić family, who owned the ground the tower was built upon. By its height and impressive volume the tower dominates the north-western high part of the city and the walls. It was built in 1319, originally as a strong four-sided fort. It was built by a local builder Nićifor Ranjina. As the fall of Constantinople in 1453 was a clear sign to the cautious citizen of Dubrovnik quickly to take ample defensive measures, the first and one of the most important tasks was to strengthen this key point. The fall of Bosnia, which followed soon in 1463, only hastened the works. The Republic invited a famous architect, Michelozzo di Bartolomeo of Florence. His work in Dubrovnik resulted in several buildings of highest importance for the defence of Dubrovnik. Among his principal activities around the middle of the 15th century was the reconstruction of the tower Minčeta. Around the earlier quadrilateral fort Michelozzo built a new round tower adapted to the new technique of warfare and joined it to the new system of low scarp walls. The walls of the new tower were full 6 metres thick and had a series of protected gun ports. The work on Minčeta was continued by the famous architect and sculptor Juraj Dalmatinac, born in Zadar. He designed and built the high narrow round tower, while the battlements are a later addition. The tower was completed in 1464, and is the symbol of the unconquerable city of Dubrovnik. Since it is the highest point of the wall, it offers an unforgettable view on the city.

*Michelozzo di Bartolomeo and Juraj Dalmatinac,
the tower Minčeta, 15th century*

The walls from the sea. Left: Fortress Lovrijenac, centre: Fortress of the Passing Bell

The Fortress of the Passing Bell

The southern section of the walls rises over steep cliffs which precipitate into the sea. This section was not much affected in the general reconstruction of fortifications in 15th and 16th centuries. Among the rare additions was the round fortress on the most outstanding point of the southern wing of the wall. The fortress was built early in the 16th century according to the plans drawn by the local builder Paskoje Milićević. Because of a large number of gun ports it was the focal point of defence between the tower Bokar and the fortress of St. John against possible danger from the sea. It was named after the bell in the nearby church of St. Peter which announced citizens' deaths.

The Fortress of St. John and Defence of the Port

    The Fortress of St. John, often called Mulo Tower, is a complex monumental building on the south-eastern side of the Old City Port, controlling and protecting its entrance. The first fort was built in mid 14th century, but it was modified on several occasions in the course of the 15th and 16th centuries, which can be seen in the triptych by the painter Nikola Božidarević in the Dominican monastery. The painting shows St. Blasius, the patron saint of Dubrovnik. In his hands he holds a scale model of Dubrovnik where the fortifications of the port can be seen clearly. The present appearance of the fortress dates from the 16th century and is mainly the work of the local builder Paskoje Miličević, whose reconstruction plans contributed considerably to the present look of the fortification of the Old Port. The side towards the sea is round and the lower part of the wall is inclined, while the part facing the has flat vertical walls. This large building, which had many gun ports for its primary function, is a cultural monument today. It houses the Maritime Museum, containing objects, paintings and documents relating to a most important activity in the history of the

Old port and the forts Revelin and St. John

city. The ground-floor houses the famous Aquarium. The monumental space of the fortress creates a special mood for visitors who can view specimens of Adriatic fauna in 27 basins of various sizes.

The opposite side of the old port was protected by the Fortress of St. Luke, built in the 14th century, and the city engineer Paskoje Miličević added a round bastion to it. Prior to the building of the breakwater the old port was closed at night by a chain and wooden beams which were stretched between the Forts of St. John and St. Luke.

Construction of the breakwater named Kaša started in 1484 from the drawings of the same engineer. This object offered protection to the port from southerly winds, and it added substantially to the safety of the anchorage against possible raids from the sea.

The Fortress Revelin

In the period of unmistakable Turkish danger and the fall of Bosnia under Turkish rule, the fortress Revelin was built to the east of the city in 1462, a detached fortress providing additional protection to the land approach to the eastern Ploče Gate. The name derives from *rivelino* (ravelin), a term in military architecture which refers to work built opposite to the city gate in order to afford better protection from enemy attack. Danger of Venetian assault suddenly increased in the times of the First Holy League, and it was necessary to strengthen this vulnerable point of the city fortifications. The Senate hired Antonio Ferramolino, an experienced builder of fortresses in the service of the Spanish admiral Doria, a trusted friend of the Republic. In 1538 the Senate approved his drawings of the new, much stronger Revelin. It took eleven years to build it, and during that time all other construction work in the city had stopped in order to finish this fortress as soon as possible. The new Revelin became the strongest city fortress, safeguarding the eastern land approach to the city. It is an irregular quadrilateral, with one of its sides descending towards the sea, and protected by a deep ditch on the other sides. One bridge crossing the protective ditch connects it to the Ploče Gate, and another connects it to the eastern suburb. The construction work was executed perfectly so that Revelin was not harmed by the devastating earthquake of 1667. As its interior is divided into three large vaulted rooms, Revelin became the administration centre of the Republic. The sessions of the Councils were held in the fortress, and the treasuries of the Republic and of the Cathedral were transferred there, and so was all other wealth which was saved from the ruins and fires following the earthquake.

The top of Revelin is a huge stone terrace, the largest in Dubrovnik, used in summer as a stage for many events of the summer festival.

The Tower Bokar

The tower Bokar (*Zvjezdan*) is among the most beautiful instances of harmonious and functional fortification architecture. It was built by the above mentioned Michelozzo of Florence while the city walls were reconstructed (from 1461 to 1463). This tower was conceived as the key point in

Fort Revelin protected the eastern gate.

the defence of the Pile Gate, i.e. the western fortified entrance to the city. Together with Minčeta this tower is the second key point in the defence of the western land approach to the city. It was built as a two-story casemate fortress, standing in front of the medieval wall face and protruding into space almost with its whole cylindrical volume. Nowadays the tower is used as a stage for events in the summer festival of Dubrovnik.

The Fortress Lovrijenac

The famous fortress was built upon a sheer rock 37 metre high over-looking the sea. This detached fortress is of prime importance for the defence of the western part of Dubrovnik, both against attack from land and the threat from the sea. The fortress was mentioned in a legend from the 11th century, but reliable data are from the 14th century, when its present form was determined. It was reconstructed several times in the centuries that followed. The main reconstruction occurred together with other fortresses: in the 15th and 16th centuries. In those times the municipal builder I. K. Zanchi of Pesaro was repairing the parapets. Having suffered damage in the earthquake of 1667, Lovrijenac was also repaired in the 17th century. Triangular in plan and following the contour of the rock on which it was built, Lovrijenac faces the western suburbs with its narrowest, highest part, and its longest wall is open towards the tower Bokar and the western wall, thus protecting the small, but also the oldest port of the city - Kolorina. The fortress has a quadrilateral court with mighty arches. As the height is uneven, it has three terraces with powerful parapets, the broadest looking south towards the sea. Lovrijenac was defended with 10 large cannons, the largest and most famous being *Gušter* (Lizard). It never fired a single shot. It was designed and cast in 1537 by master Ivan of Rab. As it is a dominant fortress whose capture could endanger the City and the Republic, its construction reveals all the wisdom and caution of the administration again. The walls exposed to enemy fire are almost 12 metres thick, but the large wall surface facing the city does not exceed 60 centimetres. The caution of the Republic was not only directed against the foreign enemy, but also against possible mutiny of the commander of the garrison of the fortress. Therefore the would-be tyrant was permanently exposed to the threat of destruction of the thinnest wall of the fortress. As caution was never sufficient, the commander of the fortress, always elected from the rank of the nobility, was replaced every month. The Republic defended freedom in every possible way. The famous inscription over the entrance to Lovrijenac: NON BENE PRO TOTO LIBERTAS VENDITUR AURO is witness to that. In translation: Freedom is not sold for all the gold in the world.

In the search for space suitable for theatre productions during the summer festival, it was observed very early that the three terraces of this fortress has great potential. It is especially suitable as the stage for Shakespeare's "Hamlet", and its production at Lovrijenac has become cultic and the trade mark of the summer festival.

The Pile Gate

The Pile Gate has been the main entrance to the city for centuries, and the whole area outside the walls was so named (from Greek *Pyle*, "gate"). The gate got its present shape in 1537 when the outer semi-circular tower with a Renaissance arch was built and the statue of St. Blasius, the patron saint of Dubrovnik, was set in a richly decorated niche. The approach to the gate is over a stone bridge and a wooden drawbridge, suspended by

The mighty fortress Lovrijenac, one of defence pillars of Dubrovnik

chains, which was lifted every evening with great ceremony. The first stone bridge was built in 1397 by Giovanni of Sienna, while the later, longer bridge with several arches, was built from the drawings of the famous architect Paskoje Miličević. This bridge spanned the deep protective ditch which was dug systematically along the city walls. The inner gate was built in the Gothic style in 1460, at the same place where the oldest gate had stood.

Pile gate

The Church of the Saviour

Between the Pile Gate and the Franciscan Monastery is a small votive church of the Saviour, built by the order of the Senate in 1520 in gratitude that the city had been spared from destruction in the earthquake which hit Dubrovnik in that time. The monumental inscription in the front testifies to this. The church was built by the architect Petar Andrijić of Korčula. It was completed in 1528. As this church was spared in the earthquake of 1667, it is preserved in its original form and is a good example of harmonious Renaissance architecture in Dubrovnik. This church has a nave with a Gothic cross-ribbed vault, and the lateral windows are also Gothic with pointed arches. Nevertheless, the front with marked Renaissance elements on the portal and the three-leaf semicircular top and the semi-circular apse reveal a clear and recognizable Renaissance concept.

The Convent of St. Clare

The convent of St. Clare is situated close to the city walls to the south of the inner Pile Gate. It was built in late 13th and early 14th centuries. It was one of the most respectable convents in the Republic. A home for foundlings was founded in this convent as early as 1434 to care for abandoned and illegitimate babies. It was one of the first institutions of its kind in the world. The children were nursed in this home up to their sixth year and than entrusted to the care of decent families.

The French authorities dissolved the convent and turned the building into ammunition depot and later into horse stable.

The Big Onofrio's Fountain

In the middle of a small but pleasant square close to Pile Gate is the Big Onofrio's fountain. It was built in 1438 by the Neapolitan builder Onofrio della Cava who was hired by the Republic to construct the urban aqueduct. While the majority of Dalmatian cities under Venetian authority solved the problem of water supply by building large cisterns for rain water, Dubrovnik decided to bring water from a well. Dubrovnik aqueduct from the late Middle Ages is an exceptional case. Onofrio tapped the well named Šumet at Rijeka Dubrovačka, 12 kilometres away from the city. He built two branches at Konali above the city itself. One branch supplied the workshops in the Pile area, and the other turned to the city at the level of the tower Minčeta. Onofrio also built a number of mills along this branch. The water thus brought to the city was accessible to the public in two places: at a large polygonal fountain with a water reservoir which he built close to the western gate, and at a smaller fountain in the east which supplied the market place at Luža square. In addition to these two main fountains there were several others: at the fish-market, in the port, in the atrium of the Rector's Palace, and in the cloister of the Franciscan Monastery. A smaller fountain for the Jewish community was also built.

*A picturesque square near the western gate, the church of the Saviour,
the Franciscan monastery and the Big Onofrio fountain*

For its form and volume, set in a small quadrilateral square, the Big
Onofrio's fountain looks like a replica of a former Romanesque baptistery
of the former cathedral in Bunić's Square. This fountain was heavily damaged by earthquake in 1667 and what we see today is a bare architectural
volume whereas the splendid sculptural ornaments are lost forever. The
original 16 masks in relief are still extant and water jets are gushing out of
their mouths.

The Franciscan Monastery

The large complex of the Franciscan monastery (Friars Minor) is situated at the very beginning of Placa, to the left of the Pile Gate. The lateral façade of the monastery church runs along the principal street of Dubrovnik, and the monastery spreads north along the walls as far as the tower Minčeta. The earliest monastery was built in the 13th century in the Pile area. As the city was threatened with war, in 14th century the friars were forced to move under the protection of the defence walls. The new monastery building was started in 1317 but work went on for a very long time. Some parts were destroyed and rebuilt several times. The large Franciscan church, one of the richest churches in Dubrovnik at the time, was destroyed in the earthquake of 1667. The only element of the former building which has been preserved is the portal on the south wall. It was probably moved from the front to the lateral wall in the course of the restoration in the 17th century. According to the contract of 1498, this portal, the most monumental one in Dubrovnik at that time, was carved in the leading local workshop owned by the brothers Leonard and Petar Petrović. The portal has all the marks of the Gothic style, but the solid volumes of the figures

Brothers Petrović, The portal of the Franciscan church, 15th century

The cloister and garden of the Franciscan monastery

show the Renaissance spirit. The figures of St. Jerome and St. John the Baptist are set above the door-posts, while the Pietŕ in relief is represented in the central Gothic lunette. The figure of the Father Creator is above the lunette. Such iconography of the portal and the choice of the patron saints are proof of the aspirations and social doctrine of the Franciscan in the political circumstances of the times. St. John the Baptist symbolizes

*Capitals shaped
like dogs
(14th century)*

Christian constancy in the face of the Turkish penetration. St. Jerome symbolizes the spiritual unity with the rest of Dalmatia. The Pietŕ symbolizes their compassion with the poorest members of the urban community who sought solace from the Franciscans anyhow, and the figure of the Creator on top should symbolize opposition to the humanist world-views of the time. The church was reconstructed in the Baroque style. The northern wall of the church closes the southern wing of one of the most beautiful cloisters of Dubrovnik. This cloister was built in late Romanesque style by master Mihoje Brajkov of Bar in 1360. The ambient is most harmonious, framed by a colonnade of double hexaphoras, each with a completely different capital. The Franciscan cloister is one of the most valuable late Romanesque creations on the Croatian shores of the Adriatic. The Franciscan monastery has another cloister built in the Gothic style, but it is for private use only and not accessible to the public.

A pharmacy was founded in the monastery 1317, the third oldest in the whole world, continuously functioning until the present day. The monastery owns one of the richest old libraries in the Croatia, famous all over the world for the value of its inventory. The collection has over 20,000 books, over 1200 of which are old manuscripts of extraordinary value and importance, 137 incunables and seven books of old church corals.

The collection of liturgical and art objects is exhibited in the large Renaissance hall, containing the inventory of the old Franciscan pharmacy, paintings by old masters, valuable specimens of gold-work and rare books.

Placa (Stradun)

Placa is the main open urban area in Dubrovnik and the most favoured promenade and gathering place. It is the venue of all popular feasts and processions, but also the main business street of the old city centre. This widest and most beautiful street divides the old city into northern and southern halves. At the same time it is the shortest communication

between the western and the eastern gates. This street was created at the close of the 11th century when the shallow channel separating the islet of Lava and the settlement upon it from the settlement on mainland was filled with earth in order to join them. Placa acquired its proper function at the close of the 12th century when both settlements were enclosed by a single city wall and became one urban whole. The name Placa is derived from the Greek and Latin *Platea*, which we translate as "street". The other name, Stradun, is a Venetian sobriquet used ironically in the sense of "Big street". The present shape was acquired after the earthquake of 1667 when Dubrovnik was hastily rebuilt after destruction and fires. The picturesque diversity of the former palaces of old Placa was replaced by planned and unified construction of two rows of stone houses built in the Baroque style, of equal height with similar fronts and similar internal arrangement. The

The square in front of Luža is one of the most picturesque places.
From left: Sponza palace, Luža, Bell Tower, House of the Main Guard,
St. Blasius'

Senate of the Republic had ruled that every house should have space for
several shops on the ground-floor, which shows that the authorities cared
about maintaining business life. Notwithstanding its modesty, this new
complex cannot be denied certain harmony or rhythm of volumes nor the
dignity of clean stone walls. In the western end of the Placa, close to the
Pile Gate, the street widens into Paskoja Miličevića Square where two
monastic houses are located - the Franciscan monastery and the convent of
the nuns of St. Clare. Close to the walls is the Renaissance church of the
Saviour, the centre of the square is adorned by the Big Onofrio's fountain,
built after the construction of the aqueduct in the 15th century. The opposite, eastern end of the Placa widens into the square named Luža.

Dubrovnik Summer Festival

The great theatre and music festival under the title of Dubrovnik Summer Festival has taken place without interruption since 1950. The programme takes place between July 10 and August 25 on 33 open-air stages

in the city. Owing to original historic places of old Dubrovnik, which are natural stages for many drama productions on account of their picturesque character, and places that become ideal for music productions on account of extraordinary acoustic properties - such the atrium of the Rector's Palace or the marvellous churches - the festival is known all over the world as a festival which attracts famous names of the theatre and music. The ambience is so much charged with historic meaning, artistic values and unmatched natural beauty that it is almost an ideal framework for artistic pleasure of the highest level. The spectacular opening of the festival on July 10 is particularly impressive. The whole city and all the visitors take part in it. The focal ceremony of this unique night takes place in Luža Square, when Festival flag is hoisted on Roland's column.

The Luža Square

The eastern widening of Placa - the Luža Square - formerly was used as market place. The famous Roland's column soars in the middle of the square and a great number of most important administrative and sacral buildings are situated around the square, such as the Baroque church of St. Blasius, the patron saint of the city of Dubrovnik, the Palace of the Major Council, the building of the Main Guard, the Little Onofrio's Fountain, the Bell Tower, the bell house Luža, and the Sponza Palace, seat of the Custom-House and the Mint. The main festivities take place on Luža square, such as the feast of St. Blasius or the opening ceremony of the summer festival.

The Church of St. Blasius

The Baroque church of St. Blasius, the patron saint of Dubrovnik, was built in 1715 in the place of the former Romanesque church which was consecrated to the same saint. This precious building was badly damaged by earthquake in 1667, and completely destroyed by fire in the night of May 24/25, 1706. The Senate hired the Venetian architect Marino Gropelli, who built the present church on the model of the Venetian church of St. Mauritius. It is a central building with an oblong cupola in the centre, a large portal with rich ornaments, and a broad flight of stairs before the entrance. The rich outer Baroque ornament is in sharp contrast with the severe, simple house fronts in Placa, but it refreshes the ambience in a way. The interior of the church is richly decorated according to the norms of its representative Baroque style. The magnificent altars built in coloured marble are most pronounced in this respect. The high altar has a precious Gothic statue of St. Blasius in gilt silver, made in the 15th century by an unknown master of the local school. Because of its high quality it is one of the most precious statues in the long history of art in Dubrovnik. In addition to its art value, this statue is also a historical document because the in his left hand saint holds a scale model of Dubrovnik showing the buildings which were later destroyed by earthquake. Of the many gold and silver statues and church vessels, this was the only statue to survive the fire, and this fact was taken as the proof of its miraculous power.

The Feast of St. Blasius

St. Blasius (Vlaho) is to Dubrovnik what St. Mark is to Venice. The feast of St. Blasius, the Patron saint, is observed every year on February 3, and it is the true feast of the whole city. It is known far and wide for its pageantry and participation of people from neighbouring villages in their picturesque costumes, for its majestic procession in which the relics of the Saint are carried, and for popular events and merrymaking. In the times of the Republic it was a custom seven days before the feast and seven days after it to release from jail prisoners who were not dangerous, and anyone who was permanently banned from the city could come back for the festivities. St. Blasius was bishop of Sebasta in Armenia, he suffered martyrdom

under emperor Diocletian, and became patron saint of Dubrovnik in the 10th century. It seems that he appeared in a dream to one Stojko, rector of the cathedral, and warned him that the Venetians, anchored near the island of Lokrum, intended to attack the city that night. After the Senate had meticulously checked Stojko's report, St. Blasius became the patron saint of the city of Dubrovnik. His statue was carved on all fortresses of the city and above all gates of Dubrovnik. St. Blasius also adorns the flag of the Republic, and the figure of the bearded bishop with mitre and pastoral staff appeared on all official seals of Dubrovnik and on coins minted in Dubrovnik.

Roland's Column

In the middle of the Luža Square is a high and slender stone column with flag-staff, decorated with the figure of the legendary medieval knight Roland. The column was set up in 1418, and the flag of the free Republic

with the image of its patron saint on white ground streamed from the column for four centuries. The column is Gothic in style and was carved by the sculptor Bonino of Milan with the help of local craftsmen. The figure of the proud knight is a fine example of monumental Gothic sculpture. It is an interesting question how this knight, the symbol of north European cities, came to southern Adriatic. Although tradition has it that this knight defended Dubrovnik from the raids of the Saracen pirates, the explanation of the riddle is of political character. Dubrovnik was in 15th century protected by Sigismund, the King of Hungary, Croatia and Bohemia, later also the German Emperor. Sigismund was also Margrave of Brandenburg, a province where such columns were common. Thus Roland of Dubrovnik is symbol of loyalty to Sigismund, whose protection was crucial in the strife against Venice. Roland formerly looked east towards the Custom-Office, but it was often moved. In 1825 the column was blown down by a gale and was kept in a store for half a century. When the column was set up again, it was turned so that Roland faces north. It is of interest that the length of his forearm was taken for a measure - the ell of Dubrovnik, which is 51.1 cm.

The Palace of the Major Council

In the space between the Rector's Palace and the bell tower stood formerly the Gothic palace of the Major Council. The earliest reference to this building is in a document from 1303. The palace was renewed and enlarged in 1487 as a Gothic and Renaissance building. As the front was designed by the local master Paskoje Miličević, it probably looked like the front of the Sponza Palace which was built by the same master. The front was decorated with valuable statues. Many foreign and local masters worked on this important public palace. Radivoje Bogosalić and Leonard Petrović constructed the building, whereas Rade Ivanov and Marin Radetić decorated the interior. Direct connection with the Rector's Palace existed on the first floor level. Over the doorway is the inscription: OBLITI PRIVATORUM PUBLICA CURATE - Forget private business, care for public affairs. In the course of the 18th century the palace was also used as a public theatre. It was completely destroyed by fire in 1816, and the new town hall was built in the same place in 1882, in Neo-Gothic style. The new theatre was built within this complex, and the City coffee house was built in the 20th century.

The House of the Main Guard

The House of the Main Guard was built in the Gothic style close to the Palace of the Major Council. This building was of a very great importance for the safety of the city, as it was the residence of the admiral, supreme commander of the armed forces. The ground-floor of the building was reconstructed in early 18th century, and the monumental Baroque portal was built between 1706 and 1708. The author of the reconstruction was the Venetian architect Marino Gropelli, who had also designed the new Baroque church of St. Blasius.

The Little Onofrio's Fountain

Close to the Guard-House is the Little Onofrio's Fountain. After the completion of the aqueduct, its builder Onofrio della Cava set two public fountains at the western and eastern ends of Placa. The Big Onofrio's Fountain, which is also a water reservoir, is at the western end close to the Pile Gate, while the Small fountain was placed at the eastern end to supply water to the market place which was in the Luža Square. The Little Onofrio's Fountain was built in 1438, and is masterly combination of function and decoration. The sculptures were made by Pietro di Martino of Milan. In the Middle Ages water had a religious significance, so this Fountain was for the use of Christians only. Close by was another fountain for the use of the Jewish community of Dubrovnik - *Žudioska česma*. This one was later shifted to the Pile Gate.

The Bell Tower

The Bell Tower with clock was built in 1444 right in the axis of the Placa. It is 31 metres high and together with the Tower Minčeta and the Roland's Column is one of the symbols of the free city state. The bell tower was built by the local masters Grubačević, Utišenović and Radončić. Prior to the construction of this tower the city clock was on the Rector's Palace. The coloured brass face of the new clock with the hand showing the phases of the moon, and the two human figures which strike the bell announcing hours, were made by Luka, son of Admiral Miho Žugrović. A new plate with ciphers was made somewhat later by the painter Matko

Junčić. The wooden figures were replaced by the famous horses, and in 1509 the noted bell-founder Ivan of Rab cast another bell with an epigraph by Ilija Lampridije Crijević. It was also hit by the earthquake, it lost its stability, it leaned and was in danger of falling. Therefore it was rebuilt in 1929 after the original drawings.

Luža

In the area between the Bell Tower and the Sponza Palace is Luža, the old bell-house. After a gunpowder explosion in the Rector's Palace the bells for summoning the Major Council were moved from the Palace to Luža. The bells at Luža were also used as alarm bells to warn citizen in case of fire or other danger. Luža was built in 1463, and generally renewed in 1952. Beneath Luža is the inner city gate, built in the Gothic style, the Customs Gate, leading from Placa towards Ploče Gate or directly to the old port through the Fish Market Gate.

The Sponza Palace

Close to Luža, on the left side of the square is the monumental Gothic-Renaissance Sponza Palace, one of the most beautiful in the city, which has preserved its original form. Its form suggests possible appearance of the majority of public and private palaces before the earthquake of 1667. Its name is derived from the word for the spot where rainwater was collected (*Spongia* - "alluvium"). In the time of the Republic this palace housed the custom office and bonded warehouse, hence it was often referred to as Divona (from *dogana* - "customs"). The palace also housed the mint, the bank, the treasury, and the armoury. The Sponza Palace was the seat of a number of state offices, important in the life of the Republic, which was based on commerce. This complex palace was designed by *protomagister* Paskoje Miličević. It is a large rectangular building with an inner courtyard. An open porch communicates with the square in front; another porch opens on the first floor towards the yard, and there is a shady porch on the first floor in front. The building is a mixture of Gothic and Renaissance styles, typical of all important palaces which were built on the east Adriatic coast at that time. The porch and the sculptural ornaments of the building were made after 1516 by the brothers Andrijić, masters from Korčula, and by other less known stone-cutters. A beautiful medal with Jesus' monogram and two angels was carved by the sculptor Beltrand Gallicus on the back wall. Individual custom bonded warehouses have names of saints inscribed in capital letters above their doors. The main inscription on the arch of the atrium from which a balance was suspended drew attention to the fact that the city measures were true: FALLERE NOSTRA VETANT; ET FALLI PONDERA: MEQUE PONDERO CVM MERCES: PONDERAT IPSE DEVS - Our weights do not permit cheating or being cheated. When I measure the commodities, the Lord measures with me. The Sponza palace was not damaged in the earthquake of 1667, and this fact probably saved the Republic. Affairs of state could continue notwithstanding heavy destruction. Members of the *Academia dei Concordi*, founded at the close of the 16th century by a group of poets, met

in the large hall on the first floor. That was Dubrovnik's first institution of literary life.

Nowadays the Sponza Palace is the home of the most important cultural institution of Dubrovnik - the Archive. Previously, in the times of the

Republic, the archives were kept in the Rector's Palace. Almost all documents that cover the period between the 12th century and the fall of the Republic are to be found there. More recent documents from the 19th and 20th centuries are also there. The wealth of records of all kinds make these archives one of the most important historical archives of the world. The archives contain 7000 volumes of manuscripts and about 100,000 of individual manuscripts. The earliest charter in the archives is from 1022. As early as 1278, the Republic introduced compulsory registration and filing of all public and private legal documents. The official languages of the documents were Latin and Italian, but many documents are in Croatian, also

Interior court in Sponza palace

in Turkish, Spanish, Russian, New Greek and Arabic. Of especial value is the collection of statutory and law books, among them the Statutes of Dubrovnik of 1272. The records of the Chancellery and the Notaries of the Republic are all preserved, together with the copies all testaments, the protocols of all the three Councils of the Republic, official correspondence, records of voyages of all ships, cargo and passenger lists, and many other precious historical data from which the political, diplomatic and economic history of the Republic can be reconstructed, as well as a wealth of materials relating to the history of other countries and nations.

The Rector's Palace

Close to the Town Hall (formerly the palace of the Major Council) is the Rector's Palace, an outstanding monument of secular architecture not only in Dubrovnik but on the whole Adriatic coast. This harmonious Gothic and Renaissance palace owes its present shape to many additions and reconstructions in its stormy history. From time to time it was destroyed or heavily damaged by fire, gunpowder explosions and earth-quake. A defence building stood at the site of the present palace in early

Middle Ages, and in the Statutes of 1272 it was referred to as *castrum*. In 1296 it was *castellum*. i.e. fortress. The term palatium - "palace" - occurs in the documents in 1349, and later the term *palazzo maggior*. As the documents sometimes specify its parts, it could be deduced that it was a building with corner towers, two wings and a high wall which enclosed the yard. The intent to embellish the building became manifest in the 15th century. This was certainly made easier because fires and gunpowder explosions had so seriously damaged the old building and its towers that it had to be rebuilt practically from the foundations. After the fire of 1435 which gutted the building and its towers, the government decided to build a new, more beautiful palace. The job was entrusted to Onofrio della Cava of Naples, master builder who had previously built the aqueduct. The Rector's palace rose as a smart and harmonious two-story Gothic building, with a pillared porch between two side towers which are slightly higher.

Capitals from the front of Rector's palace

Atrium of the Rector's palace

The column of the porch end in most beautiful capitals with figural representations. The sculptural ornaments of the palace, including the capitals, were made by master Pietro di Martino of Milan. Only a semi-capital with the figure of Aesculapius built into the southern angle of the porch, the capital with the scene of the Judgement of Solomon (which is now in the City Museum), and four figural wall brackets in the front porch have survived to the present day. Although the arrangement of the figures was Gothic, they show evidence of early Renaissance spirit. A gunpowder explosion occurred in the armoury of the palace in 1463 and heavily damaged it. The renewal was entrusted the famous architect Michelozzo of Florence who was reconstructing the city walls at the time. It appears that his plans were too much in the style of the Renaissance for the tastes of the notoriously conservative Major Council because they rejected them on May 5, 1464. Michelozzo left Dubrovnik soon after, and the work was continued by other builders. The arches in the porch were reshaped according to the principles of the Renaissance with completely new Renaissance capitals. The modernisation of the sculptural decoration was probably the work of the Florentine master Salvi di Michele who directed the reconstruction from 1467 on. The main changes of Onofrio's building were made on the western and southern fronts where the former simple windows were replaced by large biforas, eight on the western front and three on the southern front. The biforas were carved by local masters Radivoj Bogosalić and Nikola Marković, while the relief ornaments on the portal were made by master Pavko Antojević Bogičević. New damage was caused by the earthquake of 1520. One of the masters who repaired it was Petar Andrijić of Korčula. The Palace suffered major damage in 1667. The southern front with biforas broke down, and this wing was rebuilt in the Baroque style. At the same time, a new Baroque flight of stairs was built in the atrium in place of the old one which was damaged, and a bell was set up on the first floor of the atrium. Its stand is decorated with rich rococo ornaments. It was connected to a clock mechanism below which struck the hours. On the ground-floor of the atrium, between two pillars in the eastern wing, the Senate had a monument erected in 1638 to Miho Pracat, a citizen of merit. He was a rich

Rector's palace, Rector's office

shipowner from Lopud who bequeathed his wealth to the Republic, and the only citizen (a commoner at that) whom the Republic had honoured with a monument in one thousand years of its existence. The bust was

Bronze bust of Dubrovnik's benefactor Miho Pracat,
in the atrium of the Rector's palace

made by Pietro Giacometti of Recanati. The monument was damaged in the great earthquake, but it was repaired and returned to the same place in 1738. The eastern front, looking towards the harbour, underwent great changes after the earthquake. Originally representative in form, with a porch and a loggia, it was never restored to its previous shape. Owing to many misfortunes, the Rector's Palace became a unique building, harmoniously combining elements of Gothic, Renaissance and Baroque styles.

In addition to the Rector's Office and his private chambers, the reception and audience halls, the Palace was the seat of the Minor Council and of the state administration (the Secretary, the Notariate and the Cadastre), the armoury, the powder-magazine, the watch-house and the prison. The Rector, whose term of office was one month only, was not allowed to leave the Palace except on official business. He received the keys to the city gates every the evening during a ceremony for safe keeping. The ceremony was repeated every morning when he returned the keys. A row of stone benches are arranged along the western front wall under the porch. The Rector and the members of the Minor Council sat there on cushions, either to receive flag salute on St. Blasius day or to bid farewell to the ambassadors on their departure to distant countries. The Rector and his company used to watch carnival festivities from the same place too.

Rector's palace, the bell

The Rector's Palace is the home to the History Department of the Museum of Dubrovnik today. The majority of the halls have style furniture so as to recreate the original atmosphere of these rooms. In addition to style furniture, here are numerous portraits and coats of arms of the noblemen, paintings of old masters, coins minted by the Republic, the original keys of the city gates, and a number of copies of important state documents.

The Cathedral

The Cathedral of the Assumption of the Virgin was built in the 18th century after almost complete destruction in the earthquake of 1667 of the former 12th-14th century Romanesque cathedral. According to historical sources, the former cathedral was a magnificent basilica with a cupola, richly decorated with sculpture. According to tradition, part of the money to build the church was contributed as a votive gift by King Richard the Lion Heart having survived shipwreck near the island of Lokrum in 1192 on his return from the Third Crusade. During the restoration work in 1981,

foundations of an earlier cathedral were discovered. Its architectural features suggest that it was built in the 7th century. This discovery gives a new dimension to the history of Dubrovnik, proving as it does that Dubrovnik was an organized urban whole as early as the 7th century.

The Republic endeavoured to restore the ruined cathedral as soon as possible. An important role in these endeavours was played by Stjepan Gradić, one of the leading intellectuals of Dubrovnik, who was in Rome at the time employed as custodian and later rector of the Vatican library, but also in the role of unofficial ambassador of his native city of Dubrovnik to the Holy See. Gradić had many friends in Rome and he used his influence to find help for the rebuilding of his native city. His was the plan to renew the cathedral in the form of the Roman Baroque. With this in mind, he suggested that the Republic employ the famous Roman architect Andrea Buffalini of Urbino. Buffalini designed the new cathedral as a Roman Baroque

Cathedral, St. John Nepomuk's altar (1758)

church with three aisles and a cupola. The front of this church rises upon a flight of seven steps, and is articulated in a typical Baroque manner so as to emphasize the rich front and the concept of dynamic space with multiple contrasts of light. The protruding central part with the main portal is dominated by four high Corinthian columns. The upper half of the central part with a large Baroque window, shallow pillars and a strong triangular gable, rises above the attic. The left and right sides of the front have one floor only, articulated with pillars and deep niches with statues, and with a balustrade and statues of saints on top. The two smaller side entrances are

Cathedral of the Assumption of the Virgin, interior

considerably lower than the central one. The lateral walls of the church are articulated by small pillars and large semicircular Baroque windows. The aisles are separated from the nave by big columns. A slim Baroque cupola rises at the intersection of the nave and the transepts. The building of the church began in 1671 after Buffalini's plans. The first master builder was Paolo Andreotti of Genoa. He was followed by Pier Antonio Bazzi of Genoa, and friar Tommaso Napoli of Palermo. The new cathedral was finished in 1713 by the local architect Ilija Katičić. The cathedral has several fine late Baroque altars, such as the altar of St. Bernard built by Carlo degli

Frangi, or the unique altar of St. John Nepomuk built of violet marble in northern Baroque style. This altar was a gift by the bishop of Sirmium Nikola Josip Gjivović from Pelješac, who was a counsel to the Austrian queen Maria Theresa. The treasury of Dubrovnik cathedral was one of the richest on the Adriatic coast, but it was badly damaged in the earthquake. The objects which could be saved from the ruins and the sites of the con-flagration testify to the great art treasures that the churches possessed. Among the most precious objects in the treasury are the reliquaries of the head and the arm of the patron saint of Dubrovnik St. Blasius. The reli-quary of his head, in the form of the Byzantine imperial crown, is embel-lished with enamelled medals and precious stones. It is an outstanding example of goldsmith's work from 11th-12th century. The treasury has many reliquaries and church vessels from the 13th to the 18th century, some of them made by famous goldsmiths of Dubrovnik. An interesting detail testifies to the proverbial caution of the citizens. As treasury of the cathedral was also regarded as property of the Republic, access was possi-ble only if three different keys were used simultaneously: one was kept by the archbishop, one by the cathedral rector, and one by the secretary of the Republic. The treasury also has a number of paintings of extraordinary val-ue - from the Romanesque-Byzantine icon of the Virgin with Child from the 13th century to the paintings by Padovanini, Palma il Giovane, Savol-do, Parmigianino, P. Bordone and others. The big polyptych of the

Cathedral treasury, reliquary of the saint's head shaped like
the crown of the Byzantine emperors, 11th -12th century

Assumption of the Virgin which adorns the sanctuary was made in Titian's workshop, possibly in part by Titian himself. This painting was moved to the cathedral from the church of St. Lazarus in Ploče, which was destroyed.

A detached polygonal baptistery building of red and white stone stood to the west of the cathedral, close to it, in the present Bunić square. The baptistery was built in 1326, and was the only part of the old cathedral complex to survive the earthquake. It was pulled down in 1830 by an arrogant Austrian military commander because it obstructed the view from the window of his residence.

Gundulić Square

A relatively spacious, picturesque square lies to the west of the cathedral - Gundulićeva poljana, surrounded with old stone houses. In the day-

time it is a lively, coloured, rich market-place, and in the summer evenings it becomes an open-air stage for the summer festival. The square is dominated by the monument to Ivan Gundulić, the most famous poet of Dubrovnik, erected by the grateful citizens in 1892. The monument is the work of Ivan Rendić, one of the first modern Croatian sculptors. A full bronze figure of the great poet stands on a high pedestal; its four surfaces are decorated in relief with scenes from the epic poem "Osman", his most famous poem. The west side shows the old man Ljubdrag meditating upon Dubrovnik, from the eighth canto. The south side shows the priest Blaž blessing the Christian army, from the eleventh canto. The east side shows a scene from the ninth canto, in which Sunčanica, the principal woman character, is taken to the Sultan's harem, and the north side shows King Vladislav on horseback as victor over the Turks.

Ivan Rendić, relief from the monument to Ivan Gundulić

Picturesque market at Gundulić Square

The Granary Rupe

In the oldest part of Dubrovnik, the district called St. Mary which is to west of the Jesuit Church and College, is the old grain store Rupe.

Dubrovnik gave particular attention to reserves of grain - in case of siege or famine. Provisions of grain were as important as supplies of gunpowder. Therefore the city had several grain stores, Rupe ("pits") being the largest and the most interesting from the architectural point of view. This granary was built between 1542 and 1590. Fifteen deep, dry cisterns with a capacity of 150 wagons of grain were bored in the living rock, and the two-floor building above was the horizontal storage area from where grain flowed into the cisterns through a system of openings in the floor and arches, or through channels in the wall.

Besides its intrinsic interest, the building is now used as Ethnographic Museum.

The Church of St. Ignatius and the Jesuit College

A monumental Baroque flight of steps leads from the south side of Gundulić square to Ruđer Bošković square and the church of St. Ignatius and the Collegium Ragusinum, the famous Jesuit school. This urban complex is considered by many as having greatest Baroque characteristics, not only in Dubrovnik but in whole Dalmatia. Dissatisfied with many Italian teachers who often came in conflict with the citizen of Dubrovnik, bishop Beccadelli asked in 1555 the newly founded Jesuit society to establish a college in the city. The idea was not put into effect immediately. It was not until 1647 that when the legacy of the Jesuit Marin Gundulić made it finally possible to start planning. The Jesuit rector Gianbattista Canali prepared plans in 1653 to regulate this old section of the city in order to built the Jesuit church and college. His plans included pulling down a whole complex of old houses. Some of the houses were bought off, but the earthquake of 1667 stopped all further work. It was continued only at the end of the century. The famous Jesuit architect and painter Ignazio Pozzo was hired for the purpose. He started working on the church project in 1699 and finished it in 1703. The church of St. Ignatius was completed in 1725, and opened for worship in 1729. The articulation of its monumental Baroque front is reminiscent of the architectural concept which is also visible in the cathedral of Dubrovnik. The interior of the church shows similar features too. The sanctuary is decorated with illusionist Baroque frescoes by Gaetano Garcia, which display scenes of life of St. Ignatius, founder of the Jesuit society. The Jesuit College abuts at right angles against the front of the church. It was built according to the design by Ranjina and Canali and, with its neutral and severe lines, it only emphasizes the Baroque front of the church and the articulated broad flight of steps towards the city. The author of these extraordinary steps was the Roman architect Pietro Passalacqua. They were designed in 1738. Their architectural articulation and its effect it represents a far echo of the famous Roman steps leading from Piazza di Spagna towards the church Trinità dei Monti.

Prijeko and the Little Church of St. Nicholas

At right angles to Placa (Stradun) many small narrow streets run towards the north with numerous flight of steps ascending steeply to the northern section of the city walls. These picturesque little streets are cut by a long straight Prijeko street, which runs parallel to Placa. This part of the city has preserved its original picturesque outlook. Prijeko street links these urban surroundings - somewhat more humble, but equally attractive. This rather narrow but straight street is bounded in the west by the lateral wall of the Franciscan monastery and in the east the front of the church of St. Nicholas. This little church was built as early as the 11th century and is one of the oldest churches in Dubrovnik. This church of the seamen of Dubrovnik was reconstructed several times, and the present-day front is from the 16th century.

The Dominican Monastery

In the east part of the city, close to the walls is the large architectural complex of the Dominican monastery. This area is one of the most important architectural complexes of Dubrovnik and a major treasury of cultural and art heritage in Dubrovnik. The Dominicans established their monastery in Dubrovnik as early as 1225, but the building of the church and the monastery took much longer, so the church and the monastery building were completed in the 14th century. The place that the Dominicans chose for their monastery was strategically one of the most sensitive points in the defence of the city, so that as early as the 14th century the whole complex came was included within city walls, becoming their part. The church is one of the largest Gothic buildings on the east Adriatic coast. It is of simple architectural design: a hall with a pentagonal Gothic apse which is separated from the central area by three high openings with Goth-

The cistern crown and the courtyard of the Dominican monastery

ic arches. The high outer walls of the church are bare of ornaments. The portal on the southern side has certain Romanesque elements, but in 1419 Bonino of Milan added to it a frame ending in a pointed Gothic arch. The interior is rich in stone church furniture, a pulpit, gravestones and Renaissance niches. The Monastery complex acquired its final shape in the 15th century, when the vestry, the chapter house and the cloister were added. The beautiful porches of the cloister were built between 1456 and 1483., They were built by the local builders: Utišenović, Grubačević, Radmanović

The cloister of the Dominican monastery, 15th century

and others from the designs of the Florentine architect Massa di Bartolomeo. The arches of the cloisters are closed by beautiful Gothic and Renaissance triforas. In the middle of the courtyard is a richly decorated cistern crown. The vestry was built in 1485 by the famous Dubrovnik architect Paskoje Miličević. The bell-tower was started by the architect Checo of Monopoli in the 16th century, but it was finished only in the 18th century. Although the complex of the Dominican Monastery has in some of its elements different style characteristics, from the Romanesque to the

Dominican monastery, Lovro Dobričević, polyptych Baptism of Christ, 1448

Baroque, it is a harmonious and logical architectural unit, but nevertheless predominantly Gothic and early Renaissance. A special treasure of this monastery is its library with over 220 incunables, numerous illuminated manuscripts, and a rich archive with precious manuscripts and documents. The art collection is very rich, and the best paintings of Dubrovnik school of the 15th - 16th centuries have a special place among them - works by Nikola Božidarević, Lovro Dobričević and Mihajlo Hamzić. Of foreign paintings, the painted crucifix by the noted Venetian painter Paolo Veneziano from the 14th century and the altarpiece of St. Magdalene, a work of Titian and his assistants from 1550 deserve especial attention.

Of the more recent Croatian painters, the altarpiece "Miracle of St. Dominic" by Vlaho Bukovac and paintings by Ivo Dulčić also deserve attention.

Nikola Božidarević, altar-piece, detail

South portal of the Dominican church

The Ploče Gate

The eastern entrance to the city is protected by a complex of walls, towers and fortifications. As the detached fortress Revelin is also in front of the city walls, the eastern entrance consists of an outer and inner gate. The inner gate is smaller, built in the Romanesque style; it is within the zone of the city walls and is protected by the high tower Asimon (Kula od Ploča), built in the 14th century. The outer gate near the south-eastern corner of the fortress Revelin and was built by Simeone della Cava in mid 15th century. This gate was widened in the 19th century. The stone bridge over the defence ditch was built in mid 15th century.

The Gallery of Fine Arts

    A stately stone palace in Frana Supila Way to the east of Ploče, built between the two world wars inspired by the Renaissance and Gothic summer villas of the patricians, serves as the home of the Gallery of Fine Arts,

one of the richest public collections of paintings on the Croatian coast. This gallery has many paintings from the 19th and 20th centuries, and particularly it exhibits paintings by the local painters - from Vlaho Bukovac to modern colourists. This Gallery arranges many exhibitions of national and international character, and is in this respect one of the most important national institutions of its kind in Croatia.

The Arsenal

The Arsenal was situated in the port. It consisted of four separate vaulted areas where the galleys for the defence of the city were docked. Warships for immediate defence of the city were built and maintained there. The Republic owned no other warships, but their merchant ships were armed adequately. The Arsenal was often modified over the centuries, it was reconstructed or new parts were added. A fact testifying to the proverbial caution of the Republic ought to be mentioned. If a new construction or a long repair was started, the arched openings were walled in. The walls were knocked down and opened again when the vessel was completed in order to launch it. The arsenal serves nowadays as the well-known coffee house, its three semicircular arches looking towards the port.

The Lazarettos

A large building which served as a lazaretto was situated in the region named Ploče close to the sea. Its purpose was to put in quarantine foreign sailors, travellers and merchants in order to prevent the spread of contagious disease and a possible epidemic. In the course of the 15th century large lazarettos were built in the region named Danče, to the west of the city, and in the 16th century such buildings were also provided on the island Lokrum. The Lazarettos at Ploče were built from late 16th to the 18th century. They were located at a suitable position along the former Trebinje road, where caravans from the Turkish hinterland came down. The building is composed of several parallel longitudinal rooms which one enters from the courtyard. Small watch-towers face the road. The Lazaretto building is very well preserved.

The Island of Lokrum

The island of Lokrum, covered with dense greenery, is situated near the shore to the east of the city. In addition to a dense pine forest, Lokrum is rich in Mediterranean and sub-tropic vegetation, and because of extraordinary natural beauty it was declared a national park. In the south-eastern part of Lokrum, amidst dense vegetation, is an old Benedictine monastery from the 12th century, which was abolished by the French occupation during the reign of Napoleon. In 1859 the Archduke Maximilian of the House of Habsburg, the future Emperor of Mexico, converted the monastery into his summer residence, had it reconstructed in Neo-Gothic style, and added a high tower. After his death in Mexico the monastery changed many owners. Early in the 19th century the French had built Fort Royal on the highest peak of Lokrum, which now serves as a belvedere to many visitors.

Pile, Gradac, Danče

The area to the west of the city walls is named Pile, after the western entrance to the city. The area right in front of the gate is Brsalje, today important crossroad and reception point for tourists. To the west of the fortress Lovrijenac is Kolorina, the oldest port in Dubrovnik. Close to Pile is Gradac, a large park which offers full view of the city and the open sea. Under the southern wall of Gradac, in the region named Danče, lazarettos

Church of St. Mary at Danče, Nikola Božidarević,
triptych Virgin with saints, 1517

were built in the 15th century to prevent the spread of plague and other epidemics. The rules of quarantine in Dubrovnik were very strict and the isolation of the sick was very long. Close to the lazarettos is the small church of St. Mary where some of the most beautiful paintings from the 15th and 16th century Dubrovnik school are kept - a polyptych by Lovro Dobričević and a triptych by Nikola Božidarević.

Gruž

The deep and well protected bay of Gruž was formerly the site of the famous Dubrovnik shipyards, but in more recent times a new port was built there and an urban settlement developed close to it. Gruž was the suburban area where the patricians of Dubrovnik had their summer villas, many of them preserved to the present day. Three big villas are at the very end of the bay, which were built in the 16th century. The first one is the summer residence of Palatin Gundulić, built in 1527 in the Renaissance style with a chapel, a separate pavilion, gardens and a fish pond. Close to it Junije Bunić built his villa in 1550. The front of his residence with Gothic windows is one of the latest examples of conservative Gothic style in the region of Dubrovnik. The third, owned by Martin Bunić, and situated between the two above-mentioned villas, was built in the Renaissance style in 1578. These villas and others that the noblemen had built in Gruž, Lapad, Rijeka Dubrovačka, along the coast and on the islands of Koločep, Lopud and Šipan, their harmonious proportions, modesty, fine architectural details, gardens containing selected greenery, fruit trees and fish ponds - it all testifies to an exceptional culture of living in the times of the highest economic and political progress of the Republic.

Lapad

The large, forested Lapad peninsula lies to the west of the historic centre of Dubrovnik is. Its highest peak is the hill Petka. Lapad is now a suburban area with accommodation for tourists, hotels and other tourist services. In the past Lapad was the region of numerous Renaissance summer villas, of which certainly the most famous was the mansion belonging to Petar Sorkočević, situated at the very beginning of the peninsula, opposite Gruž. It is situated at the foot of a wooded hill near the sea shore. It was

Lapad, Petar Sorkočević's villa (first half of 16th century)

built in the decades between 1520 and 1580 in a mixture of Gothic and Renaissance styles. It has Renaissance characteristics on the ground-floor, but the monoforas and the trifora on the first floor are Gothic. The first floor opens to a large terrace under which is a water cistern. The residence is surrounded by a high wall. The garden with lush vegetation has two parts on different levels and a large fish pond. The villa has a small protected

A view of the Lapad peninsula

garden with a chapel. The Institute of Historical Science of the Croatian Academy of Science and Arts is housed nowadays this villa.

The well-known church of St. Michael and the old cemetery of the nobility is located in Lapad. The Church of the Virgin of Grace is a votive church and it owns a rich and interesting collection of paintings of old sailing ships.

Contents

THE WORLD'S CLASSICS
PÈRE GORIOT

HONORÉ BALZAC was born in 1799 at Tours, the son of a civil servant. Put out to nurse and sent later to boarding school, he had, except between the ages of four and eight, little contact with home. In 1814 the family moved to Paris, where Honoré continued his boarding-school education for two years, and then studied law at the Sorbonne. From 1816 to 1819 he worked in a lawyer's office, but having completed his legal training he knew he wanted to be a writer. While his family gave meagre financial support he wrote a play, *Cromwell*, but it was a complete failure. He also collaborated with other writers to produce popular novels. During the 1820s he dabbled in journalism, and tried to make money in printing and publishing ventures, whose lack of success laid the foundation for debts that plagued him for the rest of his life.

In 1829 Balzac published his first novel under his own name, *Le Dernier Chouan* (later *Les Chouans*), and the *Physiologie du mariage*. In 1830 came a collection of six stories called *Scènes de la vie privée*. Self-styled 'de Balzac', he became fashionable in the literary and social world of Paris, and over the next twenty years, as well as plays and articles, wrote more than ninety novels and stories. In 1842 many of these were published in seventeen volumes as the *Comédie humaine*. Important works were still to come, but ill-health interfered with his creativity and marred the last years of his life.

In 1832, in his extensive fan-mail, Balzac received a letter from the Polish Countess Hanska, whose elderly husband owned a vast estate in the Ukraine. The next year he met Madame Hanska in Switzerland, and in 1835 the couple agreed to marry after Count Hanski's death. For seventeen years, with intermissions, they conducted a voluminous correspondence, until their marriage finally took place in March 1850. Balzac died three months later in Paris.

A. J. KRAILSHEIMER is Emeritus Student and was Tutor in French at Christ Church, Oxford from 1957 until his retirement in 1988. His published work is mostly on the sixteenth and seventeenth centuries, but among his translations are Flaubert's *Three Tales* (also in the World's Classics), *Salammbô*, and *Bouvard et Pécuchet*.

THE WORLD'S CLASSICS

HONORÉ DE BALZAC

Père Goriot

Translated with an Introduction and Notes by
A. J. KRAILSHEIMER

Oxford   New York
OXFORD UNIVERSITY PRESS

Oxford University Press, Walton Street, Oxford OX2 6DP

Oxford New York
Athens Auckland Bangkok Bombay
Calcutta Cape Town Dar es Salaam Delhi
Florence Hong Kong Istanbul Karachi
Kuala Lumpur Madras Madrid Melbourne
Mexico City Nairobi Paris Singapore
Taipei Tokyo Toronto

and associated companies in
Berlin Ibadan

Oxford is a trade mark of Oxford University Press

Chronology © Sylvia Raphael 1990
Translation and other editorial material
© A. J. Krailsheimer 1991

First published as a World's Classics paperback 1991

British Library Cataloguing in Publication Data

Data available

Library of Congress Cataloging in Publication Data
Balzac, Honoré de, 1799-1850.
[Père Goriot/Honoré de Balzac; translated with an introduction
and notes by A. J. Krailsheimer.
p. cm.—(The World's classics)
Includes bibliographical references.
I. Krailsheimer, A. J. II. Title. III. Series.
PQ2168.A35 1991 843'.7—dc20 91-2434
ISBN 0-19-282858-4

5 7 9 10 8 6 4

Printed in Great Britain by
BPC Paperbacks Ltd.
Aylesbury, Bucks

CONTENTS

CONTENTS

INTRODUCTION

SINCE 1842 most of Balzac's novels and stories have been published under the collective title *la Comédie humaine*, and the sight of all these volumes aligned on the shelf (ten in the currently most compact edition) may well daunt the reader anxious to make Balzac's acquaintance but unsure where to begin. *Père Goriot* was written in 1834–5, well before this vast project had taken definite shape, and even the most conscientious reader should have no qualms about approaching it as an autonomous work in its own right. It is true that *Père Goriot* affords an exceptionally good introduction to many of Balzac's other novels, not only because it was the first to make extensive use of recurrent characters, but also because several of the main characters in the book are actually those which reappear elsewhere with greatest frequency. That said, the reader would be well advised to forget the complexities of the *Comédie humaine* and enjoy *Père Goriot* in the quite specific terms in which Balzac presents his work. The opening paragraph refers several times to the 'drama' that is to follow (the word 'comédie' in fact corresponds more closely to the English 'drama' or 'theatre' than to any suggestion of the comic; compare Dante's *Divine Comedy*); and claims that it is 'not fiction or romance. *All is true.*' Balzac also wonders at the outset whether anyone but a Parisian will really understand the drama, and concludes the first, and longest, of the book's four sections with the words: 'here ends the exposition of this obscure but appalling Parisian tragedy.' From exposition to denouement the tragedy of *Père Goriot* moves within clearly defined limits of time and place, focusing on the eponymous protagonist an action which is self-contained and final.

The book is not just 'a slice of life' or series of case histories, it is, just like *King Lear* with which it at once invites comparison, the story of a father and his children and of events that lead inexorably to a tragic outcome. While a goodly number of other characters appear on scene, and in the case of Vautrin dominate the action for a time, it is Goriot's fate that sustains interest and excites emotion. It is convenient to look at the work under the traditional headings of time, place and motivation (or character).

As originally conceived by Balzac the story would have begun in 1824, but he altered this to 1819, whence a few anachronisms of minor importance. More precisely, we are told that the drama begins at the end of November 1819, and it ends with Goriot's death on 18 February 1820 and his funeral the following day. Even within this brief period of three months, the action is concentrated into much briefer periods of a day or two at a time—the whole of the last section extends from the morning of 15 February to the evening of 19 February—and references to 'next day', 'that evening', or 'just at that moment' signal the passage of time rather than 'next week' or 'next month'. In other words, the feeling of impending crisis is reinforced by a series of deadlines and ultimatums. It is no doubt significant that the season of the book's composition, from late September 1834 to late January 1835, coincides with the damp and cold so often mentioned in the novel.

This relationship between time in the novel and in external reality takes on further significance from the choice of 1819, rather than the original 1824, for the fictional action. In 1819 Balzac was the same age as Rastignac, he too was living in straitened circumstances in Paris, and graduated in law that year. Balzac's own sentimental and social education began in 1822, when Madame de Berry, then at 45 twice his age, became his mistress and treated him to first-hand accounts of life at Court under Louis XVI. Three years later, in 1825, he added the Duchesse d'Abrantès (fifteen years his senior) to his amorous conquests, and from her acquired still more familiarity with aristocratic ways, private and public. Thus the sentimental and worldly education of Rastignac, the loss of his youthful innocence, the growth of his ambition, the role of older women and resentment at the constraints of poverty are all concentrated for dramatic purposes into a much shorter span than Balzac's own experience, but none the less are set in a year and state of mind which the author, fifteen years later, could readily recall. Rastignac is however not Balzac, and it would be quite wrong to seek direct autobiographical identification in this or any other Balzac novel.

The element of hindsight is not merely personal; the irony of history, fifteen years on, mocks the complacency of those whose social certainties are proved false by events and the folly of those whose financial speculations lead to ruin. Born in 1799, Balzac had lived under the rule of Napoleon, first as Consul, then as Emperor, until the battle of Waterloo brought back the Bourbons, but like Rastignac he had grown up with a parental generation for whom the *ancien régime*, the Revolution and the Terror were recent and vivid memories. By 1819, only four years after Napoleon's downfall, there were plenty of people, especially in Paris, who like the restored Bourbons and émigrés had forgotten nothing and probably learned very little. By 1834 they knew better; the July Revolution of 1830 had once more, less bloodily, sent the Bourbons on their travels. Not many had the supple versatility of a Talleyrand, and while exile or the guillotine no longer threatened those who had thrown in their lot with the losing side, professional and social ruin was all too real a danger. The unnamed Napoleonic prefect, reduced to penury at the Restoration, who steers Rastignac through his first game of roulette, Madame Couture, widow of a Commissary General, and many other minor characters are the other side of a social coin which could equally well have come down heads or tails. Finally, it is not only the young, with their heady dreams of a future full of riches and success, who are at risk, but those of riper years whose wishful thinking springs from memories of a past gone beyond recall.

In dramatic terms, place is as important as time. The first

sentence of the book introduces a geographical location of
the utmost precision, the boarding-house in the rue Neuve-
Sainte-Geneviève, between the Latin Quarter and the seedy
Faubourg Saint-Marcel, and from the first to the last sentence
of the book the geography of Paris plays a major role. At
the immediate visual level it is the décor of the Maison
Vauquer, reinforced by its smell, that is the focus of attention,
and the greater part of the action is played out within its
precincts. The Beauséant mansion, scene of two crucial
episodes, represents the opposite pole of elegance and amenity,
while further contrast is provided by descriptions of the
Restaud and Nucingen residences, and by the apartment in
the rue d'Artois which Rastignac hardly has time to use. These
various interiors are not merely a backcloth for the action,
they are part of it and intimately linked with the actors. The
zoological notion of habitat applies most obviously to the
Maison Vauquer, but to the extent that all the action is laid
in Paris, where the corruption of a great city conditions all
who live there, high and low, habitat in a physical sense is
of great importance. The claustrophobic squalor of the *pension*
is graduated, from the shared seediness of the public rooms,
through the threadbare respectability of the best apartments
to the sordid wretchedness of those occupied by Goriot and
Rastignac. The whole house, and garden, is the expression
of Madame Vauquer's personality, for she alone is permanently resident. The shifting student population is not, by
definition, at home there, it is just a staging point, but this
is true too for longer-term residents like Madame Couture
or Goriot, for whom loss of a real home, through bereavement
or other disaster, means living provisionally, but indefinitely,
in borrowed quarters, in the company of others whom they
would not have chosen and in a setting over which they have
minimal control.

At the other extreme, the opulent vulgarity of the Nucingen
residence, and the impeccable elegance of the Hôtel de Beauséant, are as much expressions of social standing and personal
taste as is the pension. It is noteworthy that Rastignac, so

eager for a place of his own, is overjoyed when presented with an apartment furnished and equipped by Delphine and her father without his knowledge. One wonders what he would have chosen if left to his own devices, and with appropriate funds.

For dramatic purposes interiors are of more immediate importance than geography, but in the wider fictional context décor and address very much go together. The shabbiness of the rue Neuve-Sainte-Geneviève, the expensive ostentation of the Chaussée-d'Antin (recalling the style of a café, and Delphine's rooms those of a courtesan, according to Balzac), the effortless perfection of the Faubourg Saint-Germain represent three different worlds whose inhabitants cannot migrate at will, if at all. As if to emphasize the social barriers, much is made of doors, open or closed. At the bottom of the scale the door of the pension is closed on the boarders at night like that of a prison (and they are indeed likened to convicts); the ex-convict Vautrin alone is allowed a master-key which enables him to enter or leave at will. Higher up the scale exclusivity replaces incarceration; Rastignac's kinship with Madame de Beauséant also opens the door of the Restaud's house, but he makes such a disastrous gaffe on his first visit that thereafter he finds the door permanently barred to him. The upstart Alsatian Baron de Nucingen, like other financiers in the Chaussée-d'Antin, may be more wealthy than the old aristocracy of the Faubourg Saint-Germain (though his wealth is insecure), yet it is only through Rastignac's intervention that Delphine (but not her husband) at last receives the coveted invitation to the Hôtel de Beauséant. The Restauds, whose lineage puts them in the Beauséant orbit, do in fact live in the rue du Helder, strictly in the Chaussée-d'Antin, but socially on another plane, so that the two sisters are neighbours only in a geographical sense. A glimpse of yet another world is offered in Goriot's past history, while he was still in trade. Living in the rue de la Jussienne, in the quartier of the Halles, he was not only happy with his family, he counted for something. Everyone knew him, had

seen him rise from labourer to prosperous merchant, and
his physical strength as well as his business acumen ensured
him respect. It is only when he and his daughters are uprooted,
when his retirement and their respective marriages remove
them only a short distance from their origins, that everything
goes wrong.

Claustrophobia and solitude are the keynotes of the book's
final section. Rejected by his daughters and fellow boarders
alike, Goriot is confined by physical collapse to his dreadful
room, attended only by two penniless students. But by an
irony that is perhaps less obvious that same final section also
includes a social death, that of Madame de Beauséant, equally
claustrophobic and solitary in every respect that matters.
Compelled by the duties of hostess to preside over a ball
arranged weeks beforehand, Madame de Beauséant is no more
able to escape than Goriot. She is, like the executioner's victim
in the place de Grève or the Roman gladiator with whom
she is compared, a spectacle for more than a thousand guests,
'all Paris', playing her part with dignity and with death in
her heart until the reception is at last over. A further twist
of irony leaves her totally isolated amid the vast and glittering
throng except for two loyal friends, one of whom is Rastignac.
The symmetry and paradox is emphasized when she leaves
'the world', her world, in her coach, and bids him farewell
last of all, whereupon he returns to the pension to attend
the last moments of Goriot. The open door of the Hôtel
de Beauséant, the hundreds of guests who had coveted an
invitation to this most exclusive event, the blaze of publicity
pin down Madame de Beauséant as cruelly as poverty, sickness,
and abandonment pin down Goriot.

The use of time and place to concentrate attention on the
inner drama is a familiar theatrical device transposed to the
novel. A third element of equal importance is the theme of
money. Again from first to last the book stresses the power
of money, the humiliation and wretchedness of having too
little, the obsession with acquiring more, the frightening vola-
tility of wealth, and the moral bankruptcy of a society where

human relations all have their own price. In the last few lines of the book Rastignac, unable to find a mere five francs to tip the gravedigger, is obliged to borrow the trifling sum from Christophe. We are told he is so upset by this that he falls into a deep depression, from which he eventually recovers to issue his resounding challenge to society. Goriot in his dying delirium raves about going to Odessa to make enough money to buy back his daughters' affection, even if it is only simulated. The dandies who win and lose thousands of francs at the gaming tables, the society women who resort to the basest expedients to make up for their chronic shortage of cash, the financiers who swindle naïve and trusting victims, police informers, thieves like Vautrin, even the clergy at Goriot's funeral, reciting only the prayers to which their fee obliges them, from top to bottom of the social scale money is what counts. There are exceptions: Madame de Beauséant is so rich she does not need to worry about money, Bianchon has an authentic medical vocation and is content at the prospect of succeeding his father in a modestly remunerated country practice, but even the most morally virtuous, like Madame Couture and Victorine, or Rastignac's female relatives, are always worried, and sometimes desperate about making both ends meet. Interest rates and bills of exchange, pawnshops and gambling houses, money inherited or money stolen, in Balzac's fictional world (as in his own life) financial dealings honeycomb society at every level. Romantic ideals of pure and disinterested love have to compete with the reality of a world where everything apparently has its price. It is not only love, however, but, at the most fundamental level, respect that is determined by money.

Goriot's carefully amassed fortune enabled him to marry his daughters to husbands of their choice. So long as he looked a likely source of further wealth his snobbish daughters and their husbands were prepared to overlook his lack of education and social graces. When he first comes to the pension his clothes, his silver and his prosperous appearance send Madame Vauquer into dreams of matchmaking. When this

plan comes to nothing, she turns against him, but only after
two years, when his financial situation has forced him to move
into a cheaper room, do she and the other boarders drop
the formal title 'Monsieur' and henceforth call him just 'Père
Goriot.' This has usually been translated as 'old Goriot',
which implies a familiarity ranging from the almost affectionate to the rudely contemptuous, but such a rendering loses
all sense of the irony implied in the literal meaning of 'father'.
His impoverishment is due to the continuous and insatiable
demands of his daughters, and though the other boarders see
the young women arrive in so many changes of costume that
two are taken for a multitude, no one believes him when
he says that they are his daughters. His lengthy and passionate
speeches on what it means to be a father, Balzac's not wholly
felicitous description of him as 'Christ of Fatherhood', the
constant emphasis throughout the book on the theme of
paternity, charge the dismissive nickname 'Père Goriot' with
an emotional load that 'Old Goriot' completely fails to convey. That is why in the title as in the text the form 'Père
Goriot' has been consistently used throughout this version.

A word should be said of Balzac's use of dramatic irony.
Characters are constantly being told the truth about their
situation only to ignore it: Madame de Beauséant dismisses
the warning of her friend the Duchesse de Langeais that her
lover, the Marquis d'Ajuda, and Mademoiselle de Rochefide
are to marry as unfounded rumour and covert malice some
weeks before it comes about, and she, like Rastignac, remains
sceptical until the very day of the marriage contract, which
happens to be that of the grand ball. Just after Poiret and
Michonneau have accepted the drug from the detective by
which Vautrin's identity is to be established, Vautrin himself
drugs Goriot and Rastignac to prevent them interfering in
the Taillefer duel, but the wine-induced merrymaking with
which he covers his treatment of these two also provokes
him into insulting Michonneau, with the result that he in
turn is given the drug next morning which she had earlier
been hesitating to administer. As the pace quickens, and the

events of the last two sections occupy only a few days, irony is intensified. Goriot's last words to Rastignac at the end of the third section are 'Tomorrow we begin our life of happiness', by moving out of the pension into the new apartment. Next morning, the visit of his daughters lays him low just as he is all ready to leave. A strange verbal coincidence makes him challenge Restaud in precisely the same words as those used by Rastignac in his final challenge to society: 'It's between the two of us!' The greatest irony of all is the delusion with which he dies, that the two weeping figures by his bedside are his daughters rather than the two students who have spent their last penny to ease his passing.

Dramatic irony arises from the blindness of the characters involved, but in the novel this blindness is of will rather than vision. The central character, Goriot, shows in his dying revelations that he has been fully aware of the essentially self-interested nature of his daughters' feelings and even that he himself has made them what they are by spoiling them uncritically from their earliest childhood. He goes so far as to admit that simply to have them at his side would make his dying moments happy, even if nothing but the lure of more money has attracted them. He is lucid, but helpless, one of those monomaniacs whom Vautrin accurately identifies, and whom reason cannot cure because the defect is one of will. His deification of fatherhood, and his disturbing appeals to God as Father, followed by bitter complaints, show a mind deranged. He starts from a natural, and admirable, principle, that of paternal love, but ends by destroying not only himself but, morally, the objects of a love, so distorted as to be terrifying—like the Inquisitor praying for the soul of the heretic he has committed to the flames. Goriot is not worried at the thought of going back to the bread and water diet of his early years, but money is the only remedy he can think of for his daughters' self-induced needs, and there they agree with him.

As for Rastignac, through whose eyes the whole drama is seen, he is as yet too young to be obsessed incurably, but we see in him the same mixture of moral lucidity and failure of will. His exploitation of his sisters, mother, and aunt is too childish to command censure, his conscience tender enough to make him plan to warn the odious Taillefer (though prevented by Vautrin's opiate), but it is soon quietened when Delphine beckons. Characters as different as Madame de Beauséant and Goriot recognize in him someone they can trust, but he is still unformed as the novel ends, and the concluding sentence leaves one with a sense of unresolved ambiguity.

Much the most impressive character is Vautrin, for whom ambiguity is a way of life. From his own mouth, as well as from the detective, we learn that for all his suggestive bravado his deepest feelings are not for women, but for handsome young men. He accepted conviction for forgery to save the true criminal, a young Italian 'of whom he was very fond', but his own criminal past and future are hardly in doubt. He gives cynically realistic advice to Rastignac, for whom his affection is clearly genuine, and is almost literally the Devil's advocate, but he is as passionately loyal to his friends as he is contemptuous of society, its laws and its establishment, including the church. His sheer energy and dignity, particularly at the moment of his arrest, compel admiration, or at least respect, but do nothing to resolve the ambiguity. It is known that Balzac modelled the character at least in part on a former convict, Vidocq, who rose to be head of a police department staffed largely by former criminals, and whom Balzac knew personally.

Delphine de Nucingen and Anastasie de Restaud continue the ambiguity. They are what they are because of their father's initial indulgence of their whims, and then because their respective marriages impose standards of social behaviour which encourage illusion and deception, eventually leading each of them into the arms of a lover as selfish, irresponsible, and silly as they are. Only when Delphine begins to feel something deeper for Rastignac do we get a hint of what she might have been, and might yet become, if exposed to the right influences for long enough, but in reality she, like her sister, leaves an impression of an inner emptiness like that of the carriages bearing their coat-of-arms at their father's funeral. We are invited from the start to see that they never had a chance, marrying out of their class into a corrupt society. Their frivolity can hardly be held against them, distasteful as its effect is dramatically.

Madame de Beauséant and Bianchon have already been noted as exceptions to the general rule concerning money and ambition, and it is useful to have such explicitly good characters in such a book as this. A more highly coloured character is Madame Vauquer, *née* de Conflans. She identifies herself with her boarding house; when it is suddenly emptied of so many lodgers she feels personally diminished. She wants to be thought well of, and combines financial carefulness with almost incredible gullibility—the very model of a confidence trickster's victim. She cannot bring herself to believe that Vautrin, the life and soul of her house and her boisterous companion, is truly a convict, any more than she can for a long time accept that Goriot could have such elegant daughters. She is superstitious rather than religious, indifferent to politics, a remote spectator of the most catastrophic public events, vain, avaricious, the stereotype Parisian bourgeois woman. With all that, one senses a crude and conformist kindness, a capacity for jollity and fun, which put her on the positive rather than the negative side of the ledger.

In *Père Goriot*, as in all his novels, Balzac is much given to moralizing in a rhetorical and often even embarrassing way. His comparison of Goriot and Christ is only the most striking of many such incongruous observations. Questions of taste apart, these remarks are not, as it were, an optional extra, a literary flourish, but must be seen in the context of his enthusiasm for scientific explanations of human behaviour. In his foreword to the first collected (but still incomplete) edition of the *Comédie humaine* Balzac wrote, 'There is only one animal. The creator used one and the same pattern for all organized being. The animal is a principle whose outward form, or, more exactly, differences in that form derive from the environment in which it is required to develop. Zoological species are the result of these differences.' He then acknowledges his debt to Geoffroy de Saint-Hilaire (to whom the Furne edition of *Père Goriot* is dedicated) for propounding and demonstrating this theory, and goes on to explain how he realized that Society in this respect resembled Nature: 'Is it not Society which makes of man, according to the environment in which he operates, as many different men as there are varieties in zoology? ... There are thus, and always will be, Social Species as there are Zoological Species.'

The relevance of this quotation hardly needs underlining. What interests Balzac is cause and effect, environment more than heredity, and behavioural rather than ethical categories. That is why Delphine and Anastasie are explained rather than condemned like another Regan and Goneril, why Goriot's obsession is traced from his early years as a labourer, why Rastignac is shown at the very moment when a pupa becomes a butterfly under the stimulus of a new environment. What in any other author would be mere preaching or judgement in Balzac is the irresistible urge to categorize individuals and their reactions with reference to better-known examples of the same species. His generalizations about 'the Southerner' or 'Parisian women', his endorsement of Gall's theory of phrenology as a guide to character and all the rest are attempts to present objectively phenomena to which the reader will be more likely to respond emotionally. The paradox is that no amount of scientific jargon can stop us feeling for Oedipus, or Lear, or Goriot, as suffering human beings rather than classic examples of species doomed by scientific logic. All is indeed true in Balzac, but the truth is rainbow-hued, not plain black and white.

NOTE ON THE TEXT

The text used for this translation is that published in the *Folio* series by Gallimard (1971), which follows that of the Furne edition (1842–8), corrected by Jean Ducourneau in his edition of 1966 and by Pierre-Georges Castex in his of 1963. The main difference from the Furne edition is the division of the novel into sections, as in the original edition of 1834–5, which Furne suppressed for reasons of economy of space but which Balzac is said to have wanted.

NOTE ON THE TEXT

The text used for this translation is that published in the Folio series by Gallimard (1971), which follows that of the Furne edition (1842–8), corrected by Jean Ducourneau in his edition of 1966 and by Pierre-Georges Castex in his of 1964. The main difference from the Furne edition is the division of the novel into sections, as in the original edition of 1841–3, which Furne suppressed for reasons of economy of space but which Balzac is said to have wanted.

SELECT BIBLIOGRAPHY

(i) *Biography*

André Maurois, *Prometheus: the Life of Balzac*, Bodley Head, London, 1965

H. J. Hunt, *Honoré de Balzac: a Biography*, Athlone Press, London, 1957; reprinted and updated, Greenwood Press, New York, 1969

(ii) *General studies*

P. Bertaut, *Balzac and the Human Comedy*, New York University Press, 1963

H. J. Hunt, *Balzac's 'Comédie humaine'*, Athlone Press, London, 1964

E. J. Oliver, *Honoré de Balzac*, Weidenfeld and Nicholson, London, 1965

F. W. J. Hemmings, *Balzac: an interpretation of la Comédie humaine*, Random House, New York, 1967

F. Marceau, *Balzac and his World*, W. H. Allen, London, 1967

V. S. Pritchett, *Balzac*, Chatto and Windus, London, 1973

D. Festa-McCormick, *Honoré de Balzac*, Twayne's World Authors Series, Boston, 1979

(iii) *On 'Père Goriot'*

Erich Auerbach, *Mimesis* (part of ch. 18, 'In the Hotel de la Môle', an analysis of a passage describing the Maison Vauquer), trans. W. Trask, Doubleday Anchor, New York, 1957

David Bellos, *Honoré de Balzac, 'Old Goriot'*, Landmarks of World Literature, Cambridge University Press, 1987

A CHRONOLOGY OF HONORÉ DE BALZAC

1799	Born at Tours, the son of Bernard-François Balzac and his wife Anne-Charlotte-Laure Sallambier. Put out to nurse till he is four.
1804	Sent as a boarder to the Pension Le Guay, Tours.
1807–13	A boarder at the Oratorian college in Vendôme.
1814	Restoration of the Bourbon monarchy in France with the accession of Louis XVIII. The Balzac family moves to Paris, where Honoré continues his education.
1815	Flight of Louis XVIII on Napoleon's escape from Elba, but second Restoration of the Bourbons after Napoleon's defeat at Waterloo.
1816	Honoré becomes a law student and works in a lawyer's office.
1819	Becomes a Bachelor of Law. The family moves to Villeparisis on the retirement of Bernard-François Balzac. Honoré stays in Paris, living frugally at the rue Lesdiguières, in an effort to start a career as a writer. He writes a tragedy, *Cromwell*, which is a failure.
1820–5	Writes various novels, some in collaboration, none of which he signs with his own name.
1822	Beginning of his liaison with forty-five-year-old Laure de Berny, who remains devoted to him till her death in 1836.
1825–8	Tries to make money by printing and publishing ventures, which fail and saddle him with debt.
1829	Publication of *Le Dernier Chouan*, the first novel he signs with his own name and the first of those to be incorporated in the *Comédie humaine*. Publication of the *Physiologie du mariage*.
1830	Publication of *Scènes de la vie privée*. Revolution in

France resulting in the abdication of Charles X and the accession of Louis-Philippe.

1831   Works hard as a writer and adopts a luxurious, society life-style which increases his debts. Publication of *La Peau de chagrin* and some of the *Contes philosophiques*.

1832   Beginning of correspondence with Madame Hanska. Publication of more 'Scènes de la vie privée' and of *Louis Lambert*. Adds 'de' to his name and becomes 'de Balzac'.

1833   Meets Madame Hanska for the first time in Neuchâtel, Switzerland, and then in Geneva. Signs a contract for *Études de mœurs au XIXᵉ siècle*, which appears in twelve volumes between 1833 and 1837, and is divided into 'Scènes de la vie privée', 'Scènes de la vie de province', and 'Scènes de la vie parisienne'. Publication of *Le Médecin de campagne* and the first 'Scènes de la vie de province', which include *Eugénie Grandet*.

1834   Publication of *La Recherche de l'absolu* and the first 'Scènes de la vie parisienne'.

1834–5 Publication of *Le Père Goriot*.

1835   Publication of collected *Études philosophiques* (1835–40). Meets Madame Hanska in Vienna, the last time for eight years.

1836   Publication of *Le Lys dans la vallée* and other works. Starts a journal, *La Chronique de Paris*, which ends in failure.

1837   Journey to Italy. Publication of *La Vieille Fille*, the first part of *Illusions perdues*, and *César Birotteau*.

1838   Publication of *La Femme supérieure* (*Les Employés*) and *La Torpille*, which becomes the first part of *Splendeurs et misères des courtisanes*.

1839   Becomes president of the Société des Gens de Lettres. Publication of six more works, including *Le Cabinet des antiques* and *Béatrix*.

1840   Publication of more works, including *Pierrette*.

1841   Makes an agreement with his publisher, Furne, and booksellers for the publication of the *Comédie humaine*. Publication of more works, including *Le Curé de village*.

1842   Publication of the *Comédie humaine*, with its important
             introduction, in seventeen volumes (1842–8); one post-
             humous volume is published in 1855. Publication of
             other works, including *Mémoires de deux jeunes mariées*,
             Ursule Mirouet, and *La Rabouilleuse*.

1843   More publications, including *La Muse du département*,
             and the completion in three parts of *Illusions perdues*.
             Visits Madame Hanska (widowed since 1841) at St
             Petersburg.

1844   Publication of *Modeste Mignon*, of the beginning of *Les
             Paysans*, of the second part of *Béatrix*, and of the second
             part of *Splendeurs et misères des courtisanes*.

1845   Travels in Europe with Madame Hanska and her
             daughter and future son-in-law.

1846   Stays in Rome and travels in Switzerland and Germany
             with Madame Hanska. A witness at the marriage of
             her daughter. Birth to Madame Hanska of a still-born
             child, who was to have been called Victor-Honoré. Pub-
             lication of *La Cousine Bette* and of the third part of
             Splendeurs et misères des courtisanes.

1847   Madame Hanska stays in Paris from February till May.
             Publication of *Le Cousin Pons* and of the last part of
             Splendeurs et misères des courtisanes.

1848   Revolution in France resulting in the abdication of
             Louis-Philippe and the establishment of the Second
             Republic. Balzac goes to the Ukraine to stay with
             Madame Hanska and remains there till the spring of
             1850.

1849   His health deteriorates seriously.

1850   Marriage of Balzac and Madame Hanska on 14 March.
             He returns with her to Paris on 20 May and dies on
             18 August.

1869–76   Definitive edition of the *Œuvres complètes* in twenty-
             four volumes, published by Michel-Lévy and then by
             Calmann-Lévy.

PÈRE GORIOT

A Family Boarding House

MADAME VAUQUER, *née* de Conflans, is an old woman who for the past forty years has run a family boarding house in the rue Neuve-Sainte-Geneviève,* between the Latin Quarter and the Faubourg Saint-Marceau. The boarding house, known as the Maison Vauquer, is open alike to men and women, young and old, but no breath of scandal has ever sullied the reputation of this respectable establishment. It is also true that for thirty years no young female person has ever been seen there, and any young man who stays there must be getting a very meagre allowance from his family. All the same, in 1819 when this drama begins an impoverished young woman was living there. However discredited the word 'drama' may have become through incorrect, strained and extravagant use in these days of harrowing literature, it must be employed here; not that this story is dramatic in the true sense of the word, but by the end of this work the reader will perhaps have shed a tear or two *intra muros* and *extra*. Will anyone understand it outside Paris? That is open to doubt. The special features of this scene, full of local colour and observations, can only be appreciated in the area lying between the heights of Montmartre and the hills of Montrouge, in that illustrious valley of flaking plasterwork and gutters black with mud; a valley full of suffering that is real, and of joy that is often false, where life is so hectic that it takes something quite extraordinary to produce feelings that last. One can however occasionally encounter sorrows to which the concentration of vice and virtue imparts a solemn grandeur. At such a sight egoism and self-interest are momentarily forgotten and give way to pity, but the impression lasts no longer than the taste

of a fruit greedily swallowed. The chariot of civilization, like
that of some juggernaut, may be briefly impeded when a heart
less easily broken than most jams its wheels, but soon crushes
it and rolls on in triumph. You will do likewise, holding
this book in soft white hands, sinking into a comfortable
armchair with the thought, 'Perhaps I'll enjoy this one.' After
reading about the secret misfortunes of Père Goriot, you will
eat your dinner with relish, blaming the author for your insen-
sibility, charging him with exaggeration, accusing him of
poetic licence, but, let me tell you, this drama is not fiction
or romance. *All is true.** So true that everyone can recognize
its elements in his own circle, perhaps in his own heart.

The boarding house is the property of Madame Vauquer.
It stands at the bottom of the rue Neuve-Sainte-Geneviève,
just where the ground slopes down towards the rue de
l'Arbalète so suddenly and steeply that horses rarely pass up
or down. This helps to preserve the habitual silence of the
streets squeezed between the dome of the Val de Grâce and
that of the Panthéon, two monuments which charge the whole
surrounding atmosphere with sombre yellow hues reflecting
the austere tones of their cupolas which overshadow everything. The paving stones there are dry, the gutters empty
of mud or water, weeds grow along the walls. All who pass
by, even the most carefree, feel depressed there, the sound
of a vehicle is an event, the houses are gloomy, the walls
like a prison. A Parisian straying there would see nothing
but boarding houses or institutions, poverty or boredom, the
old approaching death, boisterous youth condemned to toil.
No district in Paris is more forbidding, nor, it must be said,
less well known. The rue Neuve-Sainte-Geneviève in particular is like a bronze frame, the only one appropriate to this
tale, for which the mind can best prepare itself by dwelling
on dark colours and solemn thoughts; just as the visitor to
the Catacombs finds the daylight fade with every downward
step and the guide's singsong voice grow more hollow. The
comparison is realistic. How can one decide which is more
horrible to see, withered hearts or empty skulls?

The front of the house looks on to a small garden, so that the building is set at right angles to the rue Neuve-Sainte-Geneviève, where you see its depth in cross-section. Along the façade, between house and garden, runs a sunken strip of gravel a couple of yards wide, with a sandy path in front, lined with geraniums, oleanders, and pomegranate trees planted in big blue and white earthenware pots. Access to this path is by a gate, above which is a board bearing the legend: MAISON VAUQUER, and, below that, *Boarding house for persons of both sexes and others*. In the daytime an openwork gate with a clamorous bell attached allows a glimpse of a green marble arch at the end of the pathway, painted by a local artist on the wall facing the street. Under the recess simulated by this painting stands a statue representing Love. Those who are keen on symbolism might discern in the peeling varnish that covers this statue a figuration of that Parisian love for which treatment is provided not far away.* Under the plinth a half-erased inscription recalls the period from which this ornament dates, with its evident enthusiasm for Voltaire,* who returned to Paris in 1777:

> Whoever you may be, behold your master
> He is, or was, or is to be so.

At nightfall the openwork gate is replaced by a solid door. The garden, as broad as the façade is long, is enclosed by the street wall and the party wall of the house next door, completely concealed by a curtain of ivy, which catches the eye of passers-by as being rather picturesque for Paris. Each of these walls is draped with espaliers and vines, producing shrivelled dusty fruit, over which Madame Vauquer worries each year and which she discusses with her lodgers. Along each wall runs a narrow path, leading to a clump of lime trees which Madame Vauquer, though a de Conflans by birth, persists in pronouncing 'loime', despite the linguistic strictures of her guests. Between the two side paths is a bed of artichokes, with a border of sorrel, lettuce, and parsley, flanked by fruit trees cut back top and bottom. Under the limes is set a round table, painted green, with seats all round it. There, at the height of summer, guests rich enough to afford it come to enjoy a cup of coffee in a temperature hot enough to make eggs hatch. The façade, three storeys high with attics on top, is built of quarry stone and colour washed in that shade of yellow which so demeans almost all the houses in Paris. There are five windows on each floor, with small panes and fitted with blinds that are all set at different levels, spoiling the symmetry. The building is two windows deep, and these, on the ground floor, are adorned with iron bars covered in mesh. Behind the house is a yard about twenty feet wide, where pigs, chickens and rabbits consort together, and at the back stands a wood-shed. Between this shed and the kitchen window hangs the meat-safe, beneath which the greasy water from the sink runs out. There is a narrow door to this yard onto the rue Neuve-Sainte-Geneviève, through which the cook disposes of all the household rubbish, sluicing clean this dirt trap with gallons of water to prevent a noisome stench.

Naturally suited to use as a boarding house, the ground floor comprises a first room lit by the two windows on the street side, with access through a French window. This drawing-room opens on to a dining-room, separated from the kitchen by the stairwell. The stairs are wood, with coloured, polished tiles. There could be no more depressing sight than this drawing-room, with its armchairs and upright chairs covered in haircloth with alternate matt and shiny stripes. In the middle stands a round table, with a Sainte-Anne marble top, displaying one of those white china coffee sets with gold tracery almost rubbed away which you find everywhere nowadays. The floor of the room is rather badly laid; panelling extends to shoulder height, above which the walls are covered with shiny paper depicting the principal scenes from *Télémaque*,* with the classical characters in colour. The panel between the meshed windows presents the boarders with a picture of the banquet given by Calypso for Ulysses' son. For forty years this painting has provoked humorous sallies from the younger residents, who try to demonstrate their superiority by making fun of the fare to which their penury condemns them. The stone mantelpiece, beneath which a permanently clean hearth bears witness to the fact that a fire is only lit on special occasions, is adorned with two vases of ancient artificial flowers duly ranged on either side of a blue marble clock in execrable taste. This room gives off a smell for which our language has no special word; it can only be described as a *boarding house smell*. It smells stuffy, mouldy, rancid; it is chilly, clammy to breathe, permeates one's clothing; it leaves the stale taste of a room where people have been eating; it stinks of backstairs, scullery, workhouse. It could only be described if some process were invented for measuring the quantity of disgusting elementary particles contributed by each resident, young or old, from his own catarrhal and *sui generis* exhalations. Even so, despite these dull horrors, compared to the dining-room next door the drawing-room seems as elegant and sweet-smelling as a boudoir. That room, panelled throughout, was once painted in a now unidentifiable colour, over which filth has built up in layers to form weird patterns. The walls are lined with sticky sideboards bearing chipped and tarnished decanters, tinplate discs with a shimmery finish, piles of thick china plates with blue borders made in Tournai. In one corner stands a box with numbered pigeonholes in which are kept the boarders' tablenapkins, stained with food or wine. There you will find those indestructible furnishings which everyone else throws out, but which finish up here like the rejects of civilization at the Hospital for Incurables. You would see a barometer with a friar who comes out when it rains, appalling prints which spoil your appetite, all in varnished wooden frames with gilt trimmings; a tortoiseshell wall clock with copper inlay; a green stove, patent Argand lamps on which dust has stuck to the oil, a long table covered with oilcloth greasy enough for a mischievous diner to trace his name on with his fingertip, rickety chairs, pathetic little rush mats which keep unravelling without ever quite disintegrating, wretched footwarmers with broken holes, broken hinges, charred wood. Fully to convey how old, cracked, rotten, rickety, decayed, crippled, crooked, feeble, moribund this furniture is would require a description involving a digression from the interest of this story which impatient readers would find inexcusably long. The red floor-tiles are full of grooves caused by scrubbing or repainting. In a word the drabbest poverty rules supreme; a pennypinching, concentrated, threadbare poverty. Squalor may not yet have taken over, but there are patches of it; all is not yet tattered and torn, but it is rotting away.

This room can be seen in all its glory at about seven o'clock in the morning, when Madame Vauquer's cat precedes its mistress, jumps on to the sideboards, sniffs at a number of bowls of milk covered by plates, and purrs to greet the day. The widow soon appears, decked out in a tulle cap, a switch of artificial hair hanging crookedly below, shuffling along in her creased old slippers. Her nose jutting out like a parrot's beak from the middle of an aged, puffy face, her pudgy little hands, her body as plump as a presbytery cat, her baggy, outsize bodice, are well matched to this room, where misfortune oozes all around, where hope lies low, and where Madame Vauquer breathes the fetid, overheated air without a qualm. Her face, chilly as the first frost of autumn, her wrinkled eyes, whose expression ranges from the fixed smile demanded of ballet dancers to the sullen scowl of the discount broker, her whole person is an explicit comment on the boarding house, just as the boarding house is implicitly suggestive of her. Prison could not exist without warders, the one cannot be conceived of without the other. The pallid corpulence of this dumpy woman is the product of this sort of life, as typhus is caused by the effluvia of a hospital. Her knitted woollen petticoat, showing below the overskirt made from an old dress, with the padding coming out through splits in the worn material, sums up the drawing-room, the dining-room, the garden, gives an idea of the food and some inkling of the boarders. When she is there the spectacle is complete. About 50 years old, Madame Vauquer is like all *women who have been in difficulties*. She has the glassy eye, the innocent air of a bawd preparing to make a scene to get a better price, but who is also ready to do anything to improve her lot, to betray Georges or Pichegru,* were Georges or Pichegru still there to be betrayed. For all that, she is *a good woman at heart*, according to her boarders, who believe her to be without means when they hear her wheezing and coughing like themselves. What had Monsieur Vauquer been? She never discussed her late husband. How had he lost his money? 'Things went wrong', she would reply. He had treated her badly, had left her nothing but eyes for weeping, this house to live in, and the right to be hard-hearted about the misfortunes of others, since, as she would say, she had suffered all that anyone could possibly suffer. When fat Sylvie, the cook, heard her mistress on the move, she hurried to serve breakfast to the resident boarders.

Generally the regulars who did not live in, the outside boarders, signed up only for dinner, which cost thirty francs a month. At the time when this story begins the residents were seven in all. The two best apartments in the house were on the first floor. Madame Vauquer lived in the smaller of the two, and the other belonged to Madame Couture, widow of a Commissary-General of the French Republic. She had with her a very young girl, called Victorine Taillefer, to whom she acted as a mother. These two ladies paid eighteen hundred francs board and lodging. One of the two apartments on the second floor was occupied by an elderly man called Poiret, the other by a man of about 40, who wore a black wig, dyed his whiskers, claimed to have been in trade and went by the name of Monsieur Vautrin. The third floor consisted of four rooms, of which two were let, one to an elderly spinster named Mademoiselle Michonneau, the other to a former manufacturer of vermicelli, Italian pasta, and starch, who answered to the name of Père Goriot.* The two other rooms were kept for birds of passage, penurious students who, like Père Goriot and Mademoiselle Michonneau, could only put by forty-five francs a month for board and lodging, but Madame Vauquer was not too keen on having them, and only took them in when she could find nothing better; they ate too much bread. At the moment one of these two rooms belonged to a young man who had come to Paris from the Angoulême area to study law, and whose large family endured the harshest sacrifices in order to send him twelve hundred francs a year. Eugène de Rastignac, for such was his name, was one of those young men trained by poverty for hard work, who realize from their earliest youth what their parents expect of them, and from the start prepare for a successful career by working out the scope of their studies, adapting them in advance to future trends in society so that they can be the first to exploit it. Without his observant curiosity and the skill with which he contrived to enter on the Parisian social scene, this narrative would have lacked the stamp of authenticity which it surely owes to his shrewdness and his desire to probe the mysteries of a dreadful situation that was carefully concealed both by those who had created it and by the victim of it.

Above the third floor were a drying-loft and two attic rooms occupied by Christophe, the odd-job man, and fat Sylvie, the cook. Besides the seven boarders, Madame Vauquer had, on average, eight students of law or medicine, and two or three regulars who all lived nearby and signed up just for dinner. At dinner-time the dining-room contained eighteen, and could hold twenty, but in the morning there were only the seven boarders, and their breakfast together resembled a family meal. Everyone came down in slippers, and felt free to pass confidential remarks on the dress or appearance of the external regulars and the events of the previous evening, speaking out with an assurance born of intimacy. These seven boarders were Madame Vauquer's spoilt children and the attention and respect she accorded them was calculated with the accuracy of an astronomer according to the amount they paid for their board. One and the same consideration affected all these people who had been brought together by chance. The two tenants on the second floor paid only seventy-two francs a month. Such a bargain price, to be found only in

the Faubourg Saint-Marcel between the Bourbe* and the
Salpêtrière, and applying to everybody except Madame
Couture, indicated that these boarders must be labouring
under the burden of more or less obvious distress. Thus the
depressing sight presented by the interior of the house was
matched by the clothing of its equally run-down residents.
The men wore frock-coats whose original colour could only
be surmised, shoes of the kind that one finds discarded in
the gutter in smart districts, threadbare linen, clothes which
had ceased to have substance. The women wore shabby
dresses, dyed, faded once more, patched up old lace, gloves
worn smooth with use, collars that were always rusty, and
frayed fichus. If their clothes were in such a state, nearly
all of them were solidly built, with constitutions that had
stood up to the buffeting of life, and cold, hard faces rubbed
as blank as obsolete coins. Their withered mouths were armed
with sharp predatory teeth. These boarders hinted at dramas
past or present; not the dramas performed in the glare of
the footlights, against painted backcloths, but living, wordless
dramas, icy dramas to stir and sear the heart, dramas without
end.

The elderly Mademoiselle Michonneau protected her weary
eyes with a grubby green taffeta shade, edged with brass wire,
which would have scared away the angel of pity. Her shawl
with its scraggy, drooping fringes concealed a frame so angular
as to appear skeletal. What corrosive acid had stripped this
creature of all feminine form? She must once have been pretty
and shapely; was it vice, grief, greed? Had she been too generous with her love, had she been a secondhand clothes dealer,
or just a courtesan? Was she expiating the triumphs of a shame-
less youth when pleasures pressed upon her by an old age
from which passers-by recoiled? The blankness of her look
was chilling, her shrunken features full of menace. Her voice
was as shrill as a cricket calling from its bush as winter
approaches. She claimed to have looked after an old gentleman
afflicted with inflammation of the bladder, and forsaken by
his children who believed him to be penniless. This old man

had left her an income of a thousand francs a year for life, which his heirs periodically contested, making slanderous allegations against her. Although her face bore the ravages of passion, it still showed some traces of a fair, delicate complexion which might lead one to suppose that some vestiges of beauty still lingered in her body.

Monsieur Poiret was a kind of automaton. As he crept like a grey shadow along a pathway in the Jardin des Plantes, a limp old cap on his head, a stick with a discoloured ivory handle dangling in his hand, the faded skirts of his coat trailing and barely covering almost empty breeches, blue stockings on legs as shaky as those of a drunkard, displaying a dirty white waistcoat and a crumpled shirt-frill of coarse muslin, which had parted company with the tie strung round his turkey neck, the sight made many people wonder if this silhouette belonged to the same bold tribe as the sons of Japhet* fluttering along the Boulevard des Italiens. What toil could have shrivelled him up like that? What passion had darkened his bulbous features, which would have looked unreal if drawn in a caricature? What had he been? Perhaps he had worked in the Ministry of Justice, in the office to which the public executioners send notes of their expenses, their accounts for providing black veils for parricides, sawdust for the baskets, cord for the blade of the guillotine. Perhaps he had checked admissions at the doors of an abattoir, or been an assistant health inspector. In a word this man seemed to have been one of the donkeys who drive our great social wheel round, one of those Parisian rats who, as in the fable,* do not even know the monkeys who deceive them, a pivot on which public misfortunes or scandals had revolved, in fact one of those men on whom we look and say, 'We need people like that, after all.' The handsome side of Paris knows nothing of these figures of moral and physical suffering. But Paris is a veritable ocean; take as many soundings as you like, you will never know how deep it is. Travel round it, describe it, but no matter how systematic your travels or your description, how numerous and eager the explorers of that sea, there will always be some place untouched, some cave unknown, flowers, pearls, monsters, something unheard of, forgotten by the literary divers. The Maison Vauquer is one of those curious monstrosities.

Two figures stood out in striking contrast from the mass of boarders and regulars. Although Mademoiselle Victorine Taillefer had a sickly pallor like that of girls afflicted with greensickness, and blended in with the general atmosphere of wretchedness which formed the background to this picture, through her habitual melancholy, her pained demeanour and her weak and fragile air, yet her face did not look old, her movements and her voice were still full of life. In her youthful misfortune she resembled a shrub whose leaves have yellowed from being freshly planted in the wrong sort of soil. Her tawny fair hair, the complexion to go with it, her excessive slimness, expressed the kind of grace that modern poets have found in medieval statues. Her dark-flecked grey eyes expressed Christian mildness and resignation. Her simple, inexpensive clothes revealed a youthful figure. She was pretty in contrast to those around her. If she had been happy she would have been beautiful: happiness is the inner poetry of women, just as fine clothes are the mask of beauty. If the delighted excitement of a ball had made these pale features glow; if the comforts of an elegant life had filled out and coloured those already sunken cheeks; if love had brought back a sparkle to those sad eyes, Victorine could have competed with the loveliest of girls. She lacked what gives new life to any woman: dainty clothes and love letters.

Her story would have provided a good subject for a book. Her father thought he was justified in not acknowledging her, refused to let her live in his house, allowed her only six hundred francs a year, and had liquidated his estate so as to be able to leave it entirely to his son. Distantly related to Victorine's mother, who some time ago had come to her home to die of despair, Madame Couture cared for the orphan girl as though she had been her own. Unfortunately the widow of the Commissary-General of the Armies of the Republic owned nothing in the world but her dower and her pension; she might some day have to leave this poor girl, inexperienced and indigent, to the mercy of the world. The good woman took Victorine to Mass every Sunday and to confession every fortnight, so that she would at all events acquire the habits of piety. She did right; religious feelings offered some future to the disowned daughter, who loved her father, and went to his home every year to bring him her mother's forgiveness, only to find every year the door of the paternal home inexorably closed in her face. Her brother, her only intermediary, had not been to see her once in four years, and sent her no help. She begged God to open her father's eyes, to soften her brother's heart, and prayed for them without accusing them of any wrong. Madame Couture and Madame Vauquer could find no words in the dictionary of insults to describe such inhuman behaviour. When they called down curses on this infamous millionaire, Victorine spoke only kind words, like the call of a wounded dove, whose cry of pain still tells of love.

Eugène de Rastignac had the face of a real Southerner, fair complexion, dark hair, blue eyes. His bearing, his manners, his habitual posture all marked him out as the scion of a noble family, in which basic upbringing entailed only traditions of good taste. If he dressed thriftily and on ordinary days went on wearing out last year's clothes, yet he could at times go out dressed like an elegant young man. He usually wore an old frock-coat, a shabby waistcoat, the wretched, frayed, badly tied black tie of the student, trousers to match, and boots that had been resoled.

Between these two individuals and the others, Vautrin, the man of 40 with tinted whiskers, played a bridging role. He was one of those men of whom people commonly say, 'He's a bit of a lad!' He had broad shoulders, a powerful chest, bulging muscles, square, thick hands with tufts of bright red hair sprouting on the knuckles. His face, prematurely lined, indicated a hardness that his easy, friendly manner belied. He had quite a pleasing bass-baritone voice, which went well with his bluff good humour. He was obliging and cheerful. If a lock would not work he would soon have it out, put it right, oil it, file it, and replace it, with the comment, 'That's just my line.' His line in fact extended to ships, the sea, France, foreign parts, business, people, events, the law, hotels, and prisons. If anyone grumbled too much he would instantly offer his services. More than once he had lent money to Madame Vauquer and some of the boarders, but those he had obliged would rather have died than fail to repay him, for, in spite of his good-natured appearance, his way of looking hard and searchingly at people inspired fear. His very manner of spitting declared him to be imperturbably cold-blooded, one who would not shrink from crime to get out of a compromising situation. Like a harsh judge, his eyes seemed to go to the heart of every question, every conscience, every emotion. His custom was to go out after breakfast, return for dinner, disappear for the rest of the evening and come home around midnight, using a master-key which Madame Vauquer had entrusted to him. He was the only one to enjoy such a favour. But he also got on famously with the widow, whom he called 'Ma' as he grasped her round the waist, a tribute she did not fully appreciate! The good woman thought it still easy enough to do, whereas Vautrin alone had arms long enough to encircle her hefty circumference. It was typical of him to pay the handsome sum of fifteen francs a month for the coffee laced with spirits that he took after dinner. Anyone less superficial than the young people who were carried away in the whirl of Parisian life, or the elderly ones who were indifferent to anything not directly concerning them, would have wanted to look further into the dubious impression conveyed by Vautrin. He knew or guessed the business of those around him, whereas no one could penetrate his thoughts or identify his occupations. Although he had erected his ostensible affability, his constant helpfulness and good humour into a barrier between himself and others, he often allowed a glimpse into the fearful depths of his character. Often some quip worthy of Juvenal, suggesting that he revelled in flouting the law, castigating high society, convicting it of inconsistency, invited the conclusion that he bore a grudge against the social system and that some mystery lay carefully buried in his innermost life.

Attracted, perhaps unconsciously, by the older man's strength and the other's good looks, Mademoiselle Taillefer divided her furtive glances and her secret thoughts between the 40-year-old and the young student, but neither of them showed any interest in her, though from one day to the next chance might alter her situation and make her a wealthy match. Besides, none of these individuals bothered to check whether the misfortunes alleged by any one of them were true or false. They all viewed each other with a mixture of mutual indifference and distrust deriving from their respective situations. They knew that they were incapable of relieving the distress of the others, and through telling each other about it they had all emptied the cup of sympathy. Like old married couples, they had nothing left to say to each other. Nothing remained between them therefore but the automatic contacts of daily existence, the interplay of unoiled cogs. They would all no doubt walk straight past a blind man in the street, listen unmoved to the account of some disaster, and see in someone's death the solution to a problem of wretchedness which made them indifferent to the most terrible suffering.

The happiest of these desolate souls was Madame Vauquer, who presided over this private almshouse. For her alone this little garden, which silence and cold, drought and damp made as spacious as a steppe, was a laughing grove. For her alone this dreary, yellow house, with its smell of verdigris like the coins in a counting house, was full of charm. These cells belonged to her. She fed these convicts serving a life sentence, and wielded over them an authority they respected. Where else in Paris would these poor creatures have found at the price she offered sound, adequate food, and an apartment which it was up to them to make, if not elegant or comfortable, at least clean and salubrious? If she had ever allowed herself to behave with blatant injustice, the victim would have endured it without complaint.

Such a collection of people should, and indeed did, present in miniature the elements of society as a whole. Among the eighteen who ate together there was to be found, as in colleges and the wider world, one poor rejected creature, a butt for constant mockery. At the beginning of the second year this figure became for Eugène de Rastignac the most notable of all those with whom he was condemned to live for another two years. This natural victim was the former vermicelli-merchant, Père Goriot, on whose head a painter, like this historian, would have focused all the light in the picture. By what chance had this half-malevolent contempt, this half-pitying persecution, this absence of respect for misfortune, struck the oldest resident? Had he provoked it by ridiculous or eccentric behaviour of the kind that is less easily forgiven than actual vice? Such questions are very relevant to much social injustice. Perhaps it is human nature to spare no torment when the victim accepts any suffering out of genuine humility, weakness or indifference. Do not we all like proving our strength at the expense of someone or something? The feeblest creature, the street urchin, rings all the doorbells when it is freezing outside, or scrambles to write his name on a monument as yet undefiled.

Père Goriot, an old man then aged about 69, had retired to Madame Vauquer's in 1813 when he gave up his business. He had originally rented the apartment now occupied by Madame Couture, at that time paying twelve hundred francs for it, with the air of someone who considered five louis* more or less a trifle. Madame Vauquer had done up the three rooms of this apartment in return for an advance payment, supposedly covering the cost of the tatty furnishings, consisting of yellow calico curtains, armchairs of varnished wood upholstered in Utrecht velvet, some tempera paintings, and wallpaper which even suburban wineshops rejected. Perhaps the carefree generosity with which Père Goriot, at that point respectfully addressed as Monsieur Goriot, fell into the trap made her look on him as an old fool with no head for business.

Goriot arrived with an ample wardrobe, the splendid outfit of a merchant who denies himself nothing when he retires. Madame Vauquer had admired eighteen Dutch linen shirts, whose fine quality was emphasized by the fact that the former vermicelli-merchant wore on his frilly shirt-front two pins each set with a large diamond, linked with a little chain. Usually dressed in a cornflower-blue coat, he changed his white piqué waistcoat every day, and as his massive pearshaped paunch swayed beneath it, a heavy gold chain hung with trinkets bobbed up and down. His snuff-box, also gold, contained a locket full of hair, apparent trophies of more than one amorous conquest. When his hostess accused him of being one for the ladies, he did not repress the slight smirk of the solid citizen whose pet weakness has been indulged. His 'armoires' (which he pronounced 'ormoires' with a working-class accent) were full of his household silver, of which he had a great deal. The widow's eyes lit up when she lent him a helping hand with unpacking and arranging the ladles, serving spoons, knives and forks, cruets, sauce boats, several dishes, silver-gilt breakfast services, in short, more or less handsome pieces of considerable weight, which he did not want to part with. These gifts reminded him of milestones in his family life.

'This', he told Madame Vauquer as he put away a dish and a little bowl whose lid represented two turtle-doves billing and cooing, 'is the first anniversary present I had from my wife. Poor dear! It cost her all she had saved up before our marriage. Do you know, Madame, I would sooner scratch a living from the ground with my bare hands than part with it. Thanks be! Every morning for the rest of my life I can drink my coffee from this bowl. I have no cause to complain, I have enough on my plate to keep from starving for a good while yet.' In fact Madame Vauquer had seen with her own beady eyes some entries in the Register of Government Stock which roughly added up meant that this excellent Goriot had an income of some eight to ten thousand francs a year. From that day forth Madame Vauquer, née de Conflans, whose real age was then 48 but who owned only to 39, began to have ideas. Although Goriot's tear ducts were deformed, swollen and sagging, so that he had to keep wiping them, she found him personable and proper in appearance. Besides, his bulging fleshy calves, as well as his long square nose, betokened moral qualities to which the widow apparently attached importance, and were reinforced by the inane simplicity of the old chap's moon-like face. He wore his hair in pigeon-wing style, coming down in points over his low forehead and setting off his features to advantage; the barber from the École Polytechnique came in every morning to powder it. Although his looks were somewhat rustic, he was always so neatly turned out, he took such generous pinches of snuff, sniffing it up with all the assurance of one who knows that his snuffbox will always be full of macouba,* that on the evening of the very day Monsieur Goriot moved in, Madame Vauquer went to bed sizzling like a barded partridge on a spit with the desire to put off the funeral shroud of Vauquer and be reborn as Goriot. To get married, sell her boarding house, walk arm in arm with this finest flower of respectable citizenry, become a lady of note in the quarter, organize collections for the poor, go on little Sunday outings to Choisy, Soisy, Gentilly;* go to the theatre when she felt like it, and sit in a box, instead of waiting for the complimentary author's tickets which her boarders sometimes gave her in July. The Eldorado that filled her dreams was that of every humble Paris household. She had never admitted to anyone that she owned forty thousand francs, saved up sou by sou. To be sure, she considered herself, as far as wealth went, an eligible match. 'For the rest, I am as good as he is,' she told herself, turning over in her bed as if to verify personally the physical charms of which Sylvie found the massive imprint on the mattress every morning.

From then on, for about three months, the widow Vauquer took advantage of Monsieur Goriot's barber, and incurred some expense in respect to her personal appearance, which she excused on the grounds that she needed to give her establishment a certain tone appropriate to its distinguished clientèle. She schemed busily to revise the roll of her boarders, announcing her intention henceforth to accept only those of the greatest distinction in every respect. When a stranger presented himself she would boast of the preference shown to her house by Monsieur Goriot, one of the most notable and respected merchants of Paris. She distributed prospectuses headed: MAISON VAUQUER. 'It was', she said, 'one of the oldest and most esteemed family boarding houses in the Latin Quarter. It enjoyed a particularly pleasant view over the Gobe-lins valley (which could be glimpsed from the third floor) and a *charming* garden, at the end of which EXTENDED AN AVENUE of limes.' She spoke too of its pure air and privacy. This prospectus brought in Madame la Comtesse de l'Amber-mesnil, a woman of 36, who was waiting for the final liquida-tion and settlement of a pension due to her as widow of a general fallen on the battlefield. Madame Vauquer took care over her table, had a fire lit in the drawing-room for nearly six months, and fulfilled the promises made in her prospectus, *really putting her back into it*. So the comtesse told Madame Vauquer, whom she called 'my dear friend', that she would acquire for her the Baronne de Vaumerland and the widow of Colonel Comte Picquoiseau, two friends of hers who were just coming to the end of their lease in a boarding house in the Marais which was much more expensive than the Maison Vauquer. Moreover these two ladies would be very well off once the War Office had finished its work. 'But', she said, 'with ministries nothing is ever final.' The two widows would go up together to Madame Vauquer's room to have a little chat while they sipped cassis and ate delicacies reserved for the proprietress's enjoyment. Madame de l'Am-bermesnil strongly approved of her hostess's intentions regarding Goriot, admirable intentions, which in fact she had guessed from the first; she thought he was just perfect.

'Oh! dear lady, as healthy a man as you will ever find,' the widow said, 'extremely well preserved, and still well able to make a woman happy.'

The comtesse generously offered some suggestions about the way Madame Vauquer dressed, which ill accorded with her ambitions. 'You must put yourself on a war footing,' she told her. After lengthy calculations the two widows went together to the Palais-Royal, where in the Galeries de Bois they bought a feathered hat and a bonnet. The comtesse next took her friend to *La Petite Jeannette*,* where they picked out a dress and a shawl. When these weapons were deployed and the widow was armed for the fray she looked exactly like the sign of the *Bœuf à la mode*.* However she found herself so much changed for the better that she felt under an obligation to the comtesse, and though not much of a one for giving presents, she invited her to accept a twenty-franc hat. To tell the truth, she was planning to ask her to be kind enough to sound out Goriot and sing her praises to him. Madame de l'Ambermesnil lent herself most obligingly to this stratagem, and pinning down the old vermicelli-merchant managed to arrange a meeting with him. But when she found that he responded primly, not to say adversely, to approaches that were inspired by her personal desire to win him for herself, she left him, disgusted at his lack of breeding.

'My angel,' she told her dear friend, 'you'll never get anywhere with that man! He is absurdly suspicious, a miser, who will bring you nothing but unhappiness.'

What had taken place between Monsieur Goriot and Madame de l'Ambermesnil made her unwilling to stay any longer under the same roof with him. Next day she left, forgetting to pay six months' board and leaving behind cast-offs worth five francs. However keenly Madame Vauquer sought to trace her, nowhere in Paris could she obtain any information about the comtesse de l'Ambermesnil. She often spoke of this deplorable affair, complaining that she had been too trusting, although she was in fact more distrustful than a cat, but she was like so many people who mistrust those close to them and confide in the first stranger they meet. A curious, but true fact about behaviour whose origin is readily identifiable in the human heart. Perhaps certain people have nothing more to gain from those with whom they live; once they have revealed to them their inner emptiness they feel that they are being secretly judged with well-deserved severity, but, desperately craving the compliments they need, or obsessed with the desire to look as though they possess qualities which they do not, they hope to win by surprise the esteem or affection of strangers, at the risk of one day forfeiting it. There are also individuals who are born mercenary and do nothing to benefit their nearest and dearest, just because that is their duty, whereas by rendering some service to strangers they feel better pleased with themselves. The closer the circle of their friends or relatives is to them the less they like them, the wider the circle extends the more obliging they are. Madame Vauquer no doubt had something of both these natural types, essentially mean, false and detestable.

'If I had been here', Vautrin would then say, 'you would never have suffered that misfortune! I would have seen right through that joker of yours. I know those pretty faces.'

Like all narrow-minded people, Madame Vauquer habitually looked no further than the sequence taken by events, without analysing their causes. She liked to blame others for her own mistakes. When she suffered this loss she looked on the honest vermicelli-merchant as the one responsible for her misfortune, and that was the point when, as she put it, she came back to earth where he was concerned. Once she realized that her coquetry and play-acting were of no avail she did not take long to guess why. She realized then that her boarder, to use her own expression, already 'had something going on'. She finally had the proof that the hopes she had so tenderly indulged were based on sheer fantasy, and that 'she would never get anywhere with that man', to quote the brisk verdict of the comtesse, who seemed to be something of an expert. Inevitably she carried her dislike further than she had her friendship. Her hatred was not proportionate to her love, but to her disappointed expectations.

If the human heart finds time to rest as it scales the heights of love, it rarely pauses in its headlong slide into hatred. Monsieur Goriot, though, was her boarder, and so the widow was obliged to repress the outbursts of her wounded pride, to stifle her sighs of frustration and swallow her desire for revenge, like a monk angered by his prior. Petty spirits satisfy their feelings, good or bad, by constant acts of pettiness. The widow deployed all her feminine wiles in thinking up covert ways of persecuting her victim. She began by cutting out the little luxuries which had been introduced into the meals. 'No more gherkins, no more anchovies; just window-dressing!' she said to Sylvie the morning she resumed her old style of catering. Monsieur Goriot was a frugal man, in whom the niggardly ways which self-made men are compelled to practise had degenerated into a habit. Soup, boiled meat, and vegetables had been, and would always be, his favourite dinner. Thus it was very difficult for Madame Vauquer to torment her boarder, whose tastes she was quite unable to offend. In despair at being faced with someone who was unassailable, she began to run him down, thus making her aversion for Goriot something in which her other boarders could share, and they, for amusement's sake, furthered her revenge. After about a year the widow had become so suspicious that she wondered why this merchant, with a handsome income of seven or eight thousand livres, possessor of silverware and jewels as superb as those of a kept woman, should board with her, paying a sum so modest in relation to his means.

For most of the first year Goriot had often dined out once or twice a week, then, imperceptibly, he had ended up dining out only twice a month. These intimate little rendezvous of Goriot's suited Madame Vauquer's interests too well for her not to feel displeased by the increasing frequency with which her boarder dined in. These changes were attributed as much to his desire to annoy his hostess as to a gradual reduction in his resources. One of the most odious habits of such Lilliputian minds is to assume that others are as petty as they are. Unfortunately, at the end of the second year, Monsieur

Goriot made the rumours circulating about him more plaus-
ible by asking Madame Vauquer if he might move to the
second floor and reduce his rent to nine hundred francs. He
was obliged to make such stringent economies that he stopped
lighting a fire in winter. The widow Vauquer wanted to be
paid in advance, to which Monsieur Goriot agreed, and from
thenceforth she called him just Père Goriot. It was anyone's
guess what had caused this decline and fall. No easy investi-
gation! As the bogus comtesse had said, Père Goriot was a
secretive person who kept things to himself. According to
the logic of the empty-headed who disclose everything because
they have nothing to say that matters, those who do not
talk about their affairs must necessarily be doing badly. This
distinguished old merchant thus became a rogue, this ladies'
man just an old rascal. One theory, offered by Vautrin, who
came to live at the Maison Vauquer about this time, was
that Père Goriot was someone who went to the Bourse and,
to use a forceful expression from the world of finance, tried
a 'fiddle' on government stocks, which had already caused
his ruin. Another theory was that he was one of those small
gamblers who go out every evening to put on ten francs and
bring back the same amount. Again some people thought
that he was a spy working for someone high up in the police
force, but Vautrin maintained that he was not wily enough
to be 'one of them'. Père Goriot for others was a miser who
lent out money by the week, or someone who kept betting
on the same number in the lottery. He was made out to
be all the most mysterious things that vice, shame, and
impotence can produce. There was just one thing; however
vile his conduct or vices might be, the antipathy which he
aroused did not go so far as to have him thrown out: he
paid his rent. He had his uses too; everyone worked off on
him their good or bad temper with jokes or insults as the
case might be. The opinion which seemed the most likely,
and became generally accepted, was that of Madame Vauquer.
To listen to her, this well-preserved man, healthy as they
come and still well able to make a woman happy, was a liber-

tine with peculiar tastes. Here is the evidence on which Madame the widow Vauquer based her calumnies. Some months after the departure of the disastrous comtesse who had managed to live at her expense for six months, one morning before she was up she heard on the stairs outside her room the rustle of a silk dress and the dainty step of a lissom young woman going into Goriot's room, the door of which had opened in anticipation. Straight away fat Sylvie came to tell her mistress that a girl, too pretty to be good and 'dressed divinely', wearing laced prunella* boots without a speck of dirt on them, had slipped like an eel out of the street into the kitchen and asked for Monsieur Goriot's apartment. Madame Vauquer and her cook began eavesdropping and managed to pick up several words uttered in tones of affection in the course of the visit, which lasted quite some time. When Monsieur Goriot came out with his *lady*, fat Sylvie picked up her basket at once and pretended to go out shopping so that she could follow the loving couple.

'Madame,' she said to her mistress on her return, 'Monsieur Goriot must be devilish rich despite everything to keep 'em in such style. Just fancy, a superb carriage was standing on the corner of the rue de l'Estrapade, and *she* got into it.'

During dinner Madame Vauquer went to draw a curtain so that Goriot should not be troubled by the sun getting in his eyes.

'Beauty is attracted to you, Monsieur Goriot, even the sun won't leave you alone,' she said, referring to his recent visitor. 'My word, you have good taste, she was very pretty.'

'That was my daughter,' he said proudly, in a way which the other boarders took for the vanity of an old man keeping up appearances.

A month after this visit Monsieur Goriot received another. His daughter, who the first time had worn clothes suited for the morning, came after dinner all dressed up to go out. The boarders, chatting together in the drawing-room, saw a pretty blonde, slim and graceful, and looking much too distinguished to be the daughter of a Père Goriot.

'And that makes two!' said fat Sylvie, who did not recognize her.

A few days later another girl, tall and shapely, a brunette with dark hair and a lively eye, asked for Monsieur Goriot.

'That makes three!' said Sylvie.

This second girl, whose first visit to her father had also been in the morning, came some days later in the evening, dressed for a ball and in a carriage.

'Now it's four!' said Madame Vauquer and fat Sylvie, who failed to recognize in this fine lady any trace of the simply dressed girl who had paid her first visit in the morning.

Goriot was still paying twelve hundred francs rent. Madame Vauquer found it perfectly natural that a rich man should have four or five mistresses, and she even thought it was very astute of him to pass them off as his daughters. She did not mind him summoning them to the Maison Vauquer. However, since these visits explained her lodger's indifference towards her, at the beginning of the second year she went so far as to call him 'an old tomcat'. Finally, when his rent went down to nine hundred francs, she very rudely asked what sort of house he thought it was, as she saw one of these ladies leaving. Père Goriot replied that the lady in question was his elder daughter.

'So you have three dozen daughters, do you?' Madame Vauquer sourly remarked.

'I only have two,' her lodger replied in the mild tones of a man who has been ruined and meekly accepts the constraints of poverty.

Towards the end of the third year Père Goriot still further reduced his expenses by moving up to the third floor and paying forty-five francs a month. He gave up snuff, sent his barber away and stopped powdering his hair. The first time Père Goriot appeared without powder his hostess let out a gasp of surprise at the colour of his hair, which was a dirty greenish-grey. His face, which secret sorrows had made gradually more mournful day by day, looked more woebegone than any of those round the table. There was no more room for doubt. Père Goriot was an old rake who but for his doctor's skill would have lost his sight from the ill-effects of the treatment required for his diseases. The disgusting colour of his hair was the result of his excesses and the drugs he took in order to continue them. The old fellow's physical and moral condition supported such nonsensical theories. When his wardrobe wore out he bought calico at fourteen sous* an ell to replace his fine linen. His diamonds, his gold snuff-box, his chain, his jewels disappeared one by one. He had abandoned his cornflower-blue coat and his whole expensive-looking outfit, and now wore, summer and winter, a dark brown frock-coat of coarse cloth, a goat-hair waistcoat and hard-wearing grey woollen trousers. He lost more and more weight, his calves shrank away, his face, once fleshy from the satisfactions of material prosperity, became excessively gaunt, his brow was furrowed with wrinkles, his jaw protruded. During the fourth year of his residence in the rue Neuve-Sainte-Geneviève he changed beyond recognition. The good vermicelli-merchant of 62 who looked no more than 40, the plump, well-fed gentleman who looked as fresh and simple as a child, whose roguish ways were the delight of all who met him and whose smile was still youthful, now looked like a man in his seventies, confused, shaky and wan. His blue eyes, once so lively, had gone a dull, metallic grey; they had faded, and no longer watered, but their red rims seemed to exude drops of blood. Some found him repulsive, others pitiful. Some young medical students, observing his drooping lower lip and the slope of his facial angle, pronounced him a victim of cretinism, after they had bullied him for a long time without provoking any reaction. One evening after dinner Madame Vauquer said mockingly, 'So those daughters of yours don't come to see you any more?', implying that he was not their father, at which Père Goriot started as though she had stabbed him.

'They do come sometimes,' he replied with obvious emotion.

'Ha! So you still see them sometimes!' the students

exclaimed. 'Bravo, Père Goriot!'

But the old man did not hear the quips provoked by his reply, he had relapsed into a state of meditation which his superficial observers took for senile torpor due to mental deficiency. If they had really known him they might have been keenly interested in the problem presented by his physical and moral situation, but there was no easy way to that knowledge. Although it was easy to find out whether Goriot had really been a vermicelli-merchant, and what he was worth, the elderly people whose curiosity he had aroused never went beyond their own neighbourhood and lived in the boarding house like oysters on a rock. As for the others, as soon as they left the rue Neuve-Sainte-Geneviève the special allurements of Parisian life made them forget all about the poor old man they mocked. For these narrow-minded people, as for the heedless youth, the arid wretchedness of Père Goriot and his dumb passivity were incompatible with any sort of wealth or ability. As for the women whom he called daughters, everyone agreed with Madame Vauquer, who would say with the strict logic which habitual conjecture imparts to old women who spend their evenings gossiping: 'If Père Goriot had daughters as rich as all the women who come to see him appear to be, he would not be living in my house, on the third floor, at forty-five francs a month, and he would not dress like a pauper.' Her conclusions were irrefutable. Thus, towards the end of November 1819, when this drama broke, everyone in the boarding house had definite views about the poor old man. He had never had a daughter or a wife; a life of debauchery had turned him into a slug, an anthropomorphic mollusc of the species of *Capifers*,* said a man from the Natural History Museum, a regular with a style of his own. Poiret was an eagle, a gentleman compared to Goriot. Poiret could speak, argue, reply; in fact he never said anything when he spoke, argued or replied, for it was his habit to repeat in other words what others said, but he did contribute to the conversation, he was alive and seemed to be sentient, whereas Père Goriot, again according to the man from the Museum, permanently registered zero on the Réaumur scale.

Eugène de Rastignac had come back to Paris in a state of mind familiar to all young men of superior talents, or those momentarily inspired by a crisis to rise above the common run. During the first year of his stay in Paris the work for his preliminary qualifications in the Faculty had been so un-demanding that it left him free to enjoy the manifest material delights of Paris. A student will be pressed for time if he tries to become familiar with the repertory of all the theatres, find his way round the Parisian maze, know the capital's ways, learn its language, and become accustomed to its special attractions; searching out both good and bad spots, attending lectures that interest him, and inspecting the treasures in its museums. Then it is that a student is fired by passion for foolish things which he finds impressive. He has his great man, a professor at the Collège de France, paid to perform at a level appropriate to his audience. He adjusts his cravat and poses for the women in the front galleries of the Opéra-Comique. In the course of these successive initiations he sheds his greenness, broadens his horizons and ends up understand-ing the different strata of humanity that make up society. If he began by admiring the carriages parading down the Champs-Élysées on a fine sunny day, he soon comes to envy them. Eugène had already served this apprenticeship without realizing it when he left for the vacation after passing his baccalaureate in arts and in law. His boyish illusions, his prov-incial ideas had disappeared. His more critical intelligence and lofty ambition enabled him to see things clearly once he was back in the ancestral home in the bosom of his family. His father and mother, his two brothers, two sisters and an aunt who owned nothing but annuities, lived on the modest property of Rastignac. The estate brought in about three thou-sand francs a year, subject to the fluctuations to which the industrial product of the vineyard is always liable, and yet out of that twelve hundred francs a year had to be found for him. The sight of his family in such constant distress,

which they had generously kept from him, the comparison
he was forced to make between his sisters, who had seemed
so lovely when he was a child, and the Parisian women who
were the living fulfilment of his earlier dreams of beauty,
the precarious future of this large family which depended
on him, the penny-pinching care with which he saw them
save every scrap and crumb, and drink the dregs from the
wine press, in a word numerous circumstances which it would
be pointless to relate, vastly increased his desire for success
and made him crave distinction. As happens with great souls,
he wanted nothing he had not deserved. But his temperament
was very much that of the Southerner; when it came to carrying things out, his decisions were thus subject to the kind
of hesitation that afflicts young men on the open sea, unsure
where to apply their energies or at what angle to set their
sails. If at first he wanted to throw himself wholeheartedly
into his work, he was soon diverted by the need to make
social contacts, and noticing how influential women are in
social life, he suddenly took it into his head to launch out
into the world so that he could win some feminine patronage.
Could such patronage fail to reward an ardent and witty
young man, whose wit and ardour were enhanced by an
elegant bearing and the kind of wiry good looks to which
women willingly succumb? These ideas beset him during
walks through the fields with his sisters, who found him much
changed from the cheery companion of former days. His aunt,
Madame de Marcillac, who had once been presented at Court,
had known there the cream of the aristocracy. Suddenly the
ambitious young man recognized in the reminiscences with
which his aunt had so often lulled him to sleep the basis
for a number of social conquests at least as important as those
which he was pursuing at Law School; he questioned her
about family connections which might still be resumed. The
old lady shook the branches of the genealogical tree, and considered that of all the self-centred clan of rich relations who
could help her nephew, Madame la Vicomtesse de Beauséant
was the person least likely to be awkward about it. She wrote

this young woman a letter in the old style, and handing it over to Eugène told him that if he were successful with the vicomtesse, she would put him in touch with his other relatives. Some days after his return to Paris Rastignac sent his aunt's letter to Madame de Beauséant. The vicomtesse replied by inviting him to a ball for the following day.

Such was the general situation in the boarding house at the end of November 1819. A few days later Eugène had attended Madame de Beauséant's ball, and had come home at about two in the morning. To make up for lost time the resolute student had promised himself, as he danced, to work through until the morning. For the first time he was about to sit up all night in the heart of this silent neighbourhood, for the sight of such social splendour had so enthralled him that he felt deceptively energetic. He had not dined at Madame Vauquer's, so the other boarders might well not expect him back from the ball until early the following morning, as had sometimes happened when he returned from a gala at the Prado or a ball at the Odéon,* his silk stockings spattered with dirt and his pumps trodden out of shape. Before bolting the door Christophe had opened it to look out into the street. Just at that moment Rastignac arrived, and was able to go up to his room without making a noise, followed by Christophe, who made a lot. Eugène undressed, put on slippers and a shabby old coat, lit his peat fire, and briskly got ready for work, while Christophe's heavy boots made such a din as to cover the young man's barely audible preparations. Eugène stayed pensive for a few moments before plunging into his law books. He had just realized that Madame la Vicomtesse de Beauséant was one of the leaders of Paris fashion, and that her house was acknowledged as the most agreeable in the Faubourg Saint-Germain. Besides, both her name and her fortune made her one of the top people in aristocratic society. Thanks to his aunt de Marcillac the poor student had been welcomed in that house, without appreciating the extent of such a favour. Admittance to these gilded salons was as good as a certificate of the highest nobility.

By showing himself in such society, the most exclusive of all, he had won the right to go anywhere. Dazzled by the glittering assembly, exchanging only a few words with the vicomtesse, Eugène had been content to pick out from the crowd of Parisian goddesses thronging together in this 'rout' one of those women whom a young man is bound to worship from the first. Comtesse Anastasie de Restaud, tall and shapely, was considered to have one of the prettiest figures in Paris. Imagine large dark eyes, superb hands, dainty feet, mettlesome movements, a woman whom the Marquis de Ronquerolles called a thoroughbred filly. Such fine-tuned sensitivity in no way impaired her natural assets; her figure was generously curved, although no one could accuse her of being too plump. 'Thoroughbred', 'good bloodline', such expressions for women were beginning to replace the angels from heaven, the Ossianic* figures, all the old amorous mythology spurned by the new dandies. But for Rastignac Madame Anastasie de Restaud was the very type of woman to be desired. He had contrived to put himself down twice on the list of partners written on her fan, and had been able to speak to her during the first quadrille.

'Where can I meet you again, Madame?' he had blurted out with the passionate urgency that women like so much.

'Why,' she said, 'in the Bois, at the Bouffons,* in my own house, anywhere.'

And the intrepid Southerner had made every effort to strike up a relationship with this delightful comtesse, in so far as any young man can do so with a woman in the course of a quadrille and a waltz. By saying that he was a cousin of Madame de Beauséant he secured an invitation from this woman, whom he took for a great lady, which permitted him to call on her. Her parting smile convinced Rastignac that he had to pay her a visit. He had been lucky enough to meet a man who had not laughed at his ignorance, considered a fatal defect among the high-born, arrogant fops of the time, such as Maulincourt, Ronquerolles, Maxime de Trailles, de Marsay, Ajuda-Pinto, Vandenesse, who were there in all their conceited vainglory, mingling with the most elegant women, Lady Brandon, the Duchesse de Langeais, the Còmtesse de Kergarouët, Madame de Serisy, the Duchesse de Carigliano, the Comtesse Ferraud, Madame de Lanty, the Marquise d'Aiglemont, Madame Firmiani, the Marquise de Listomère, and the Marquise d'Espard, the Duchesse de Maufrigneuse and the Grandlieus. Fortunately, then, the naïve student happened on the Marquis de Montriveau,* a general and the Duchesse de Langeais's lover, a man of childlike simplicity, who told him that the Comtesse de Restaud lived in the rue du Helder.

To be young, thirsting after the world, consumed by desire for a woman, and then find two great houses opening their doors! To have a foot in the Faubourg Saint-Germain, at the Vicomtesse de Beauséant's, and a knee in the Chaussée-d'Antin bowed before the Comtesse de Restaud! To review the salons of Paris arrayed before one's gaze, and to believe oneself handsome enough to find there aid and protection in a woman's heart! To feel ambitious enough to kick disdainfully at the tightrope on which one must walk with all the assurance of an acrobat who is not going to fall, and to have found in a charming woman the best possible balancing-pole! With such thoughts, dreaming of that sublime woman, in that setting, beside a peat fire, amid law books and penury, who would not, like Eugène, have mused on what the future held in store, who would not have filled it with success? His wandering thoughts anticipated such abundant joys to come that he was in imagination by Madame de Restaud's side, when a sigh like some Saint Joseph* grunting with effort disturbed the silence of the night, echoing in the young man's heart so that he took it for the last gasp of a dying man. He quietly opened the door, went out into the corridor and spied a bar of light shining beneath Père Goriot's door. Eugène was afraid that his neighbour might be indisposed. He put his eye to the keyhole, looked into the room and saw the old man hard at work of so apparently criminal a kind that he thought he would only be rendering society a service if

he examined closely just what the so-called vermicelli-merchant was up to in the middle of the night. Père Goriot,
who had somehow fastened to the crossbar of an upturned
table a dish and a kind of soup bowl in silver-gilt, was winding
some sort of cable round these richly tooled objects so tightly
and with such force that it looked as though he was twisting
them into ingots.

'Goodness! What a man!' Rastignac said to himself as he
watched the old man's muscular arm, with the help of the
cord, noiselessly kneading the silver-gilt as if it were dough.

Was he then a thief or a fence, pretending to be stupid
and feeble, living like a beggar, so that he could ply his trade
in greater security? said Eugène to himself as he stood up
for a moment. Then the student once more applied his eye
to the keyhole. Père Goriot had now unrolled his cable. He
took the lump of silver, spread a blanket over the table, put
the silver on it and rolled it about until it was shaped into
a round bar, performing the whole operation with amazing
ease.

'He must be as strong as King Augustus of Poland!'* thought
Eugène when the round bar was more or less completed.

Père Goriot looked sadly at his handiwork, with tears running from his eyes. He blew out the wax taper by whose
light he had twisted the silver-gilt, and Eugène heard him
sigh deeply as he got into bed.

'He is crazy,' thought the student.

'Poor child!' Père Goriot said aloud.

At these words Rastignac decided it would be wise to keep
quiet about this incident and not condemn his neighbour
too hastily. He was about to return to his room when he
suddenly heard a sound hard to describe, like that of men
in thick cloth slippers coming upstairs. Eugène listened, and
did indeed identify the sound of two men breathing in turn.
Without hearing the door creak or the men's footsteps, he
suddenly saw a dim glow on the second floor, coming from
Monsieur Vautrin's room.

'What a lot of mysterious goings-on for a family boarding

house!' he said to himself. He went down a few steps, began to listen and caught the sound of gold chinking. Soon the light went out, the two sets of breathing could be heard again, though the door had not creaked, and then, as the two men went down the stairs, the sound died away.

'Who's there?' cried Madame Vauquer, opening her bedroom window.

'It's only me coming in, Ma Vauquer,' said Vautrin in his deep voice.

'That's odd! Christophe had bolted the door,' Eugène said to himself as he went back to his room. 'You need to stay up all night if you want to know what is going on around you in Paris!' Diverted by these minor incidents from his ambitiously amorous fantasies, Eugène got down to his work, but distracted by his suspicions regarding Père Goriot, and still more distracted by the figure of Madame Restaud, who kept appearing before him to announce a brilliant destiny, he finally lay down and slept like a log. For every ten nights that young men pledge themselves to work, they spend seven asleep. You need to be over 20 to stay awake.

Next morning found Paris shrouded in one of those dense fogs which make everything so dark that even the most punctual of people mistake the time. Business appointments are missed, everyone thinks it is only eight o'clock when it is striking twelve. At half-past nine Madame Vauquer had not yet stirred from her bed. Christophe and fat Sylvie were late too, and were peacefully drinking their coffee, prepared with the top of the milk intended for the boarders, which Sylvie kept on the boil for a long time so that Madame Vauquer would not notice the levy which had been thus illegally extracted.

'Sylvie,' said Christophe, dipping his first piece of toast, 'Monsieur Vautrin, who's a good chap for all that, had two fellows come to see him again last night. If Madame gets bothered about it, best say nothing.'

'Did he give you something?'

'He gave me a hundred sous for myself this month, like

he was telling me to keep quiet.'

'Except for him and Madame Couture, who aren't stingy, the others would like to take away with their left hand what they give us with the right on New Year's Day,' said Sylvie.

'Come to that, what do they give?' said Christophe. 'A lousy five-franc piece. For the past two years Père Goriot has been cleaning his own shoes. That skinflint Poiret does without polish, and he'd rather drink the stuff than put it on his rotten old boots. As for that runt of a student, he gives me forty sous. Forty sous doesn't even pay for my brushes, and on top of that he sells his old clothes. What a dump!'

'Well!' said Sylvie sipping her coffee, 'We have still got the best jobs going round here; we do pretty well. But talking of that big fellow Vautrin, has anyone said anything to you?'

'Yes, a few days ago I met a gent in the street who says, "Don't you have a big gentleman who dyes his whiskers staying at your place?" I says to him: "No, sir, he doesn't dye them. A bright spark like him don't have the time." So I tells Monsieur Vautrin about it, and he says to me, "You did the right thing, my lad! Always answer like that. There's nothing nastier than having other people know your weaknesses. It can wreck your marriage prospects."'

'Well! When I was out shopping someone tried to get me to say whether I ever saw him putting on his shirt. Such nonsense! My word,' she said, interrupting herself, 'that's quarter to ten striking at Val-de-Grâce and nobody's stirring.'

'What of it! Madame Couture and her young lady went off to Mass at Saint-Étienne at eight o'clock. Père Goriot went out with a parcel. The student won't be back until after his lecture, at ten. I saw them go out while I was doing the stairs; Père Goriot knocked into me with whatever he was carrying and it was hard as iron. What's he up to, that old fellow? The others make sport of him, but he's a decent sort of chap all the same, and worth more than the lot of them. What he gives you isn't much, but the ladies he sends me to sometimes hand out fat tips and wear some fine clothes.'

'The ones he calls his daughters, you mean? There are a dozen of them.'

'I've never gone but to the two of them, the same who've been here.'

'There's Madame moving about; she'll raise Cain. I'll have to go up to her. You keep an eye on the milk, Christophe, look out for the cat.'

'Goodness, Sylvie, it's quarter to ten and you have let me sleep like a dormouse! I've never heard of such a thing!'

'It's the fog. You could cut it with a knife.'

'What about breakfast?'

'Something must have got into your lodgers. They all pushed off at cracker-dawn.'

'Do talk properly, Sylvie,' said Madame Vauquer reprovingly, 'you should say cocker-crow.'

'All right, Madame, I'll say whatever you like. The fact remains you can have your breakfast at ten. Michonnette and Poiret haven't stirred. They are the only ones left in the house, and they are sleeping like logs.'

'But, Sylvie, you bracket the two of them together as if . . .'

'As if what?' asked Sylvie with a loud silly giggle. 'Two make a pair, don't they?'

'It's odd, Sylvie; how did Monsieur Vautrin get in last night after Christophe had bolted the door?'

'It's the other way round, Madame. He heard Monsieur Vautrin and went down to open the door for him. And there you are, thinking . . .'

'Give me my bodice, and hurry down to see to breakfast. Do up the remains of the mutton with some potatoes, and give them some stewed pears, the ones that cost half a sou each.'

A few minutes later Madame Vauquer arrived downstairs at the very moment when her cat had knocked off with its paw the plate covering a bowl of milk, and was lapping it up as fast as it could.

'Mistigris!' she cried. The cat ran off, then came back to rub against her legs. 'That's right, try making up to me, you old coward!' she said. 'Sylvie! Sylvie!'

'Yes, what is it, Madame?'

'Just look at how much the cat has drunk.'

'It's that blockhead Christophe's fault. I told him to lay the table. Where's he gone? Don't you worry, Madame, it will do for Père Goriot's coffee. I'll put some water in it, he'll never notice. He doesn't pay attention to anything, not even what he's eating.'

'Where has he gone then, that rum old boy?' asked Madame Vauquer, setting out the plates.

'Who knows? He's got all kinds of queer deals going on.'

'I have had too much sleep,' said Madame Vauquer.

'But Madame is fresh as a daisy . . .'

At that moment the bell tinkled and Vautrin came into the drawing-room, singing in his deep voice:

> 'I've roamed the world for many a year
> And I've been seen in many lands . . .'

'Oho! Good morning, Madame Vauquer,' he said, noticing his hostess, whom he gallantly clasped in his arms.

'Now, now, you can stop that!'

'Tell me off for being cheeky,' he replied. 'Go on, say it. Won't you please say it? Half a moment, I'll help you lay the table. Oh! aren't I kind?'

> 'Wooing the girls, dark or fair,
> Loving, sighing . . .'

'I have just seen something odd.'

> '. . . as chance commands.'

'What's that?' asked the widow.

'At half-past eight this morning Père Goriot was in the rue Dauphine at the goldsmith's, where they buy old plate and gold braid. He got a good price for a bit of plate he sold them, a piece of silver-gilt, quite nicely twisted for someone who is not in the trade.'

'Really?'

'Yes. I was coming back here from seeing off one of my friends who is going overseas on one of the Royal Mail boats. I waited for Père Goriot just to see; for a bit of fun like. He came back to this neighbourhood, to the rue des Grès,* and went into the house of a well-known moneylender, name of Gobseck, a right villain, quite capable of turning his father's bones into dominoes; a Jew, an Arab, a Greek, a Gipsy. You'd have a job robbing him; he keeps his cash in the Bank.'

'What's our Père Goriot setting up, then?'

'He's not setting anything up,' said Vautrin, 'he's upsetting. He's a poor fool silly enough to ruin himself for the love of girls who . . .'

'Here he comes!' said Sylvie.

'Christophe,' cried Père Goriot, 'come upstairs with me.'

Christophe followed Père Goriot and soon came down again.

'Where are you going?' Madame Vauquer asked her servant.

'An errand for Monsieur Goriot.'

'What's that?' said Vautrin, snatching from Christophe's hands a letter on which he read: *To Madame la comtesse Anastasie de Restaud.* 'And where are you going?' he went on, handing Christophe back the letter.

'Rue du Helder. My orders are to give it to Madame la comtesse and nobody else.'

'What's inside?' asked Vautrin, holding the letter up to the light, 'a banknote? No.' He partly opened the envelope. 'A receipted account,' he cried. 'Dammit! There's a gallant old rake for you. Off you go, you old rogue,' he said planting his great hand on Christophe's head and spinning him round like a top, 'you'll get a good tip.'

The table was laid. Sylvie was boiling the milk, Madame Vauquer was lighting the stove, helped by Vautrin, who went on humming:

> 'I've roamed the world for many a year
> And I've been seen in many lands . . .'

When everything was ready Madame Couture and

Mademoiselle Taillefer came in.

'Where have you been so bright and early, dear lady?'
Madame Vauquer asked Madame Couture.

'We have been at our devotions at Saint-Étienne-du-Mont,
for we are due to visit Monsieur Taillefer today. Poor child,
she's shaking like a leaf,' Madame Couture went on, sitting
down in front of the stove and warming her shoes until they
steamed.

'Have a warm, Victorine,' said Madame Vauquer.

'You're right, Mademoiselle, to pray the good Lord to soften
your father's heart,' said Vautrin, pushing a chair forward
for the motherless girl, 'but that's not enough. What you
need is a friend to take on the job of telling a few home
truths to that old swine, a real barbarian, who they say is
worth three million francs but won't give you a dowry.
A pretty girl needs a dowry in times like these.'

'Poor child,' said Madame Vauquer. 'Come, come, my pet,
your monster of a father will bring a heap of misfortune
on his head.'

At these words Victorine's eyes filled with tears, and at
a sign from Madame Couture the widow stopped at that.

'If we could only see him, if I could speak to him, show
him his wife's last letter,' went on the Commissary-General's
widow. 'I have never dared risk sending it by post; he knows
my writing...'

'*O innocent, unhappy, persecuted women,*'* cried Vautrin,
breaking in, 'so that is what you have come to? In a few
days' time I'll take a hand in your affairs and everything will
be all right.'

'Oh Monsieur,' said Victorine, looking at Vautrin with
ardent eyes, still full of tears, while he remained unmoved,
'if you could find some way of reaching my father, make
sure you tell him that his affection and my mother's love
are dearer to me than all the riches in the world. If you could
get him to unbend in any way I would offer up my prayers
for you. You can be sure of our gratitude...'

'I've roamed the world...' sang Vautrin in ironic tones.

At that moment Goriot, Mademoiselle Michonneau, Poiret came downstairs, perhaps attracted by the smell of the sauce that Sylvie was making to go with the remains of the mutton. Just as the seven boarders sat down to table with an exchange of greetings ten o'clock struck, and they heard the student's footsteps out in the street.

'That's good, Monsieur Eugène,' said Sylvie, 'today you'll be having breakfast with all the others.'

The student greeted the other boarders and sat down next to Père Goriot.

'I've just had a rather strange adventure,' he said, helping himself to a generous portion of mutton and cutting a chunk of bread which Madame Vauquer was still weighing up by eye.

'An adventure!' said Poiret.

'Well, why should you find that surprising, old boy?' Vautrin asked Poiret. 'Monsieur de Rastignac is the right sort of person to have one.'

Mademoiselle Taillefer glanced shyly at the young student.

'Tell us about your adventure,' Madame Vauquer ordered.

'I went yesterday to the ball given by Madame la Vicomtesse de Beauséant, a cousin of mine; she has a magnificent house, silk-hung apartments, in short she entertained us royally, and I enjoyed myself like a king ...'

'–fisher,' said Vautrin, rudely interrupting.

'Sir,' Eugène shot back, 'what do you mean?'

'I say "fisher" because kingfishers enjoy themselves a lot more than kings.'

'That's true; I would rather be that carefree little bird than a king because ...' observed Poiret, the constant echo.

'Well,' continued the student, cutting him short, 'there I was, dancing with one of the most beautiful women at the ball, a charming comtesse, the most delightful creature I have ever seen. She had peach-blossom in her hair and at her side wore the loveliest bouquet, real flowers full of fragrance. But, my word, you should have seen her. There's no describing a woman caught up in all the animation of a dance. Well, this morning I met this divine comtesse, at about nine o'clock, on foot in the rue des Grès. How my heart beat! I imagined ...'

'That she was coming here,' said Vautrin with a searching look at the student. 'She was probably going to old Gobseck, the moneylender. If you ever probe the hearts of Parisian women you'll find the moneylender there before the lover. The name of your comtesse is Anastasie de Restaud, and she lives in the rue du Helder.'

At the sound of that name the student stared at Vautrin. Père Goriot suddenly raised his head and gave the two of them a look of such lucidity and concern that the other boarders were surprised.

'Christophe will arrive too late. She will have gone there already,' Goriot cried in anguish.

'I guessed right,' said Vautrin, leaning over to whisper in Madame Vauquer's ear.

Goriot went on eating automatically, unaware of what he was eating. He had never looked more bemused and pre-occupied than at that moment.

'Who the devil told you her name, Monsieur Vautrin?' asked Eugène.

'Ah, that's the point,' Vautrin replied. 'Père Goriot knew it, didn't he? Why shouldn't I?'

'Monsieur Goriot!' cried the student.

'Eh!' said the poor old man. 'She looked really beautiful yesterday, did she?'

'Who?'

'Madame de Restaud.'

'Just look at the old miser,' Madame Vauquer said to Vautrin, 'how his eyes light up!'

'Is he keeping her then?' Mademoiselle Michonneau asked the student in a low voice.

'Oh yes, she was incredibly beautiful,' Eugène went on, while Père Goriot never took his eyes off him. 'If Madame de Beauséant had not been there, my divine comtesse would have been the queen of the ball. The young men didn't look at anyone else. I was twelfth on her list; she danced all the quadrilles. The other women were furious. If anyone was happy yesterday, she was. It is certainly true what they say: there's no finer sight than a frigate in full sail, a horse galloping, and a woman dancing.'

'Yesterday at the top of Fortune's wheel, guest of a duchesse,' said Vautrin. 'This morning down at the bottom, visiting a usurer; that's Parisian women for you! If their husbands can't afford their wild extravagance, they sell themselves. If they can't sell themselves, they would rip open their own mothers to find some way to shine. They will go to any lengths. That's well known, well known!'

Père Goriot's face, which had lit up like the sun on a fine day as he listened to the student, clouded over at Vautrin's cruel remark.

'Well!' said Madame Vauquer, 'what about your adventure? Did you speak to her? Did you ask her if she wanted to study law?'

'She didn't see me,' said Eugène. 'But meeting one of the prettiest women in Paris in the rue des Grès at nine in the morning, and a woman who can't have left the ball before two a.m., isn't that odd? Such adventures could only happen here in Paris.'

'There are funnier ones than that,' cried Vautrin.

Mademoiselle Taillefer had hardly been listening, so preoccupied was she by what she was about to attempt. Madame Couture gave her the signal to leave the table and get dressed. When the two ladies went out, Père Goriot did the same.

'Well, now! Did you see that?' said Madame Vauquer to Vautrin and her other boarders. 'It is obvious that he has ruined himself on those women's account.'

'No one will ever convince me,' cried the student, 'that the beautiful Comtesse de Restaud belongs to Père Goriot.'

'But', interrupted Vautrin, 'we are not trying to convince you. You are still too young to know Paris properly; you'll come to learn that what we call "men with obsessive passions" are to be found there ...' (At these words Mademoiselle

Michonneau gave Vautrin a knowing look, like a cavalry horse
hearing the bugle sound.) 'Ah ha!' said Vautrin, breaking off
to give her a searching glance, 'we have had our little passions
too, have we?' (The old maid lowered her eyes like a nun
before a statue.) 'Well,' he went on, 'once such men get an
idea in their heads they won't let go. They thirst only for
a particular water, from a particular fountain, often stagnant
at that, and for a drink of it they would sell their wives and
children; they would sell their very souls to the devil. For
some men the fountain is gambling, the Stock Exchange,
music, collecting pictures, or insects, for others it is a woman
who knows just how to whet their appetites. You could offer
them all the women in the world and it would leave them
cold. The only one they want is the one who satisfies their
obsession. The woman in question often does not love them
at all, treats them harshly, makes them pay dearly for their
crumbs of satisfaction. These jokers never give up, though,
and would pawn their last blanket to be able to give her
their last penny. Père Goriot is one of those people. The
comtesse exploits him because he is discreet. That's high
society for you! The poor old chap thinks of nothing but
her. Apart from his obsession, as you see, he's just a dumb
animal. Get him going on that subject and his face sparkles
like a diamond. It's not difficult to guess that secret. This
morning he took some silver-plate to be melted down, and
I saw him going into Uncle Gobseck's in the rue des Grès.
Mark what follows! When he came back here he sent that
ninny Christophe round to the Comtesse de Restaud. Christophe showed us the address on the letter which contained
a receipted account. Obviously if the comtesse was also going
to see the old usurer the matter was urgent. Père Goriot was
gallant enough to find the funds for her. You don't need
to put two and two together to get the picture. There's proof
for you, my young student, that all the time your comtesse
was laughing, dancing, larking about, with her peach-blossom
waving and her dress gathered up, she was like a cat on hot
bricks, as they say, at the thought that her bills of exchange,

or her lover's, might not be honoured ...'

'You make me desperately anxious to know the truth. I will go and call on Madame de Restaud tomorrow,' cried Eugène.

'Yes,' said Poiret, 'you must call on Madame de Restaud tomorrow.'

'Perhaps you'll find old Goriot there, come to collect payment for all his gallant deeds.'

'But', said Eugène with an air of distaste, 'that Paris of yours must be a proper muckheap.'

'And a pretty funny muckheap,' Vautrin replied. 'Those who get spattered in their carriages are respectable people, those who do so on foot are rogues. Just have the bad luck to pinch something or other and you'll be pointed out as a curiosity outside the Law Courts. Steal a million and you'll be held up as an example of virtue in the salons. You pay thirty millions to the police and the lawcourts to support that kind of morality. Nice, isn't it?'

'What!' cried Madame Vauquer, 'you mean Père Goriot has taken his silver-gilt breakfast set to be melted down?'

'Weren't there two turtle-doves on the lid?' asked Eugène.

'That's right.'

'He was very attached to it then, and he wept when he had squeezed the bowl and dish into an ingot. I happened to see it,' said Eugène.

'It was as dear to him as life itself,' the widow answered.

'Just look at the poor fellow, how obsessed he is,' cried Vautrin. 'That woman knows how to tickle his soul.'

The student went up to his room. Vautrin went out. A few minutes later Madame Couture and Victorine got into a cab that Sylvie had gone to fetch for them. Poiret offered his arm to Mademoiselle Michonneau and the two of them went off to walk round the Jardin des Plantes for the only two fine hours of the day.

'Well, there they are, good as married,' said fat Sylvie. 'This is the first time they have been out together. They are both so dry that if they bump together they'll burst into flame like a tinderbox.'

'Look out for Mademoiselle Michonneau's shawl,' said
Madame Vauquer with a smile, 'it will catch like touchwood.'

At four in the afternoon, when Goriot returned, he saw
by the light of two smoky lamps that Victorine's eyes were
red. Madame Vauquer was listening to an account of their
fruitless call that morning on Monsieur Taillefer. Annoyed
by a visit from his daughter and the old woman, Taillefer
had allowed them into his presence so that he could have
things out with them.

'Dear lady,' Madame Couture was saying to Madame
Vauquer, 'just imagine, he didn't even invite Victorine to
sit down; she remained standing throughout. As for me, he
told me, with no sign of temper, quite coldly, that we should
save ourselves the trouble of calling on him; that Mademoiselle
(whom he did not even call his daughter) was only doing
herself harm in his eyes by being so importunate (once a
year, the monster!); that as Victorine's mother had been
married off without a penny she had no claims on him; in
a word he said the cruellest things and made the poor child
burst into tears. Then she threw herself at her father's feet,
and bravely told him that she persisted only for her mother's
sake, that she would do his bidding without a murmur, but
she implored him to read the poor woman's final testament.
She took out the letter and handed it to him with the most
beautiful words you can imagine, straight from the heart.
I don't know where she found such eloquence; God must
have put it into her mouth, for the poor child was so inspired
that I wept like an idiot to hear her. Do you know what
that monster did? He went on cutting his nails, then he took
the letter that poor Madame Taillefer had soaked with her
tears, and threw it into the fireplace, saying, 'That will do
then!' He tried to pull his daughter to her feet, while she
seized his hands to kiss them, but he pulled them away. Did
you ever hear of anything so scandalous? His great dolt of
a son came in without even greeting his sister.'

'Are they monsters then?' said Père Goriot.

'And then', said Madame Couture, taking no notice of the old fellow's exclamation, 'father and son went off, taking their leave of me and asking me to excuse them, but they had urgent matters to attend to. That is how our visit went. At least he saw his daughter. I don't know how he can disown her, they are as alike as two peas.'

The boarders, resident and non-resident, came in one by one, exchanging greetings and those trifles which, in certain circles in Paris, pass for wit, though their main component is foolishness, and their merit consists above all in gesture and pronunciation. This sort of slang changes all the time. The catchword on which it is based never lasts more than a month. A political event, a high Court trial, a street song, an actor's antics, anything can provide material for this form of humour which consists above all in taking ideas and words like shuttlecocks and batting them to and fro. The recent invention of the Diorama, carrying optical illusion a stage further than the Panoramas, had prompted the comic practice in some artists' studios of adding '*rama*' to words and a young painter who frequented the Maison Vauquer had injected the infection there.

'Well! *Monsieurre* Poiret,' said the Museum man, rolling his r's, 'how is your delicate *healthorama*?' Then, without waiting for an answer, 'Ladies, something must have upset you,' he said to Madame Couture and Victorine.

'Are we going to have *dinnairrr*?' cried Horace Bianchon, a medical student and friend of Rastignac, 'my tummy has sunk *usque ad talones*.'*

'It's devilish *coltorama*!' said Vautrin. 'Move over, Père Goriot! Devil take it! Your foot is blocking all the heat from the stove.'

'Illustrious Monsieur Vautrin,' said Bianchon, 'why do you say *coltorama*? That's wrong, it's *coldorama*.'

'No,' said the Museum man, 'it's *coltorama* according to the rules: I have *colt toes*.'

'Ha! ha!'

'Here is his excellency the Marquis de Rastignac, Doctor

of Jurisimprudence,' cried Bianchon, grasping Eugène by the neck and squeezing the breath out of him. 'Hey! you others, hey there!'

Mademoiselle Michonneau came in quietly, acknowledging the others without speaking and took her place with the other three women.

'She always gives me the shivers, that old bat,' Bianchon muttered to Vautrin, indicating Mademoiselle Michonneau. 'To a student of Gall's system like myself it is obvious that she has the bumps of Judas.'

'Did you know him then, Monsieur?' said Vautrin.

'Who hasn't come across him!' exclaimed Bianchon. 'Upon my honour, that pallid old maid looks exactly like one of those long worms that gnaw right through a wooden beam.'

'That's just it, young man,' said the man of forty, combing his whiskers.

> A rose, she lived as long as roses live
> Just one brief morning . . .'*

'Ah, there's a fine *souporama*,' said Poiret, seeing Christophe coming in respectfully carrying the soup.

'Excuse me, Monsieur,' said Madame Vauquer, 'it's cabbage soup.'

All the young men roared with laughter.

'You're licked, Poiret!'

'Poirrrrette is licked!'

'Mark two points up to Ma Vauquer,' said Vautrin.

'Did anyone notice the fog this morning?' asked the Museum man.

'It was', Bianchon said, 'a frenetic, unprecedented fog, a mournful, melancholy, peasoupy, wheezing fog, a Goriot fog.'

'*Goriorama*,' said the painter, 'because it was impenetrable.'

'Hey, Lord Gaoriotte, they be talking 'bout yew.'

Sitting at the bottom end of the table, near the service door, Père Goriot raised his head and sniffed at a bit of bread which he had under his napkin, an old business habit to which he sometimes reverted.

'Well then,' cried Madame Vauquer in a shrill voice which rose above the noise of spoons and plates and others talking, 'isn't the bread to your liking?'

'Quite the contrary, Madame,' he replied, 'it is made from Étampes flour of the finest quality.'

'How can you tell that?' Eugène asked.

'From its whiteness, and its taste.'

'From its smell, rather, since you are just sniffing it,' said Madame Vauquer. 'You are becoming so thrifty that you will end up finding some way of living just on the air you breathe from the kitchen.'

'Then you must take out a patent,' cried the Museum man, 'you'll make a fortune.'

'Let him be, he is doing that to convince us he used to be in the vermicelli business,' said the painter.

'So your nose is a kind of corn-still?' went on the Museum man.

'Corn what?' said Bianchon.

'Cornet.'—'Cornel.'—'Cornelian.'—'Cornice.'—'Cornishman.'—'Corncrake.'—'Cawnpore.'—'*Cornorama*.'

These eight answers shot from every corner of the room as rapidly as a volley of musketry, and caused all the more hilarity in that poor Père Goriot looked at the other diners with a bemused expression, like someone trying to follow a foreign language.

'Corn?' he asked Vautrin, who was sitting next to him.

'Corn on the foot, old chap!' said Vautrin, giving Père Goriot a bang on the head that pushed his hat down over his eyes.

The poor old man, stunned by this sudden assault, stayed quite still for a moment. Christophe cleared away Goriot's plate, thinking that he had finished his soup, with the result that when he had pushed his hat up again and picked up his spoon to eat he just struck the table. All the diners roared with laughter.

'Monsieur,' said the old man, 'you play some nasty tricks, and if you take the liberty of banging my hat down again like that ...'

'Then what, Dad?' Vautrin interrupted.

'Then you will pay dearly for it one day ...'

'In hell, no doubt?' said the painter, 'In that dark little corner where naughty children are sent!'

'Well now! Mademoiselle,' Vautrin said to Victorine, 'you are not eating. So your dad wouldn't budge?'

'A horrible man,' said Madame Couture.

'He'll have to be made to see reason,' said Vautrin.

'But', said Rastignac, who was sitting quite near Bianchon, 'Mademoiselle could start proceedings for subsistence, since she is not eating anything. But look at how Père Goriot is staring at Mademoiselle Victorine.'

The old man forgot to eat as he watched the unfortunate girl, whose face expressed genuine grief, the grief of a rejected child who loves its father.

'My dear fellow,' Rastignac said in a low voice, 'we were wrong about Père Goriot. He is not an idiot, and he is not without feelings. Apply your phrenology system to him and tell me what you find. Last night I saw him twist a silver-gilt dish as if it were wax, and at that moment his expression betrayed some very extraordinary emotions. His life seems so full of mystery that it would be well worth investigating. Yes, Bianchon, laugh as you may, I am not joking.'

'The man is a medical case, I agree,' said Bianchon, 'I'll dissect him, if he is willing.'

'No, just feel his head.'

'All right, perhaps his stupidity is catching.'

Next day Rastignac dressed up very elegantly and set off at about three in the afternoon to visit Madame de Restaud, on the way indulging in those absurdly wild hopes which so enrich the emotional lives of young people. At such times they ignore obstacles and dangers, they see themselves succeeding at everything, just by exercising their imagination they romanticize their lives and make themselves miserable or gloomy when plans are frustrated which never had any reality outside their fevered wishful thinking; if they were not also ignorant and shy, social life would prove impossible. Eugène walked with the greatest care to avoid the slightest splash of mud, but as he walked he was thinking what he was going to say to Madame de Restaud, he was stocking up with witticisms, inventing repartee for an imaginary conversation, preparing epigrams as subtle as Talleyrand's,* assuming always that circumstances would be favourable to the declaration on which he was basing his future. The student did however pick up some mud stains and was obliged to have his boots shined and his trousers brushed at the Palais-Royal. 'If I were rich,' he said to himself as he changed a thirty-sou coin which he had taken with him in case of emergency, 'I would have gone in a carriage and I could have mused at leisure.'

Finally he reached the rue du Helder and asked for the Comtesse de Restaud. With the cold fury of a man confident of eventual victory, he registered the scornful looks of the servants who had seen him crossing the courtyard on foot, but had not heard a carriage draw up at the gate. He felt these looks all the more keenly, for his inferiority had been brought home to him when he came into the courtyard and saw a fine horse pawing the ground, harnessed to one of those smart cabriolets which proclaim a life of extravagant luxury and imply familiarity with all the pleasures Paris has to offer. He began to feel at odds with himself. The open compartments in his mind which he expected to find full of wit slammed shut, he became stupid. As he waited for a response from the comtesse, to whom a manservant had gone to announce the visitor's name, Eugène stood on one foot in front of a window in the anteroom, resting his elbow on the catch and looking absently into the courtyard. He found time passing slowly and would have left but for that Southern tenacity which produces amazing results when its path lies straight ahead.

'Monsieur,' said the manservant, 'Madame is in her boudoir and very busy. She did not answer, but if Monsieur would care to go through to the salon, there is already someone there.'

While marvelling at the awesome power of these people who with a word can accuse or pass judgement on their masters, Rastignac with deliberation opened the door through which the servant had left, evidently so that these insolent servants would think he knew his way about the house, but emerged, feeling very foolish, into a room containing lamps, sideboards, a towel-warmer, and leading to a dark passage and a concealed staircase. The muffled laughter he heard coming from the anteroom completed his embarrassment.

'Monsieur, the salon is this way,' said the servant with that feigned respect which seems to add insult to injury.

Eugène turned on his heel in such haste that he knocked into a bathtub, but luckily caught his hat before it could fall into the bath. At that moment a door opened at the end of the long corridor which was lit by a small lamp. Rastignac heard simultaneously the voices of Madame de Restaud and of Père Goriot, and the sound of a kiss. He entered the dining-room, went through it, following the servant, and came to a reception-room, where he remained standing in front of the window, which he noticed looked out on to the courtyard. He wanted to see if this Père Goriot really was *his* Père Goriot. His heart beat strangely; Vautrin's dreadful remarks came back to him. The servant was waiting for Eugène at the door of the salon, but an elegant young man came out, saying impatiently: 'I'm off, Maurice. You can tell Madame la comtesse I waited more than half an hour for her.' This arrogant person, who was no doubt entitled to be so, hummed an Italian roulade as he walked over to the window where Eugène stood, as much to see the student's face as to look into the courtyard.

'Monsieur le comte would do better to wait another few minutes. Madame has finished,' said Maurice, coming back into the room.

At that moment Père Goriot was emerging from where the small staircase came out near the carriage entrance. The old man was pulling out his umbrella and preparing to open it without noticing that the main gate had been opened to admit a tilbury driven by a young man, wearing some decoration. Père Goriot barely had time to leap back to avoid being run over. The umbrella had frightened the horse, which shied slightly as it ran on towards the steps. The young man glanced round angrily, looked at Père Goriot and acknowledged him before he left with a gesture expressing the forced courtesy one pays to a usurer of whom one is in need, or the minimum respect demanded by a man with some defect, for which one will blush later. Père Goriot returned the courtesy with a friendly wave, full of goodwill. These events occurred with lightning speed. Too absorbed in watching to realize that he was not alone, Eugène suddenly heard the comtesse's voice;

'Oh, Maxime, you were leaving!' she said reproachfully, with a hint of annoyance.

The comtesse had not noticed the tilbury's arrival. Rastignac turned round sharply and saw the comtesse in a fetching white cashmere negligée with pink bows, her hair carelessly arranged, as is the way with Parisian women in the morning. She smelt of fragrant scent, having no doubt just had a bath, and her beauty seemed more voluptuous for being, as it were, more relaxed. Young men's eyes take everything in; their spirits react to the radiation given off by a woman as a plant breathes in from the air the substances it needs. Thus Eugène sensed the bloom of this woman's hands without needing to touch them. Through the cashmere he could see the rosy flesh tints which the loosely tied gown exposed from time to time and on which he feasted his eyes. The comtesse's figure needed no artificial support, a belt alone defined her slender waist, her neck was an invitation to love, her slippered feet were charming. Only when Maxime took her hand to kiss it did Eugène become aware of Maxime and the comtesse of Eugène.

'Oh, it's you, Monsieur de Rastignac. I am delighted to see you,' she said in a tone to which anyone of sensibility would have responded suitably.

Maxime looked from Eugène to the comtesse meaningfully enough to send the intruder on his way. 'As for that, my dear, I hope you will show this odd fellow the door!' In some such phrase lay the clear and evident message conveyed by the looks cast by the arrogant and haughty young man whom Comtesse Anastasie had called Maxime, and whose features she was scanning with that willing submissiveness by which a woman unwittingly betrays all her secrets. Rastignac felt a wave of violent hatred for this young man. In the first place Maxime's handsome, fair, well-curled hair showed him how messy his own was. Then Maxime's boots were elegant and clean, while his own, despite all the care he had taken on his walk, bore a light coating of mud. Finally Maxime wore a frock-coat most elegantly fitted round the waist, which made him look like a pretty woman, while at half-past two in the afternoon Eugène was wearing a black evening coat. The intelligent son of the Charente felt the superiority which fine clothes gave to this tall, slim, clear-eyed, fair-skinned dandy, one of those men who are quite capable of bringing about an orphan's ruin. Without waiting for Eugène's reply, Madame de Restaud sped off into the other room, the skirts of her gown fluttering up and down so that she looked like a butterfly. Maxime followed her. In a fury Eugène followed Maxime and the comtesse. These three then confronted each other by the fireplace in the centre of the great drawing-room. The student was well aware that he was going to be a nuisance to the odious Maxime, but at the risk of displeasing Madame de Restaud he wanted to be a nuisance to the dandy. Suddenly, remembering that he had seen the young man at Madame de Beauséant's ball, he guessed Maxime's relationship to Madame de Restaud, and with that boldness which can lead the young into the silliest errors or the greatest success, he said to himself: 'That's my rival, I will defeat him.' Unwise as he was, he did not know that Comte Maxime de Trailles liked to provoke insults, fire first and kill his man. Eugène was a good shot, but he had not yet knocked down twenty dolls out of twenty-two in a shooting gallery. The young comte flung himself into an easy chair by the fireside, took the tongs and raked the fire with such angry violence that

Anastasie's lovely face suddenly clouded with distress. The young woman turned to Eugène, and looked at him coldly as if to ask: 'But why don't you leave?' in such a way that well-bred people would at once start composing those phrases known as exit lines.

Eugène put on his most agreeable look and said, 'Madame I was in a hurry to see you to ...'

He stopped short. A door opened. The gentleman who had been driving the tilbury suddenly appeared, bare-headed, did not greet the comtesse, cast a worried glance at Eugène, and held out his hand to Maxime, saying 'Good day' with a friendly expression which peculiarly surprised Eugène. Young men from the provinces know nothing of the pleasures of a triangular relationship.

'Monsieur de Restaud,' the comtesse said to the student, indicating her husband.

Eugène bowed low.

'Monsieur,' she went on, introducing Eugène to the Comte de Restaud, 'is Monsieur de Rastignac, and is related to Madame la Vicomtesse de Beauséant through the Marcillacs. I had the pleasure of meeting him at her last ball.'

'Related to Madame la Vicomtesse de Beauséant through the Marcillacs!' These words which the comtesse had stressed almost unduly, prompted by the sort of pride with which a hostess proves that only persons of distinction are to be found in her house, produced a magical effect. The comte dropped his coldly formal manner and bowed to the student.

'Delighted, Monsieur, to make your acquaintance.'

Comte Maxime de Trailles himself glanced uneasily at Eugène and suddenly dropped his arrogant manner. This wave of a magic wand, effected by the potent mention of a name, opened up all the closed compartments of our Southerner's brain and restored the ready wit which he had earlier prepared. A flash of light suddenly gave him clear insight into what had so far been for him the murky atmosphere of Parisian high society. The Maison Vauquer and Père Goriot were at that moment far from his thoughts.

'I thought the Marcillacs had died out?' said the Comte de Restaud to Eugène.

'Yes, Monsieur,' he replied, 'My great-uncle, the Chevalier de Rastignac, married the heiress of the Marcillacs. He had just one daughter, who married the Maréchal de Clarimbault, maternal grandfather of Madame de Beauséant. We are the junior branch, made all the poorer by the fact that my great-uncle, a vice-admiral, lost everything in the King's service. The revolutionary government refused to recognize us as creditors when it liquidated the Compagnie des Indes.'

'Didn't your great-uncle command the *Vengeur* before 1789?'

'Just so.'

'Then he knew my grandfather, in command of the *Warwick*.'

Maxime gave a slight shrug of the shoulders as he looked over at Madame de Restaud, as if to say: 'If he starts talking naval shop with that fellow we're in trouble.' Anastasie read Monsieur de Traille's look. With that remarkable ability with which women are endowed she said with a smile: 'Come along, Maxime; I want to ask you something. Gentlemen we'll leave you to sail in convoy on the *Warwick* and the *Vengeur*.' She rose, and beckoned in derisive complicity to Maxime, who went off with her in the direction of her boudoir. The *morganatic* pair, to use a neat German expression for which there is no accepted native equivalent, had scarcely reached the door when the comte broke off his conversation with Eugène.

'Anastasie! Do stay with us, my dear,' he cried in vexation, 'you know very well ...'

'I'll only be a moment,' she interrupted, 'I need only a moment to tell Maxime what I want him to do for me.'

She came back very soon. Like any woman who is compelled to study her husband's character so that she can behave as she pleases, and knows just how far she can go without forfeiting his precious trust, thus never provoking a clash on minor issues, the comtesse had realized from her husband's tone of voice that it would not be safe for her to remain in her boudoir. This contretemps was Eugène's doing, as the comtesse indicated to Maxime with a look and gesture of annoyance directed at the student. Maxime then said very pointedly to the comte, his wife and Eugène, 'Listen, you are all busy, I don't want to be in the way. Goodbye,' and took his leave.

'But you must stay, Maxime!' cried the comte.

'Come to dinner,' said the comtesse, once more leaving Eugène with the comte and following Maxime into the ante-room, where they stayed together long enough to expect that Monsieur de Restaud would be seeing Eugène off.

Rastignac heard them successively laugh loudly, chat, fall silent; but the crafty student was entertaining Monsieur de Restaud, flattering him, launching him into discussions, so that he could see the comtesse again and find out the nature of her relationship with Père Goriot. This woman, who was obviously in love with Maxime, who dominated her husband, and was secretly connected with the old vermicelli-merchant, seemed a total mystery to him. He wanted to solve this mystery, hoping thereby to acquire sovereign power over a woman so eminently Parisian.

'Anastasie,' said her husband, calling his wife once more.

'Come now, my poor Maxime,' she said to the young man, 'we must just resign ourselves. Until this evening . . .'

'I hope, Nasie,' he whispered in her ear, 'that you'll send that young man packing. His eyes glowed like live coals whenever your robe fell open. He might well declare his passion and compromise you, and then you would oblige me to kill him.'

'Are you crazy, Maxime?' she said. 'On the contrary, don't you see that these little students make excellent lightning conductors? I'll certainly set Restaud against him.'

Maxime roared with laughter and left, followed by the comtesse, who stood by the window to watch him take his seat in the carriage, his horse prancing as he flourished his whip. She stayed there until the main gate closed behind him.

'Just think, my dear,' cried the comte when she rejoined

them, 'this gentleman's family estate is not far from Verteuil, on the Charente. His great-uncle and my grandfather were acquainted.'

'I'm delighted to be among friends,' said the comtesse absently.

'More so than you think,' said Eugène in a low voice.

'What do you mean?' she asked sharply.

'Well,' the student went on, 'I have just seen a gentleman leaving here who lives next door to me in the same boarding house: Père Goriot.'

Hearing this name embellished with the word 'Père' the comte, who was poking the fire, threw down the tongs as if they had burnt his hands and stood up.

'Monsieur, you might have said *Monsieur* Goriot!' he cried.

At first the comtesse went pale on seeing her husband's irritation, then she flushed in obvious embarrassment. She answered in a voice which she tried to make sound natural, and with an expression of apparent indifference, 'You could not be acquainted with anyone of whom we are fonder ...' She broke off, looked at her piano, as if taken by a passing fancy, and said, 'Are you fond of music, Monsieur?'

'Very much so,' answered Eugène, blushing and feeling foolish with a vague impression that he had committed some major blunder.

'Do you sing?' she cried, going across to the piano and running her fingers rapidly over the keys from one end of the scale to the other. Rrrrah!

'No, Madame.'

The Comte de Restaud paced up and down.

'What a pity; that deprives you of a very good way to get on in life.—*Ca-a-ro, ca-a-ro, ca-a-a-ro, non dubitare,*' sang the comtesse.

By pronouncing the name of Père Goriot Eugène had again waved the magic wand, but this time with an effect quite contrary to that produced by the words 'related to Madame de Beauséant'. He was in the situation of someone admitted as a favour into the house of a curio collector who inadvertently knocks into a cabinet full of sculptured figures, breaking off three or four insecurely fastened heads. He wished the earth would swallow him up. Madame de Restaud's gaze was cold and hard, her eyes showed only indifference and avoided those of the luckless student.

'Madame,' he said, 'you have things to discuss with Monsieur de Restaud, allow me most respectfully . . .'

'Any time that you come', the comtesse said hurriedly, stopping Eugène with a gesture, 'you can be sure of giving both Monsieur de Restaud and myself the greatest pleasure.'

Eugène bowed deeply to the couple and went out, followed by Monsieur de Restaud, who despite his protests saw him out as far as the anteroom.

'Any time that gentleman calls,' the comte said to Maurice, 'Madame and I are not at home.'

When Eugène came out on to the steps he realized it was raining. 'Well now,' he said to himself, 'all I have done by coming here is to give offence, I don't know how or how seriously. On top of that I'm going to ruin my coat and hat. I ought to sit in a corner swotting up the law, and simply aim at becoming a magistrate with no social graces. How can I move in society when to manage it properly you need a fleet of cabriolets, polished boots, essential tackle like gold chains, white doeskin gloves at six francs a pair for the daytime, and yellow gloves every evening? Père Goriot, you old rascal, to blazes with you!'

When he came to the street door, a cab driver, who had obviously just set down a pair of newlyweds and asked nothing better than to cheat his master out of a few undeclared fares, saw Eugène without an umbrella, in a black coat, white waistcoat, yellow gloves and polished boots, and signalled to him. Eugène, gripped by the kind of subdued rage which drives a young man ever deeper into the pit into which he has fallen, as if he could hope to find there some happy outcome, nodded assent to the cabby's invitation. With no more than twenty-two sous in his pocket he climbed into the cab, where some traces of orange-blossom and threads of tinsel bore witness to the earlier presence of the bridal couple.

'Where to, sir?' asked the cabby, who had already taken off his white gloves.

'Dammit!' Eugène said to himself, 'since I'm in so deep I might at least do myself a bit of good.—To the Hôtel de Beauséant,' he added aloud.

'Which one?' asked the driver.

Such an exalted question left Eugène speechless. Our aspiring man about town did not know that there were two Hôtels de Beauséant, nor how well endowed he was with relatives who never spared him a thought.

'The Vicomte de Beauséant, rue . . .'

'De Grenelle,' said the driver, nodding his head as he interrupted. 'You see there is the Hôtel of the Comte and the Marquis de Beauséant as well, in the rue Saint-Dominique,' he added, pulling up the step.

'Yes, of course,' Eugène answered drily. 'So everyone is laughing at me today!' he said, flinging his hat on to the cushions in front. 'This trip is going to cost me a king's ransom, but at least I'll be calling on my so-called cousin in thoroughly aristocratic style. Père Goriot has already cost me at least ten francs, the old scoundrel! By Jove! I'll tell Madame de Beauséant all about my adventure; perhaps it will amuse her. She is bound to know all about the mysterious criminal connections between that tailless old rat and that beautiful woman. Pleasing my cousin will do me more good than hammering away at that hussy, who looks pretty expensive to me. If the beautiful vicomtesse's name is so powerful, how much more weight must she carry in person? Let's go to the top. When you are storming heaven, it's God you must aim at!'

These words are a brief summary of the thousand and one thoughts running through his mind. He felt a little calmer and more confident as he watched the rain fall. He told himself that if he was going to squander two of his remaining precious five-franc pieces they would be well spent protecting his coat, boots and hat. He felt really cheerful when he heard the driver crying 'Gate, gate, open the gate please!' A doorman in red and gold swung the gate open on protesting hinges, and it gave Rastignac sweet satisfaction to see his carriage pass beneath the porch, then into the courtyard, and stop beneath the awning over the steps. The driver in his vast blue coat with red borders came to let down the step. Eugène heard muffled laughter from under the peristyle. Three or four servants had already been joking about this vulgar bridal carriage. Their laughter brought the student back to reality the moment he compared his vehicle to one of the most elegant broughams in Paris, drawn by two frisky horses, with roses at their ears, champing at the bit, while a coachman with powdered wig and smart cravat reined them in as though they were trying to bolt. At the Chaussée-d'Antin in Madame de Restaud's courtyard there had been the smart cabriolet of a man of 26. At the Faubourg Saint-Germain waited the luxury of a great nobleman, a carriage and horses which must have cost well over thirty thousand francs.

'But who can that be?' wondered Eugène, realizing rather late that there must be very few women in Paris without a full-time relationship and that the conquest of one of these queens required more than blue blood. 'Devil take it! I suppose my cousin too has her Maxime!'

He went up the steps with death in his heart. The glass door opened as he appeared; he found the servants all straight-faced and serious. The ball he had attended had been held in the great reception-rooms on the ground floor of the Hôtel de Beauséant. Having had no time between the invitation and the ball to pay a formal call on his cousin, he had so far not entered Madame de Beauséant's private apartments. He was thus about to see for himself for the first time the wonders of that personal elegance which reveals the soul and standards of a woman of distinction. He was all the more curious to study this for having Madame de Restaud's salon as a basis of comparison. At half-past four the vicomtesse might be seen, five minutes earlier she would not have received her cousin. Eugène, who knew nothing of these details of

Parisian etiquette, was conducted by way of a grand white staircase, with a gilded banister, red carpet, and masses of flowers, into Madame de Beauséant's presence. He knew nothing of her biography, one of those ever-changing stories recounted in confidence every evening in Parisian salons.

For the past three years the vicomtesse had been having a relationship with one of the richest and most famous of Portuguese noblemen, the Marquis d'Ajuda-Pinto. It was one of those innocent relationships which those involved find so attractive that they cannot bear the presence of a third party. The Vicomte de Beauséant had therefore himself set a public example by respecting, whether he liked it or not, this morganatic union. In the early days of this friendship people who came to see the vicomtesse at two in the afternoon found the Marquis d'Ajuda-Pinto there. Madame de Beauséant, unable to close her door to callers, which would have been most unseemly, received them so coolly and stared so intently at the ceiling that they all understood how unwelcome they were. When it became common knowledge in Paris that Madame de Beauséant did not welcome visitors between two and four in the afternoon people left her entirely alone. She would go to the Bouffons or the Opera* accompanied by Monsieur de Beauséant and Monsieur d'Ajuda-Pinto, but, being a gentleman of refinement, Monsieur de Beauséant always left his wife and the Portuguese once they had taken their seats. Monsieur d'Ajuda had decided to get married. His bride was to be a Mademoiselle de Rochefide. There was only one person in the whole of high society who did not yet know about this wedding, and that was Madame de Beauséant. Some of her friends had indeed talked about it vaguely, but she had only laughed, thinking that these women only wanted to spoil a happiness they envied. Meanwhile the banns were about to be published. Although he had come to inform the vicomtesse about the wedding, the handsome Portuguese had so far not dared to breathe a word. Why? There is probably nothing harder than conveying such an ultimatum to a woman. Some men feel more at ease faced with a swordsman who is threatening to run them through than with a woman who laments for two hours and then begins to swoon and ask for smelling salts. At that moment then Monsieur d'Ajuda-Pinto was acutely uncomfortable, and intending to leave, telling himself that Madame de Beauséant would somehow learn the news, he would write to her, it would be more convenient to kill off their romance by letter than by telling her to her face. When the vicomtesse's servant announced Monsieur Eugène de Rastignac he made the Marquis d'Ajuda-Pinto start for joy. Make no mistake, a woman in love is even more ingenious in finding grounds for suspicion than in varying the means of pleasure. When she is about to be abandoned she is quicker at interpreting a gesture than Virgil's steed in detecting the distant scent of an amorous encounter. You can be sure then that Madame de Beauséant caught this involuntary start, slight, but frightening in its very innocence. Eugène did not know that you should never pay a call on anyone in Paris without first hearing from their friends the personal stories of husband, wife, and children, in order to avoid one of those social pitfalls which prompt the picturesque Polish expression 'Yoke five oxen to your cart!', no doubt to pull you out of the mire in which you are stuck. If these conversational mishaps still have no specific name in France, it must be because they are assumed to be impossible, as a result of the vast publicity there afforded to malicious gossip. After getting bogged down with Madame de Restaud, who had not even given him time to yoke the five oxen to his cart, no one but Eugène could have plodded on again down the same track by presenting himself to Madame de Beauséant. But if he had proved a terrible embarrassment to Madame de Restaud and Monsieur de Trailles, his arrival rescued Monsieur d'Ajuda from an awkward situation.

'Goodbye,' said the Portuguese, hurrying to the door as Eugène came into a charming little pink and grey drawing-room, in which luxury simply looked elegant.

'But only until this evening,' said Madame de Beauséant, turning round to look at the marquis. 'Aren't we going to the Bouffons?'

'I can't come,' he said, with his hand on the doorknob.

Madame de Beauséant stood up and called him back without taking the least notice of Eugène, who was standing there dazzled by all the wonderful treasures sparkling before him, and ready to believe that the stories of the Arabian Nights were true, but not knowing what to do with himself in the presence of this woman who seemed unaware of him. The vicomtesse had raised her right index finger, and elegantly beckoned the marquis to a place in front of her. The gesture revealed a passion so violent and tyrannical that the marquis took his hand off the doorknob and came. Eugène watched him not without envy.

'That', he said to himself, 'is the man with the brougham! So you need frisky horses, liveried servants, and streams of gold to win the attention of a woman in Paris!'

The demon of luxury gnawed at his heart, the frenzied desire to make money gripped him, the thirst for gold made his throat dry. He had a hundred and thirty francs a quarter to live on. His father, mother, brothers, sisters, aunt did not spend two hundred francs a month between them. This rapid comparison between his present situation and the goal he had set himself contributed to his state of shock.

'Why', asked the vicomtesse with a smile, '*are you unable* to come to the Italiens?'

'Business! I am dining at the English Ambassador's.'

'You can drop your business.'

Once a man starts deceiving he is irresistibly compelled to heap one lie on top of another. So Monsieur d'Ajuda asked with a laugh, 'You insist?'

'Yes, I do.'

'That's just what I wanted to hear,' he replied with a keen look which would have reassured any other woman. He took the vicomtesse's hand, kissed it and left.

Eugène smoothed his hair and contorted himself in preparation for a bow, expecting Madame de Beauséant to turn her thoughts to him. Suddenly she sprang up, rushed through the gallery, ran to the window and watched Monsieur d'Ajuda climb into his carriage; she listened out intently for his instructions and heard the footman repeat to the coachman: 'To Monsieur de Rochefide's!'

These words, and the way d'Ajuda leaped into his carriage, struck this woman like thunder and lightning, and she came back racked with the most deadly misgivings. That is how the most awful calamities are in high society. The vicomtesse went into her bedroom, sat at her table and took an elegant sheet of notepaper.

'Since', she wrote, 'you are dining with the Rochefides and not at the English Embassy you owe me an explanation, which I await.'

Correcting a few mistakes in her writing, caused by the convulsive trembling of her hand, she added a C, signifying Claire de Bourgogne, and rang a bell.

'Jacques,' she said to the servant who came at once, 'you will go at half-past seven to Monsieur de Rochefide's house and ask for the Marquis d'Ajuda. If the marquis is there, you will see to it that this note reaches him without waiting for an answer; if he is not there, you will return and give me back my letter.'

'Madame la vicomtesse has someone in her salon.'

'Oh, so I have,' she said, opening the door.

Eugène was beginning to feel very ill at ease, but at last he saw the vicomtesse, who said to him in tones that plucked at his heartstrings, 'Forgive me, Monsieur, I had a note to write. Now I am at your disposal.' She did not know anything she was saying, for her thoughts ran something like this: 'Ha! he intends to marry Mademoiselle de Rochefide. But is he really free? This evening he will break off the match or ... But there will be no question of that tomorrow.'

'Cousin ...' said Eugène.

'Eh?' said the vicomtesse, freezing the student with the arrogance of her look. Eugène understood her exclamation. He had learned so much in the past three hours that he was on his guard.

'Madame,' he went on, going red. He hesitated and then continued, 'Forgive me; I am in such need of protection that even a distant family connection would not come amiss.'

Madame de Beauséant smiled, but sadly; she already sensed the disaster rumbling like thunder around her.

'If you knew the situation of my family,' he went on, 'you would want to play the part of one of those fairy godmothers who enjoyed clearing away the obstacles facing their godsons.'

'Very well, cousin,' she said with a smile, 'how can I help you?'

'I don't really know. The fact that we are connected by a vague family relationship is already worth a fortune. You have confused me, and I forget what I came to tell you. You are the only person I know in Paris. Ah! I wanted to consult you and ask you to accept me as a poor child who wants to cling to your apron-strings and would be ready to die for you.'

'Would you kill someone for my sake?'

'Twice over,' said Eugène.

'Child! Yes, you are a child,' she said holding back her tears, 'you at least would be sincere in your love!'

'Oh yes!' he said, nodding his head.

The vicomtesse found the student's bold answer extremely interesting. For the first time the Southerner had become calculating. Between Madame de Restaud's blue boudoir and Madame de Beauséant's pink salon he had taken an Honours course in that *Parisian Law* which is never mentioned, although it constitutes an advanced social jurisprudence which, well learned and well practised, opens every door.

'Ah, now I've got it,' said Eugène, 'I had noticed Madame de Restaud at your ball and called on her this morning.'

'You must have caused her some embarrassment,' said Madame de Beauséant with a smile.

'Yes, indeed. I am so ignorant that I'll set everyone against me if you refuse to help. I think it is very hard to meet a young, beautiful, rich, elegant woman in Paris who is fancy-free, and I need one to teach me what you women explain so well: life. I shall find a Monsieur de Trailles everywhere. So I came to ask you to solve a puzzle for me and to tell me what sort of blunder I committed. I mentioned a Père ...'

'Madame la Duchesse de Langeais,' Jacques announced, interrupting the student, who made a gesture of extreme annoyance.

'If you want to succeed,' said the vicomtesse in a low voice, 'start by not showing your feelings so plainly.'

'How are you, my dear,' she went on, rising to meet the duchesse and press her hands with as much effusive affection as she would have shown a sister, to which the duchesse responded with the fondest embraces.

'They are two good friends,' said Rastignac to himself. 'That means I shall have two women to protect me. These two must have the same friends, and the duchesse will surely take an interest in me.'

'To what happy thought do I owe the pleasure of seeing you, my dear Antoinette?' said Madame de Beauséant.

'I saw Monsieur d'Ajuda-Pinto going into Monsieur de Rochefide's house, so I thought you would be alone.'

Madame de Beauséant did not tighten her lips, she did not flush, her gaze did not waver, her brow seemed unruffled as the duchesse uttered these fateful words.

'If I had known you were engaged ...' added the duchesse, turning towards Eugène.

'This is Monsieur Eugène de Rastignac, a cousin of mine,' said the vicomtesse. 'Have you had any news of General Montriveau?' she asked. 'Sérisy told me yesterday that no one sees him any more. Has he been to your house today?'

The duchesse, who had reputedly been deserted by Monsieur de Montriveau, with whom she was madly in love, felt the question like a stab in the heart, and went red as she answered. 'He was at the Élysée yesterday.'

'On duty,' said Madame de Beauséant.

'Clara, I am sure you know,' the duchesse went on, looking daggers, 'that the banns are to be published tomorrow between Monsieur d'Ajuda-Pinto and Mademoiselle de Rochefide?'

The blow was too violent. The vicomtesse went pale and answered with a laugh, 'One of those rumours that silly people enjoy spreading. Why should Monsieur d'Ajuda bring one of the finest names in Portugal into the Rochefide family? The Rochefide title is hardly older than yesterday.'

'But Berthe will have two hundred thousand livres a year in all, they say.'

'Monsieur d'Ajuda is too rich to bother about that sort of thing.'

'But, my dear, Mademoiselle de Rochefide is charming.'

'Ah!'

'Anyhow he is dining there this evening, all the arrangements have been agreed. I am most surprised that you know so little about it.'

'What was this blunder of yours, then, Monsieur?' said Madame de Beauséant. 'This poor boy is such a novice in the ways of the world that he doesn't understand a word we are saying, my dear Antoinette. Let's be kind to him and put off talking about this matter until tomorrow. Tomorrow, you see, it will surely all be official, and you can retail your unofficial information with confidence.'

The duchesse treated Eugène to one of those arrogant looks which scan a man from top to toe and leave him feeling squashed and worthless. 'Madame, I unwittingly plunged a dagger into Madame de Restaud's heart. Where I went wrong was doing it unwittingly,' said the student, whose intelligence had served him well and who had perceived the wounding shafts concealed beneath the affectionate words of the two women. 'You go on seeing, and perhaps you fear people who know perfectly well how much they are hurting you, while someone who wounds without knowing how deeply he has wounded is regarded as a fool so clumsy that he wastes every opportunity and is despised by all.'

Madame de Beauséant gave the student a melting look, managing to combine gratitude and dignity as befits great souls. Her look was balm to soothe the wound inflicted on the student's heart a moment before by the duchesse as she estimated his value at a glance like an auctioneer.

'Just imagine,' continued Eugène, 'I had just secured the goodwill of the Comte de Restaud; for', turning to the duchesse with an expression both humble and mischievous, 'you should know, Madame, that I am still just a poor devil of a student, very lonely, very poor . . .'

'Don't say such a thing, Monsieur de Rastignac. We women never want anything that nobody else wants.'

'Bah!' said Eugène, 'I am only 22, and one must learn to put up with the misfortunes of whatever age one is. Besides, I am making my confession, and no one could be kneeling in a prettier confessional; it makes you commit the sins of which you accuse yourself in the conventional one.'

The duchesse's expression grew chilly at this irreverent speech. She condemned its poor taste by saying to the vicomtesse:

'This gentleman has only just arrived . . .'

Madame de Beauséant began to laugh openly both at her cousin and at the duchesse.

'He has just arrived, my dear, and is looking for a woman to teach him good taste.'

'Madame la duchesse,' Eugène went on, 'isn't it natural to want to be initiated into the mysteries of things that charm us?' ('Come now,' he said inwardly, 'I am sure this is the sort of sententious talk they get from their hairdresser.')

'But Madame de Restaud is, I believe, the pupil of Monsieur de Trailles,' said the duchesse.

'I didn't know about that,' the student went on, 'so I stupidly flung myself between them. In fact I was getting on rather well with the husband, I was being tolerated for a while by the wife, when I took it into my head to mention that I knew a man whom I had just seen leaving by a concealed staircase, after he had kissed the comtesse at the end of a corridor.'

'Who is that?' said the two women.

'An old man who pays two louis a month to live in the depths of the Faubourg Saint-Marcel, like me, a poor student; a real old wretch everyone makes fun of. We call him Père Goriot.'

'But child that you are,' cried the vicomtesse, 'Madame de Restaud was a Mademoiselle Goriot.'

'A vermicelli-merchant's daughter,' the duchesse added, 'an ordinary little woman who was presented at Court the same day as a pastrycook's daughter. Don't you remember, Clara? The King began laughing, and made some Latin joke about flour. People, how does it go then? People ...

'*Ejusdem farinae*,'* said Eugène.

'That's it,' said the duchesse.

'Oh, so he is her father,' said the student with a gesture of horror.

'Yes indeed. The old fellow had two daughters, and he is almost crazy about them, though both of them have pretty well disowned him.'

'Isn't the second daughter', said the vicomtesse, looking at Madame de Langeais, 'married to a banker with a German name, a Baron de Nucingen? Isn't her name Delphine? Isn't she a blonde with a side box at the Opera, who goes to the Bouffons too, and talks loudly so that people will look at her?'

The duchesse said with a smile, 'My dear, I am surprised at you. Why are you so interested in those people? Only someone madly in love, as Restaud was, could have fallen so heavily for the floury Mademoiselle Anastasie. Oh! He won't find her a very good bargain! She is in the hands of Monsieur de Trailles, who will be the ruin of her.'

'They have disowned their father,' Eugène repeated.

'They have indeed. Their father, the father, a father,' replied the vicomtesse, 'a good father who is said to have given each of them five or six hundred thousand francs to ensure their happiness by marrying them well, and only kept back eight or ten thousand livres a year for himself. He thought that his daughters would remain his daughters and that in their homes he had created two places where he would be able to live, two houses where he would be adored and spoilt. Within two years his sons-in-law had banished him from their society as if he were the most wretched of wretches . . .'

Tears welled up in Eugène's eyes. He had only recently found refreshment in the pure and holy affections of his family, he was still under the spell of youthful beliefs, and was still experiencing his first day on the battlefield of Parisian civilization. Genuine emotions are so readily communicated that for a moment the three of them looked at each other in silence.

'Ah! dear me, yes,' said Madame de Langeais, 'it all seems quite dreadful, and yet we see it every day. Isn't there a reason for it? Tell me, my dear, have you ever thought what a son-in-law is? A son-in-law is a man for whose sake you and I will bring up a dear little creature, to whom we are attached by countless ties, who for seventeen years will be the family's joy, its "pure white soul", as Lamartine would say, and who will one day become its scourge. When this man takes her from us he will begin by clutching her love like an axe with which to cut into the heart and living flesh of this angel and sever all the emotional ties which bound her to her family. Yesterday our daughter meant everything to us, and we to her; the day after she becomes our enemy. Don't we see this tragedy played out every day? Here, a daughter-in-law who treats with total disdain the father-in-law who sacrificed everything for his son. There, a son-in-law who evicts his mother-in-law. I hear people asking what is dramatic about the life we lead today; but the drama of the son-in-law is appalling, not to mention our marriages which have become a mere farce. I understand perfectly what has befallen this old vermicelli-merchant. I seem to remember that this Foriot . . .'

'Goriot, Madame.'

'Yes, this Moriot was president of his section during the Revolution. He had inside information about the famous food shortage and began to make his fortune at that time by selling flour at ten times what it cost him. He could get as much as he wanted. My grandmother's steward sold him vast amounts. This Goriot probably went shares, like all those sort of people, with the Committee of Public Safety. I remember that the steward used to tell my grandmother that she would be quite safe staying at Granvilliers, because her wheat was an excellent certificate of good citizenship. Well! This Loriot, who sold wheat to those murderers, only ever had one passion; he worships his daughters, they say. He found the elder one a perch in the Restaud house, and grafted the other on to the Baron de Nucingen's family tree, that rich banker who is ostensibly royalist. You can understand that under the Empire the two sons-in-law did not make too much fuss about receiving in their homes the old revolutionary of '93;* it was still all right under Buonaparte. But when the Bourbons came back, the old chap was an embarrassment to Monsieur de Restaud, and still more so to the banker. The daughters, who may perhaps still have been fond of their father, tried to play a double game, keeping their father and their husbands sweet at the same time. They would receive Goriot when they had no one else there; they thought up affectionate pretexts for doing so "Papa, do come, it will be so much more comfortable with just the two of us!" etc. Personally, my dear, I believe that genuine feelings are neither blind nor stupid, so the poor old 93er's heart must have bled. He saw that his daughters were ashamed of him; that if they loved their husbands he was harming his sons-in-law. So there was nothing for it but to sacrifice himself. He made the sacrifice because he was a father; he kept away of his own accord. Seeing his daughters happy, he realized he had done the right thing. Father and children colluded in this little crime. That is the sort of thing you see everywhere. Wouldn't this Père Doriot just have been completely out of place in his daughters' salons? He would have been an embarrassment to them, and would have been bored to death. What happened to this father can happen to the prettiest of women with the man she loves most: if he finds her love boring he will leave her, he will stoop to anything to escape. All our emotions are like that. Our heart is a treasure chest, and if you suddenly empty it out you are ruined. We don't forgive someone for revealing the full depth of their feelings, any more than someone without a penny of his own. This father had given away all he had. For twenty years he had given his whole heart, his love, he had given away his whole fortune in a single day. When they had squeezed the lemon dry his daughters flung the peel into the gutter.'

'What a loathsome world,' said the vicomtesse, fidgeting with her shawl, her eyes still downcast, for she was cut to the quick by some of the things Madame de Langeais had said for her benefit as she related the story.

'Loathsome! no,' replied the duchesse, 'it follows its course, that's all. If I talk to you like that it's just to show that I am not taken in by the world. I think like you,' she said, pressing the vicomtesse's hand. 'The world is a quagmire, let's try to remain above it.' She rose, kissed Madame de Beauséant on the forehead and said, 'You are looking very beautiful at this moment, my dear, I have never seen such a pretty colour in your face.' Then she went out, with a slight nod in the cousin's direction.

'Père Goriot is sublime!' said Eugène, as he remembered seeing him twisting his silver plate that night.

Madame de Beauséant did not hear; she was deep in thought. Some moments went by in silence, and the poor student, paralysed with confusion, did not dare leave, or stay, or speak.

'The world is loathsome and wicked,' the vicomtesse said at last. 'As soon as some misfortune befalls us there is always a friend ready to come and tell us about it, probing our heart with a dagger while inviting us to admire the handle. Sarcasm and mockery already! Ha! I will defend myself.' She raised her head like the great lady she was, and her proud eyes flashed.

'Oh!' she cried, seeing Eugène, 'you are still there!'

'Yes,' he said pathetically.

'Well, Monsieur de Rastignac, treat the world as it deserves. You want to get on, I will help you. You will plumb the

depths of women's corruption, you will measure the extent
of men's miserable vanity. Although I am well read in the
book of this world, there were yet some pages unknown to
me. Now I know it all. The more coldly calculating you
are, the further you will go. Strike without pity and people
will fear you. Accept men and women as mere post horses
to be left worn out at every stage and you will reach the
summit of your ambitions. Don't forget that you will be
nothing here unless you have a woman to take an interest
in you. You need one who is young, rich, elegant. But if
you have any genuine feelings, hide them like a treasure; never
let anyone suspect them, or you will be lost. You would
cease to be the executioner and would become the victim.
If you ever fall in love, keep your secret well! Do not reveal
it until you know extremely well to whom you are opening
your heart. To preserve in advance this love as yet unborn
learn to distrust the world. Listen to me, Miguel ...' (in her
innocence she used the wrong name without noticing), 'There
is something even more appalling than two daughters aban-
doning their father and wishing him dead and that is the
mutual rivalry of the two sisters. Restaud is of noble birth,
his wife has been accepted socially and presented at Court,
but her sister, her own sister, the beautiful Madame Delphine
de Nucingen, wife of a man made of money, is dying of disappointment. She is devoured by jealousy, she and her sister
are worlds apart, her sister is no longer her sister; the two
women disown each other just as they disown their father.
So Madame de Nucingen would lap up all the mud between
the rue Saint-Lazare and the rue de Grenelle* to be admitted
to my salon. She thought that de Marsay would enable her
to reach that goal, so she became de Marsay's slave. She bores
him to death. De Marsay hardly cares about her. If you introduce her to me you will be her Benjamin, she will adore
you. Love her afterwards if you can, otherwise just use her.
I will see her once or twice at some big evening party where
there is a crowd, but I will never receive her in the daytime.
I will greet her and that will be enough. You have shut the

comtesse's door against you by mentioning the name of Père Goriot. Oh yes, my dear boy, you could call on Madame de Restaud any number of times, you would always find her "not at home". You have been banned. All right, let Père Goriot win you admission to Madame Delphine de Nucingen's house. The beautiful Madame de Nucingen will be the standard you bear. Enjoy the marks of her favour and women will dote on you. Her rivals, her friends, her closest friends will try to take you away from her. There are women who love the man someone else has chosen, just as there are poor middle-class women who hope to acquire our manners by copying our hats. You will be very successful. In Paris success is everything, it is the key to power. If women believe you to have wit and talent, so will men, unless you disillusion them. Then you can set your heart on anything, every door will be open to you. Then you will learn what the world is really like: an assembly of dupes and knaves. Don't be counted with either. I am giving you my name to use like Ariadne's thread in this labyrinth. Don't compromise it,' she said, arching her neck with a regal glance at the student, 'give it back to me unsullied. Go now, leave me alone. We women too have our battles to fight.'

'Supposing you needed a volunteer to set off a mine?' said Eugène, interrupting her.

'Well?' she said.

He struck his heart, returned his cousin's smile and left. It was five o'clock. Eugène was hungry and afraid of arriving late for dinner. This fear made him appreciate the joy of being swiftly transported about Paris, and this purely automatic pleasure allowed him to give free rein to the thoughts which assailed him. When a young man of his age is wounded by contempt he loses his temper, rages, shakes his fist at the whole of society, thirsts for vengeance, but is also filled with self-doubt. At that moment Rastignac was devastated by the words: 'You have shut the comtesse's door against you!'

'I'll go there!' he said to himself, 'and if Madame de Beauséant is right, if I am banned ... I ... Madame de Restaud will come across me in all the salons she goes to. I will learn fencing, pistol shooting, I'll kill that Maxime of hers!'—'And what about money?' cried out his conscience, 'Where will you find that?'

Suddenly all the wealth displayed in the Comtesse de Restaud's house glittered before his eyes. He had seen the luxury on which a Mademoiselle Goriot was bound to set her heart, the gilding, the ostentatious display of expensive possessions, the indiscriminate luxury of the upstart, the extravagance of the kept woman. This fascinating picture was suddenly obliterated by the magnificence of the Hôtel de Beauséant. His imagination, soaring into the upper reaches of Parisian society, filled his heart with a host of morbid thoughts, while broadening his mind and his conscience. He saw the world as it is: laws and morality unavailing with the rich, wealth the *ultima ratio mundi*.* 'Vautrin is right, wealth is virtue,' he said to himself.

When he reached the rue Neuve-Sainte-Geneviève he ran up to his room, came down with ten francs for the cabby, and went into the disgusting dining-room, where he saw the eighteen diners feeding like animals at a trough. He was revolted at the sight of such wretchedness and the appearance of the room. The transition was too abrupt, the contrast too complete, not to arouse in him cravings of boundless ambition. On the one hand the fresh and charming images of the most elegant society, young and lively figures in a setting composed of marvels of art and luxury, minds fired with passion and poetry; on the other, dismal pictures edged with grime, faces on which passions had left behind only their strings and mechanism. The lesson which the fury of a woman scorned had wrung from Madame de Beauséant, her specious offers came back into his memory, and this misery was commentary enough. Rastignac resolved to open up two parallel lines of advance in his assault on fortune, to rely both on knowledge and love, to be a learned doctor of law and a man of fashion. He was still very much a child! These two lines are asymptotes which can never meet.

'You seem very gloomy, Monsieur le Marquis,' Vautrin said to him, giving him one of those looks with which he seemed able to penetrate the innermost secrets of the heart.

'I am not disposed to endure the witticisms of those who call me Monsieur le Marquis,' he answered. 'Here, to be a real marquis, you need a hundred thousand livres a year and living in the Maison Vauquer does not exactly make you Fortune's favourite.'

Vautrin looked at Rastignac with an air of paternal contempt, as if to say: 'What a brat! I'd gobble him up in one mouthful!' Then he replied, 'You're in a bad mood, maybe because you had no success with the lovely Comtesse de Restaud.'

'She has closed her door to me for saying that her father eats at our table,' cried Rastignac.

The diners all looked at each other. Père Goriot lowered his eyes and turned away to wipe them.

'You flicked some of your snuff in my eye,' he said to his neighbour.

'From now on anyone bothering Père Goriot will be attacking me,' answered Eugène, looking at the former vermicelli-merchant's neighbour, 'He is worth more than the lot of us. I am not speaking of the ladies,' he added, turning towards Mademoiselle Taillefer.

These words were conclusive. Eugène had uttered them in such a way that the diners were forced into silence. Vautrin alone said mockingly, 'If you're going to take Père Goriot under your wing and make yourself responsible for him, you'll need to learn how to use a sword and a pistol properly.'

'That's just what I'm going to do,' said Eugène.

'So your campaign started today?'

'Maybe,' answered Rastignac, 'but I'm not accountable to anyone for my affairs, considering that I don't try to guess what others get up to at night.'

Vautrin looked askance at Rastignac.

'If you don't want to be taken in by puppets, my lad, you've got to go right behind the scenes and not be content just to peep through the holes in the curtain. Enough said,' he added, seeing that Eugène was about to make a fuss. 'We'll have a few words together whenever you like.'

A chilly gloom fell on the dinner-table. Père Goriot was so absorbed by the deep sorrow caused by the student's words that he did not realize that the others' attitude to him had changed, and that a young man had come to his defence who was quite capable of silencing his persecutors.

'So Monsieur Goriot', said Madame Vauquer in a low voice, 'turns out right now to be father of a comtesse?'

'And of a baronne,' Rastignac replied.

'That's what he was cut out for,' Bianchon said to Rastignac, 'I examined his head: there's just one bump, the one meaning paternity. He'll be an Eternal Father.'

Eugène was in too serious a mood to be amused by Bianchon's jest. He wanted to turn Madame Beauséant's advice to good account, and was wondering where and how to get hold of some money. He began to worry as he saw the world's wide open spaces stretching out before him, empty and full at the same time. When dinner was over the others went out one by one, leaving him alone in the room.

'So you saw my daughter?' said Goriot with obvious emotion.

Roused from his reverie by the old man, Eugène clasped his hand and gazed at him with a kind of sympathy. 'You are a good, decent man,' he answered. 'We'll talk about your daughters later.' He stood up without waiting to hear what Père Goriot might say and retired to his room, where he wrote his mother the following letter:

My dear Mother,

After all you have already given me, see if you cannot draw on some fresh source to help me. I am in a position to become wealthy very quickly. I need twelve hundred francs, and I must have that sum at any price. Do not tell my father of my request, he might object; if I do not obtain this money I shall be plunged into such despair as to make me blow my brains out. I shall explain my reasons as soon as I see you, for it would take volumes to convey to you in writing the situation in which I find myself. I have not been gambling, dear Mother. I am not in debt, but if you care about preserving the life you gave me, you must find this sum for me. In short, I am going to be calling on the Vicomtesse de Beauséant, who has taken me under her wing. I shall have to go about in high society, and I do not have a penny for decent gloves. I can manage to live on just bread and water, and if need be even go hungry, but I cannot do without the implements used by the workers in this particular vineyard. It is a question of making my way or sticking in the mud. I know all the hopes you have invested in me, and intend to fulfil them without delay. Dear Mother, sell some of your old jewellery, I will soon replace it. I know our family situation well enough to realize just how much such sacrifices cost, and you must believe that I am not asking you to make them in vain, for that would make me a monster. You must see in my request a cry prompted by the most compelling urgency. Our whole future depends on this subsidy, which I need in order to open my campaign, for life in Paris is a constant battle. If there is no other way to make up the sum than to sell my aunt's lace, tell her that I will send her some that is even finer, etc.

He wrote to each of his sisters to ask them for their savings, and in order to extract from them a sacrifice which they would be only too happy to make for him, while ensuring that they did not mention it to the family, he appealed to their discretion by playing on the theme of honour, which always strikes a sensitive and resonant chord in the hearts of the young. When he had written these letters he none the less felt an involuntary tremor, his heart beat faster and he was shaking. This ambitious young man knew the spotless nobility of these souls buried away in their solitude, he knew what grief he would cause his two sisters, and also what joy; how they would delight in going to some distant corner of the vineyard to discuss their brother in secret. His awakened conscience showed him a bright vision of them counting their modest treasure in secret, he saw them employing all the ingenious ruses of young girls to send him this money under cover, using deceit for the first time and achieving sublimity. 'A sister's heart is diamond-pure and inexhaustibly tender,' he told himself. He was ashamed of what he had written. How intense would be their heartfelt wishes for him, how pure their fervent prayers to heaven! How they would delight in their self-sacrifices! How his mother would grieve if she could not send the whole sum! He would use such fine sentiments, such fearful sacrifices as rungs in a ladder to reach Delphine de Nucingen. Tears, a last few grains of incense cast on the sacred altar of the family, fell from his eyes. He paced up and down in agitation and despair. Père Goriot saw him in this state through the half-open door, and asked: 'What is the matter, Monsieur?'

'Ah, my good neighbour, I am still a son and a brother, just as you are a father. You are right to tremble for the Comtesse Anastasie. She belongs to a Monsieur Maxime de Trailles, and he will be her ruin.'

Père Goriot withdrew, mumbling some words which made no sense to Eugène. Next day Rastignac went to post his letters. He hesitated up to the last moment, but finally threw them in the box, saying, 'I am going to succeed!' The words of the gambler, the great soldier, fatal words which ruin more men than they redeem.

A few days later Eugène called on Madame de Restaud and was not received. He went back three times, and three times he found the door closed, although he chose hours when Comte Maxime de Trailles was not there. The vicomtesse had been right. The student had stopped studying. He attended lectures to answer the roll-call, and once he had attested his presence, he would make off. He had reasoned as most students do. Studies could wait until the time came for sitting his examinations; he had resolved to let his second- and third-year class enrolments simply accumulate, then to work seriously at learning law in a single burst at the last moment. That left him with fifteen months' leisure for sailing over the Parisian ocean, exploiting women or fishing up his fortune. During that week he saw Madame de Beauséant twice, visiting her only at the moment when the Marquis d'Ajuda's carriage was leaving. For a few more days that illustrious woman, the most romantic figure of the Faubourg Saint-Germain, held the advantage and succeeded in postponing the wedding of Mademoiselle de Rochefide and the Marquis d'Ajuda-Pinto, but these last few days, which fear of losing her happiness made the most passionate of all, could only hasten the disaster. The Marquis d'Ajuda agreed with the Rochefides in viewing this quarrel and reconciliation as a favourable turn of events. They hoped that Madame de Beauséant would become used to the idea of this marriage and would end up by sacrificing her afternoon meetings to a future such as was only to be expected in the life of any man. Despite the most faithful promises, duly renewed every day, Monsieur d'Ajuda was thus simply play-acting, with the vicomtesse enjoying the deception. 'Instead of nobly leaping out of the window, she let herself roll down the stairs,' said the Duchesse de Langeais, her best friend. Nevertheless these last embers glowed long enough for the vicomtesse to remain in Paris and help her young relative, for whom she felt a kind of superstitious affection. Eugène had shown her abundant devotion and sympathy in a situation where women find no pity or true consolation in anyone's eyes. If a man speaks kindly to them at such times it is in the hope of gain.

Seeking to master the whole layout on the board before approaching Nucingen's house, Rastignac wanted to familiarize himself with Père Goriot's earlier life and collected a quantity of reliable information, which may be thus summarized.

Jean-Joachim Goriot was, before the Revolution, an ordinary workman in the vermicelli trade, able, thrifty and sufficiently enterprising to buy up his employer's business when he chanced to fall victim to the first uprising in 1789. He had set himself up in the rue de la Jussienne, near the Corn Exchange, and had the great good sense to accept the presidency of his section* in order to have his business protected by those who wielded most influence in that dangerous period. This wise move laid the foundations of his fortune, which began with the shortage, genuine or otherwise, as a result of which grain fetched an enormous price in Paris. Ordinary people were killing each other in fights outside bakeries, while certain individuals went undisturbed to collect Italian pasta from grocers' shops. In the course of that year citizen Goriot amassed the capital which later enabled him to conduct his business from the position of superiority which a large amount of cash confers on its possessor. What happened to him is what happens to any man whose ability is only relative; his mediocrity saved him. Besides, from the fact that his wealth became known only when it was no longer dangerous to be rich, he aroused no envy. The grain trade seemed to have absorbed all his intelligence. When it came to wheat, flour, middlings, recognizing their quality or origin, seeing to their storage, forecasting whether harvests would be abundant or meagre, acquiring cereals cheaply, bringing in stocks from Sicily or the Ukraine, Goriot was unrivalled. To see him transacting his business, explaining the laws governing export or import of grain, analysing the thinking behind them, grasping their defects, anyone would have judged him able enough to be a Minister of State. Patient, active, energetic, consistent, prompt to deliver, he had an eagle eye, anticipated everything, foresaw, knew, concealed everything. He had the perspicacity of a diplomat, the stamina of a foot soldier. Away from his speciality, from the simple, obscure trading-place where he spent his leisure hours leaning on the doorpost at the entrance, he reverted to being the dull, uncouth workman, incapable of following an argument, impervious to all the pleasures of the mind, who would fall asleep at the theatre, one of those Parisian Dolibans* who excel only in stupidity. Such characters are almost all alike. In almost all their hearts you will find some exalted sentiment. Two exclusive emotions had filled the vermicelli-merchant's heart, had absorbed its vital fluids, just as the grain trade drew all the intelligence from his brain. His wife, only daughter of a rich farmer from Brie, was the object of his devout admiration and boundless love. Goriot had admired in her a nature at once fragile and strong, sensitive and graceful, contrasting powerfully with his own. If any feeling is innate in all men's hearts, is it not pride in affording protection to a weaker being? To that add love, the deep gratitude felt by all straightforward souls for the source of their pleasure, and you will understand many odd features of human behaviour. After seven years of unclouded happiness, Goriot, most unfortunately for him, lost his wife. She was just beginning to influence him outside the realm of the emotions. She might have given this lump of clay some form, she might have imparted some understanding of the wider world and of life. In such a situation Goriot's paternal emotions intensified to the point of insanity. All the affection of whose object death had deprived him was lavished on his two daughters, who at first satisfied all his emotional needs. However attractive the proposals made to him by merchants or farmers eager to offer him their daughters, he chose to remain a widower. His father-in-law, the only man for whom he had ever had any liking, claimed to know for a fact that Goriot had sworn never to be unfaithful to his wife, dead though she was. The men in the Corn Exchange, unable to comprehend such sublime folly, made jokes about it, and gave Goriot a ludicrous nickname. The first of them who took it into his head to utter it as he drank to a bargain took such a punch on the shoulder from the vermicelli-merchant that it sent him reeling headlong against a kerbstone in the rue Oblin. Goriot's unquestioning devotion, his sensitive and touchy love for his daughters was so well known that one day one of his competitors, wanting Goriot out of the way so that he himself might have a free hand with the dealing, told him that Delphine had just been run over by a cab. The vermicelli-merchant, white as a sheet, left the Exchange at once. He was ill for several days as a reaction to the conflicting emotions aroused by this false alarm. Though he did not strike this man one of his lethal blows, he did drive him from the Exchange by forcing him into bankruptcy at a crucial moment. The education of his two daughters naturally defied all reason. With an income of more than sixty thousand livres a year, and spending less than twelve hundred francs on himself, Goriot's only joy was to satisfy his daughters' whims. The most outstanding teachers were given the task of endowing them with all the talents which mark a good education. They had a lady companion, who fortunately for them was a woman of taste and intelligence. They rode, they had a carriage, they lived in the style of a rich nobleman's mistress. They had only to express the most expensive wishes to see their father hasten to gratify them; in return for his presents all he asked for was a hug. Goriot ranked his daughters with the angels, inevitably above himself, poor man! He even loved the pain they caused him.

When his daughters came of marriageable age they were in a position to pick husbands to suit their tastes. Each was to have half their father's fortune as dowry. Courted for her beauty by the Comte de Restaud, Anastasie had aristocratic aspirations which led her to leave her father's home and launch out into higher social spheres. Delphine loved money; she married Nucingen, a banker of German origin who became a baron of the Holy Roman Empire. Goriot remained in the vermicelli trade. His daughters and his sons-in-law were soon shocked to see him still engaged in this trade, although it was his whole life. After putting up with their entreaties for five years, he finally agreed to retire on the proceeds from selling his business and the profits of those years. This capital was estimated by Madame Vauquer, in whose house he had installed himself, to bring in eight to ten thousand livres a year. He resorted to this boarding house in a fit of despair, seeing his two daughters obliged by their husbands to refuse not only to give him a home with them, but even to receive him openly as a visitor.

This was all the information about Père Goriot known to a Monsieur Muret, who had bought his business. The theories which Rastignac had heard from the Duchesse de Langeais were thus confirmed. Here ends the exposition of this obscure but appalling Parisian tragedy.

2

Entry on the Social Scene

TOWARDS the end of that first week in December Rastignac received two letters, one from his mother, the other from his elder sister. The sight of the familiar handwriting set his heart beating with joy and at the same time made him tremble with terror. These two flimsy documents contained a sentence of life or death for his hopes. If he felt apprehension as he recalled his parents' straitened circumstances, he had enjoyed too many marks of their favour not to fear that he might have sucked their veins dry. His mother's letter read as follows:

My dear boy, I am sending you what you asked for. Make good use of this money, for even if it were a question of saving your life, I could not find so considerable a sum again without your father's knowledge, and that could only cause discord between us. To obtain more we should be obliged to pledge our land as security. I cannot possibly pass judgement on plans I know nothing about, but what kind of plans must they be if you are afraid of confiding in me? An explanation would not require volumes; a mere word is all that a mother needs, and a word would have spared me the anguish of uncertainty. I cannot conceal the painful impression caused by your letter. My dear son, what is this emotion that compelled you to strike such dread into my heart? You must have found it very painful to write me such a letter, for it was very painful for me to read it. What course is this on which you are embarking? Your life and happiness dependent on appearing to be what you are not, on seeing a world which you could only frequent by spending money you cannot afford, on wasting precious time from your studies? My good Eugène, believe your mother's heart, crooked paths do not lead to greatness. Patience and resignation are the proper virtues for young men in your position. I am not scolding you, I should not wish our offering to be accompanied by the slightest bitterness. I speak as a mother who trusts you and cares for you. If you know your obligations, for my part I know how pure your heart is, how excellent your intentions, and so I can say to you without fear: Go on, my beloved boy, press ahead! I tremble because I am a mother; but every step you take will be accompanied by our prayers and blessings. Take care, dear boy, you must show a man's wisdom. The fate of five people who are dear to you rests in your hands. Yes, the fortunes of all of us are invested in you, just as your happiness is ours. We all pray that you will have God's help in what you undertake. On this occasion your aunt Marcillac has been amazingly kind; she went so far as to appreciate what you told me about your gloves. But she has a weakness for my eldest, as she cheerfully admitted. You should really love your aunt, Eugène. I will not tell you what she has done for you until you have succeeded, otherwise her money would burn your fingers. Children do not know what it means to sacrifice keepsakes. But what sacrifice would we not be willing to make for you? She bids me tell you that she sends you a kiss on the forehead, and with this kiss would like to endow you with the power of being often happy. This excellent good woman would have written to you herself but for the gout she has in her fingers. Your father is well. The 1819 harvest has surpassed all our hopes. Farewell, dear boy. I will not say anything about your sisters; Laure is writing to you. I will leave to her the pleasure of passing on all the gossip about the little events within the family. May heaven grant you success! Oh, yes, you must succeed, Eugène, you have caused me too much pain for me to bear it all over again. I learned what it means to be poor when I longed to have riches to give my child. Farewell again. Do not leave us without news; your mother sends you a loving kiss.

By the time Eugène finished reading this letter he was in tears. He thought of Père Goriot flattening out his silver gilt and selling it to pay off his daughter's bill of exchange.

'Your mother has sacrificed her jewellery!' he told himself. 'Your aunt must have wept at selling some of her relics! What right do you have to condemn Anastasie? What she did for her lover's sake you have just imitated out of selfish concern for your own future! Are you any better than she is?'

The student felt himself inwardly consumed as though by

intolerable heat. He wanted to renounce the world, not to accept the money. He felt the secret pangs of fine and noble remorse, whose merit is seldom given full weight when men judge their fellows and which often wins absolution from angels in heaven for the criminal convicted by lawyers on earth. Rastignac opened his sister's letter. It was expressed in terms of such innocence and grace that it brought cheer to his heart.

Your letter came just at the right time, dear brother. Agathe and I wanted to spend our money in so many different ways that finally we could not make up our minds what to buy. You did what the King of Spain's servant did when he knocked over his master's clocks; you made us agree. Truly, we were always quarrelling over which of our desires should have priority, and we had found no way, dear Eugène, of satisfying all our wishes. Agathe jumped for joy. In fact we both behaved like mad things throughout that day, 'so conspicuously' (my aunt's style) that Mother asked us in her severest tone: 'Whatever is the matter with you young ladies?' If we had been scolded the least little bit I think we should have been still better pleased. A woman must suffer gladly for the one she loves! In the midst of my joy I was alone in feeling twinges of regret. I will surely make a bad wife, I am too extravagant. I had bought myself two sashes, a neat bodkin for piercing eyelets in my corsets, fripperies, so that I had less money than that great lump Agathe, who is so thrifty and hoards her pennies like a magpie. She had two hundred francs! All I have, my poor dear, is a hundred and fifty. I have been properly punished. I could throw my sash down the well; I shall never be able to wear it without feeling guilty. I have robbed you. Agathe was sweet. She said, 'Let's send him the three hundred and fifty francs from us both!' But I could not help telling you everything just as it happened. Do you know what we did in obedience to your orders? We took our glorious wealth, we went out for a walk together, and once we reached the main road rushed on to Ruffec, where we quite simply gave the whole lot to Monsieur Grimbert, the postmaster. We flew back light as larks. 'Can it be happiness that makes us feel so light?' Agathe asked me. We said lots of things which I will not repeat to you, Monsieur le Parisien, because they concerned you too closely. Oh, dear brother, we love you so dearly. There you have it in a nutshell.

As for secrecy, according to my aunt, little minxes like us are capable of anything, even keeping quiet. Mother made a mysterious trip to Angoulême with my aunt, and they both kept silent about the high politics of their journey, which only took place after lengthy conferences, from which we were excluded, and Monsieur le baron too. Minds in the State of Rastignac are busy with conjecture. The muslin dress sprigged with openwork flowers which the Infantas are embroidering for Her Majesty the Queen is going ahead in absolute secrecy. There are just two widths still to be done. It has been decided not to build a wall on the Verteuil side; there is going to be a hedge there. The common people will lose some fruit and espaliers, but strangers will gain a fine view. If the heir presumptive were in need of handkerchiefs, he is advised that the Dowager de Marcillac, while rummaging in her treasure chests and trunks, known by the name of Pompeii and Herculaneum, discovered a fine piece of cambric which she did not know she had: Princesses Agathe and Laure await his orders with their needle, thread and hands that are always rather too red. The two young Princes, Don Henri and Don Gabriel, still have the deplorable habit of stuffing themselves on grape jelly, infuriating their sisters, never wanting to learn, amusing themselves with bird-nesting, creating a din and, against the laws of the State, cutting themselves osiers to make switches. The Papal Nuncio, commonly called Monsieur le Curé, threatens to excommunicate them if they continue to neglect the sacred canons of grammar for the warlike cannons of the elder tree, vulgarly known as peashooters. Farewell, dear brother, no letter has ever brought so many prayers for your happiness, or so much love requited. You will have a lot to tell us when you come home! You must tell me everything, because I am the elder. My aunt has given us reason to suspect that you have had some social success.

'*They speak of a lady and keep silent about the rest.*' With us, of course!

By the way, Eugène, we could do without handkerchiefs if you like and make you some shirts. Give me a quick answer on that. If you needed fine, well-sewn shirts quite soon, we should have to get started on them at once. If there are fashions in Paris which we would not know, send us a pattern, particularly for the cuffs. Farewell, farewell! I kiss the left side of your forehead, on the temple that belongs exclusively to me. I am leaving the other sheet of paper to Agathe who has promised not to read anything of what I have told you, but to make assurance doubly sure I will stay by her while she writes to you.

Your loving sister, L. de Rastignac.

'Oh yes!' Eugène said to himself, 'I must make my fortune at any price now! Treasuries could not repay such devotion, I wish I could bring them every happiness at once. Fifteen hundred and fifty francs!' he said after a pause, 'Every penny must count! Laure is right, what a woman! My shirts are all of coarse cloth. For the sake of another's happiness a young girl becomes as crafty as a thief. Innocent for herself and far-sighted for me, she is like the angel from heaven feigning earthly faults without understanding them.'

The world was his! His tailor had already been summoned, sounded out, conquered. The sight of Monsieur de Trailles had made Rastignac realize what influence tailors have over the lives of young men. Alas! There is no middle term between the two extremes; when he sends in his bill for skilled work a tailor is either your mortal enemy or loyal friend. In his own tailor Eugène found a man who understood the paternal aspect of his trade, and saw himself as a link between young men's present and future. So, in his gratitude, Rastignac ensured the man's fortune with one of those witty remarks at which he was later to excel: 'I know of two pairs of his trousers', he would say, 'which resulted in matches worth twenty thousand a year.'

Fifteen hundred francs and all the clothes he wanted! At that moment the impecunious Southerner had no more doubts, and went down to breakfast with the indefinable air of any young man in funds. The moment money slips into a student's pocket, an imaginary pillar rises within him to give him support. He walks more briskly than before, he feels that he has a firm base from which to exert pressure, he looks people full and straight in the eye, he moves more nimbly. Humble and shy the day before, he would have taken a hiding; the following day he would inflict one on a prime minister. The most phenomenal changes take place within him. His aspirations are as boundless as his ability to achieve them. He desires everything and anything, he is gay, generous and expansive. In short the bird which only yesterday had no wings has now spread them in full flight. The penniless student snaps up a crumb of pleasure like a dog snatching a bone amid countless perils. He breaks it, sucks out the marrow, and keeps running, but the young man who for a fleeting moment has a few gold coins to jingle in his pocket savours his pleasures, counts them one by one, revels in them, sails through the air, has forgotten the meaning of the word 'poverty'. Paris is all his. At that age everything glows, sparkles and flashes! Age of joyful strength, which no one, man or woman, ever turns to full account! Age of debts and anxious fears which increase every pleasure! Anyone who does not know the Left Bank of the Seine, between the rue Saint-Jacques and the rue des Saints-Pères* knows nothing of human life!

'Ah! If only the women of Paris knew!' Rastignac said to himself, as he devoured the stewed pears bought for a farthing apiece served up by Madame Vauquer. 'They would come here to find a lover.' At that moment a postal messenger appeared in the dining-room, after ringing at the wicket-gate. He asked for Monsieur Eugène de Rastignac, and then handed him two bags and a register to sign. At that point Rastignac felt Vautrin's piercing stare strike him like a whiplash.

'Now you'll be able to afford fencing lessons and pistol practice,' said Vautrin.

'The treasure fleet has come in,' Madame Vauquer said to him, looking at the bags.

Mademoiselle Michonneau was afraid to look at the money for fear of betraying her greed for it.

'You have a good mother,' said Madame Couture.

'Monsieur has a good mother,' repeated Poiret.

'Yes, your mum has bled herself white,' said Vautrin. 'Now you'll be able to have your fun, go around in high society, fish for dowries, and dance with comtesses who wear peach-blossom in their hair. But, believe me, young man, practise shooting.'

Vautrin mimed a man aiming at his adversary. Rastignac wanted to give the messenger a tip, but found he had nothing in his pocket. Vautrin dug into his own, and threw the man a five-franc piece.

'Your credit is good,' he went on, looking at the student.

Rastignac was obliged to thank him, although ever since the sharp exchange of words on the day he had been to see Madame de Beauséant he could not bear the man. Throughout that week Eugène and Vautrin had remained silent in each other's company, and had been watching one another. The student vainly wondered why. No doubt ideas are projected in direct proportion to the force with which they are conceived, and strike where the brain directs them, by a mathematical law which may be compared to that governing the bombs shot out of a mortar. Their effects are varied. If there are sensitive characters in whom ideas lodge and wreak havoc, there are also armour-plated characters, skulls with bronze ramparts against which the will of others is flattened out and drops like bullets against a wall. Then again there are flabby, woolly characters on whom the ideas of others fall spent like cannon-balls harmlessly absorbed by the soft earth of the redoubt. Rastignac's head was one of those that are filled with gunpowder and explode at the slightest shock. He had too much youthful intensity to be impervious to this projection of ideas, this contagion of feelings which strike us in so many curious ways without our realizing it. His moral vision had the same range and acuity as his lynx-eyed physical sight. Each of his twofold senses had the mysterious outreach, the elasticity of advance and retreat at which we marvel in exceptional men, swordsmen swift to find the chink in any armour. Besides, in the past month Eugène had developed as many virtues as faults. His faults were prompted by society and the need to fulfil his increasing desires. Among his virtues was that Southern impetuosity which tries to resolve problems by confronting them head-on, and does not allow a man from South of the Loire to remain undecided about anything, a virtue which Northerners call a fault. In their eyes, if this was the origin of Murat's* success, it was also the cause of his death. From this one should conclude that a Southerner who manages to combine the artfulness of the North with the dashing bravery of the South is a complete man, and remains secure as the King of Sweden.* Rastignac could therefore not stay long under fire from Vautrin's batteries without learning whether this man was his friend or foe. From one moment to the next this singular individual seemed able to discern his feelings and read his heart, while himself remaining so hermetically sealed that he seemed to have the deep immobility of a sphinx who knows and sees everything but never utters a word. Reassured by the feel of money in his pocket, Eugène rebelled.

'Be good enough to wait a moment,' he said to Vautrin, who had stood up ready to go out, after drinking up his coffee with relish to the last drop.

'Why?' retorted the man of 40 putting on his wide-brimmed hat and picking up a swordstick which he often whirled round, like a man facing undaunted an attack by four robbers at once.

'I'm going to pay you back,' answered Rastignac, swiftly undoing a bag and counting out a hundred and forty francs to Madame Vauquer. 'Prompt settlement makes for good friends,' he said to the widow, 'That makes us quits until New Year's Day. Change me this five-franc piece, will you please.'

'Good friends make prompt settlements,' Poiret repeated, looking at Vautrin.

'Here are your twenty sous,' handing over a coin to the sphinx in a wig.

'Anyone would think you were afraid of being in my debt!' exclaimed Vautrin, reading the young man's inmost thoughts with a searching look, and giving him one of those mocking, cynical leers which all but made Eugène lose his temper a hundred times over.

'Well ... yes,' answered the student, who had stood up,

the two bags in his hand, ready to go up to his room.

Vautrin went out by the door through to the drawing-room and the student was about to take the one leading to the stairs.

'You know, Monsieur le marquis de *Rastignacorama*, what you just said was not exactly polite,' said Vautrin, pushing the drawing-room door shut and coming up to the student, who looked at him coldly.

Rastignac closed the dining-room door, and took Vautrin to the foot of the stairs, to the space between dining-room and kitchen, where there was a long window, fitted with iron bars above a solid door leading out into the garden. There the student said in front of Sylvie, who emerged from her kitchen, 'Monsieur Vautrin, I am not a marquis and my name is not *Rastignacorama*.'

'They are going to fight,' said Mademoiselle Michonneau with an air of indifference.

'Fight!' Poiret repeated.

'I hope not,' replied Madame Vauquer, fondling her heap of coins.

'But there they go, under the limes,' cried Mademoiselle Victorine standing up to see out into the garden. 'That poor young man is quite right, though.'

'Come upstairs, dear girl,' said Madame Couture, 'this is none of our business.'

Madame Couture and Victorine stood up to go and were blocked at the door by fat Sylvie.

'What's going on then?' she asked. 'Monsieur Vautrin said to Monsieur Eugène, "Let's get things straight!" Then he took him by the arm, and there they are, walking through our artichokes.'

At that moment Vautrin appeared. 'Ma Vauquer,' he said with a smile, 'don't be alarmed, I am going to try out my pistols under the lime trees.'

'Oh! Monsieur,' said Victorine, clasping her hands together, 'Why do you want to kill Monsieur Eugène?'

Vautrin took two steps back and gazed at Victorine.

'So here's another story!' he cried in a mocking voice, which made the poor girl blush. 'He's a very nice young man, isn't he?' he went on. 'You have given me an idea. I'll see that you are both happy, my lovely lass.'

Madame Couture took her ward's arm and led her away, saying in her ear: 'Why, Victorine, you are quite incredible this morning.'

'I don't want anyone firing pistols on my property,' said Madame Vauquer. 'You'll frighten the neighbours and bring the police here, at this time of day!'

'Come now, take it easy, Ma Vauquer,' Vautrin answered. 'There, there, it's quite all right, we're going to practise shooting.' He rejoined Rastignac and took his arm in a friendly way.

'Even if I proved to you that I can hit the ace of spades with five successive shots, at thirty-five paces, that wouldn't quench your ardour. It looks to me as if you have pretty well lost your temper, and are trying to get yourself killed like an idiot.'

'You are backing down,' said Eugène.

'Now don't aggravate me,' replied Vautrin. 'It isn't cold this morning, come and sit down over here,' he said, pointing to the green-painted garden seats. 'There, no one can overhear us. I want to talk to you. You're a good lad, and I wish you no harm. I like you, as true as my name's Death—(damn and blast!) Vautrin. I'll tell you why I like you. I know you as well as if I had made you myself, and I'll prove it. Put your bags there,' he went on, pointing to the round table.

Rastignac put his moneybags on the table and sat down, his curiosity fully aroused by the sudden change in the behaviour of this man who first spoke of killing him and then played the role of protector.

'You are very keen to know who I am, what I have done and what I do now,' Vautrin continued. 'You want to know too much, my boy. Now, keep calm. There's a lot more to come! I have had my share of bad luck. Hear me out first, then you can say your piece. Here is my past life in three words. Who am I? Vautrin. What do I do? What I like. Let's leave it at that. Do you want to know my character? I am good to those who are good to me, or whose hearts speak to mine. Such people can take any liberty, they can kick me in the shins without my saying "Watch it!" But, by jingo, I can be devilish nasty to those that annoy me or whose faces don't fit. And it's as well for you to know that I don't care *that* about killing someone!', spitting as he said it. 'The only thing is I try to kill cleanly when I've absolutely got to. I'm what you might call an artist. I've read the *Memoirs* of Benvenuto Cellini,* as sure as you're looking at me now, and in Italian, what's more! That chap, a pretty bright spark, taught me to imitate Providence, which kills us all at random, and to love beauty wherever it may be found. Anyhow, isn't it a fine game to be all alone against the rest and be lucky? I have thought a lot about the present components of your social disorder. My boy, duelling is a childish game, plain silly. When one of two men is bound to lose his life only an idiot would leave it to chance. Duelling? Heads or tails! That's it. I can put five successive shots into an ace of spades, one on top of another, and at thirty-five paces at that! When you've got the knack you think you can be sure of hitting your man. Well! I once shot at a man at twenty paces and missed. The fellow had never handled a pistol in his life. Look!' said this extraordinary man, undoing his waistcoat and baring a chest as shaggy as a bear's back, but with a tangle of tawny hair which provoked revulsion mixed with fear, 'That novice singed my hair,' he added, guiding Rastignac's finger to feel a bullet-hole in his breast. 'But at that time I was only a boy, your age, twenty-one. I still believed in something, in a woman's love, that load of rubbish you are going to get bogged down in. We would have fought, wouldn't we? You might have killed me. Supposing I was dead and buried, where would that leave you? You'd have to clear out, run off to Switzerland, eat up dad's money, and that's little enough.

'I'm going to spell out your situation to you, but I'm going to do it with the advantage of a man who has examined the things of this world and realized that there are only two options open: dumb obedience or revolt. I don't obey anyone or anything, is that clear? As for you, do you know what you would need at the rate you're going? A million, and right away. Otherwise, scatterbrained as you are, we might find ourselves drifting down into the nets at Saint-Cloud* to find out if a Supreme Being exists. As for the million, I'll give it to you.'

He paused and looked at Eugène. 'Ha! Now you're not looking so cross with little Papa Vautrin. Hearing that makes you like a girl who has been told "see you this evening", dolling herself up and licking her lips like a cat drinking milk. Very well! Right then, it's up to the two of us. This is where we stand, young man. Back home we have dad, mum, great-aunt, two sisters, aged eighteen and seventeen, two young brothers aged fifteen and ten. That's the crew list. Auntie is bringing up your sisters. The curé comes in to give the two brothers Latin lessons. The family eats more chestnut gruel than white bread, dad is careful not to wear out his breeches, mum barely allows herself one new dress for winter and one for summer, our sisters manage as best they can. I know it all. I have been in the South. That's how things are at your home, if they send you twelve hundred francs a year and the bit of land brings in only three thousand. We have a cook and a manservant; one must keep up appearances, dad is a baron after all. As for ourselves, we are ambitious, we are related to the Beauséants, but we go about on foot. We want to be rich, and we don't have a penny. We eat Ma Vauquer's cheap stew, and we like the fine dinners in the Faubourg Saint-Germain. We sleep on a pallet and would like a mansion in town! I don't blame you for wanting these things. It is not given to everyone, my pet, to have ambition. Ask any woman what sort of man she is after: it's the man with ambition. The ambitious have more power in their loins, more iron in their blood, more fire in their belly than other men. A woman feels so happy and beautiful at her moments of strength that she prefers above all others the man whose strength is huge, even at the risk of being broken by him.

'I'm making a catalogue of all your ambitions so that I can ask you a question. It's this: we are ravenously hungry, we have sharp little teeth, how are we going to set about stocking the pot? First we have to digest the law. It's deadly dull and teaches us nothing, but it has to be done. We make ourselves into advocates so that we can become assize judges, and send down poor devils who are better men than we are to have TF* branded on their shoulders, in order to convince the rich that they can sleep in peace. It's no fun and it takes a long time. First two years kicking our heels in Paris, watching, but not touching, all the dainties we fancy. You get tired of always wanting and never being satisfied. If you were pale and sluggish you would have nothing to fear; but we are hot-blooded as lions and have appetite enough to drive us to commit a score of follies every day. So you will be exposed to this torment, the most appalling to be found in God's hell. Suppose you are good as gold, drink milk and write elegies. For someone as generous as you, it means starting, after enough trouble and hardship to drive a dog mad, by becoming some joker's deputy, in some dismal town where the government will toss you a salary of a thousand francs like a sop to a butcher's dog. Bark at thieves, defend the rich, send men of spirit to the scaffold. Thanks very much! Unless you have protection you'll rot away in your provincial lawcourt. When you are about thirty you'll be a judge at twelve hundred francs a year, if you haven't chucked it all up first. When you get to forty you'll marry some miller's daughter, with an income of around six thousand a year. Thank you. With protection you'll be Crown Counsel at thirty, with a salary of three thousand francs, and you'll marry the mayor's daughter. If you stoop to petty political tricks, like reading Villèle for Manuel* on a bulletin—well, they do sort of rhyme, enough to set your conscience at rest—at forty you'll be Procureur-Général, and may be a deputy. Note, dear boy, that our tender conscience may get a bit bruised, that it will cost twenty years of trouble and secret wretched-ness, and that our sisters will be left on the shelf. I have the honour moreover to draw your attention to the fact that there are only twenty posts of Procureur-Général in France, and twenty thousand candidates, including some customers who would sell their families to go up a notch. If such a career puts you off, let's look at something else.

'Baron de Rastignac would like to be an advocate? Fine. You have ten years hardship, you need to spend a thousand a month, have a library, chambers, lead a social life, kiss the hem of some solicitor's gown to get briefs, lick up the dust of the lawcourt with your tongue. If such a career led to anything worthwhile I wouldn't say no, but try to find five advocates in Paris earning more than fifty thousand a year at fifty! Bah! I'd rather take to piracy than be reduced to that. Besides, where would you find the money? It's all very depressing. One possibility is a wife's dowry. Do you want to get married? It means a millstone round your neck, and, then, if you marry for money, what happens to our sense of honour, our nobility? You might as well start rebelling against human conventions from today. It would mean always having to crawl like a reptile in front of a wife, licking her mother's feet, doing deeds vile enough to turn a sow's stomach. Pah! If it only brought you happiness, but you would be as wretched as the stones in a gutter with a wife you'd married for that reason. Better wage war on men than quarrel with your wife.

'You stand at the crossroads of your life, young man, you must choose. You have already made one choice; you went to see your Beauséant cousin and had a taste of luxury. You went to visit Madame de Restaud, Père Goriot's daughter, and had a taste of how Parisian women live. That day you came back with a word marked on your forehead, and one I could read easily enough: *Succeed!* succeed at any price. Bravo! I said, there's a lad after my own heart. You needed money. Where could you find it? You bled your sisters white. All brothers more or less *swindle* their sisters. The fifteen hundred francs extracted, God knows how! from land that yields more chestnuts than five-franc pieces will vanish from sight, like soldiers on the prowl. And then what will you do? Work? Work, as you understand it at the moment, provides fellows like Poiret with a room at Ma Vauquer's for their old age. Fifty thousand young men in the same position as you are all trying to solve the problem of how to get rich quick. You are just one of all that number. Imagine the efforts that will demand and how bitter the struggle will be. You'll have to devour each other like crabs in a pot, since there aren't fifty thousand decent jobs going. Do you know the way to get on here? Through brilliant intelligence or skilful corruption. Either plough into the mass of mankind like a cannon-ball, or infiltrate them like a plague. It's no good being honest. Men yield to the power of intelligence, though they hate it and try to decry it, because it takes but does not share. But they yield if it is persistent. In a word they kneel before it in worship once they have failed to bury it in mud. Corruption thrives, talent is rare, so corruption is the weapon of the mediocre majority, and you will feel it pricking you wherever you go. You will see women whose husbands earn sixty thousand francs all told spending more than ten thousand on clothes. You will see clerks on twelve hundred a year buying land. You will see women selling themselves so that they can ride in a carriage with the son of a peer of the realm and go bowling off to Longchamp* down the middle of the road. You have seen that poor old ninny Père Goriot obliged to pay off the bill of exchange endorsed by his daughter, whose husband has an income of fifty thousand a year. I defy you to go two steps in Paris without running across some diabolical fiddle. I wager my head against one of those lettuces that you will be stirring up a hornets' nest with the first woman who takes your fancy, however rich, beautiful, or young she may be. They are all chafing at legal constraints, at odds with their husbands about everything. There would be no end to it if I had to describe all the deals done for

lovers, for clothes, for children, for the household, or for
vanity, but seldom for virtue, you can be sure of that. So
an honest man is the common enemy. But what do you think
an honest man is? In Paris he is a man who does not talk
and refuses to share. I'm not talking about those wretched
drudges who do all the rotten jobs without any fair reward
for their labours, the ones I call God's own awkward squad.
To be sure, that is virtue with its stupidity in full bloom,
but that's where wretchedness is too. I can just see how sick
those good people would look if God played the dirty trick
of not turning up for the Last Judgement. So if you want
to get rich quick you have either to be rich already or you
must appear rich. To get rich here you've got to pull off
something big, otherwise you're just a petty thief, and then
it's goodbye! If among a hundred professions you might take
up there are ten men who rise to the top quickly, the public
calls them robbers. Draw your own conclusions. That's the
way things are. It's no better than the kitchen, the stink is
just as bad and you have to get your hands dirty if you want
to cook something up; just learn how to get them clean again.
That's the only morality nowadays.

'If I am talking to you about the world like this, it's the
world that's given me the right to do so. I know it. You
think I condemn it? Not at all. It has always been like that.
Moralizing will never change it. Man is imperfect. At times
he is more or less of a hypocrite, and then fools say he is
moral or immoral. I am not accusing the rich in favour of
the masses. Man is the same at the top, at the bottom, in
the middle. In every million of this herd of cattle you will
find ten fellows who put themselves above everyone else, even
above the law. I am one. As for you, if you are an exceptional
man, walk straight with your head high. But you will have
to fight envy, slander, mediocrity, fight everyone. Napoleon
ran up against a War Minister called Aubry* who very nearly
succeeded in shipping him off to the colonies. Take your
own measure! See if you can rise every morning more determined than you were the night before.

'In the present circumstances I am going to make you an offer which no one could refuse. Listen. You see, I have an idea. My idea is to go off and live like a patriarch in the middle of some big estate, a hundred thousand acres for example, in the United States, in the South. I want to become a planter out there, own slaves, earn a cool few million from the sale of my cattle, tobacco, and timber, living like a king, doing whatever I want, leading the sort of life you can't imagine here, where people hide away in burrows made of plaster. I am a great poet. My poetry is not something I write down, it is composed of actions and emotions. At this moment I possess fifty thousand francs, which would hardly buy me forty niggers. I need two hundred thousand, because I want two hundred niggers to satisfy my taste for the patriarchal life. Niggers, do you see? They are children, but fully grown, and you can do what you like with them without some inquisitive Public Prosecutor coming along to ask you questions. Such a capital of blacks would give me three or four millions in ten years. If I am successful no one will ask, "You there, who are you?" I will be Mr Four-Millions, United States citizen. I shall be fifty years old, not yet decrepit. I shall amuse myself in my own way. In a nutshell, if I get you a dowry of a million francs, will you give me two hundred thousand? Twenty per cent commission, eh! Is that too dear? You will make your little wife love you. Once you are married you will show signs of disquiet, remorse, you will go around for a fortnight looking gloomy. One night, after a bit of fooling about, between two tender kisses, you will confess to your wife that you are in debt to the tune of two hundred thousand francs, calling her "My love!" This sort of farce is acted out every day by the most distinguished young men. A young woman does not refuse her purse to the man who steals her heart away. Do you think you'll lose? No. You'll find a way of winning back your two hundred thousand in some business deal. With your money and your brains you'll collect as handsome a fortune as you could wish. *Ergo*, in the space of six months you will have brought happiness to yourself, to a charming wife and to your old Papa Vautrin, not to mention your family, who have to blow on their fingers in winter because they have no logs to put on the fire. Don't be surprised at what I am offering, or at what I'm asking of you! Out of any sixty society weddings taking place in Paris there are forty-seven based on transactions of this kind. The Chambre des Notaires forced Monsieur ...'

'What do I have to do?' said Rastignac, eagerly interrupting Vautrin.

'Hardly anything,' replied the latter, unable to contain a movement of pleasure like the silent reaction of an angler feeling a fish tug at the end of his line. 'Listen to me. The heart of a poor unfortunate, wretched girl absorbs love as greedily as the driest sponge; it swells up at the first touch of a drop of emotion. Paying court to a young woman you meet when she is lonely, penniless, and in despair, without the least idea of the fortune that is to be hers! Dammit! It's like having a run of five cards and fourteen points in your hand at piquet, like knowing in advance the winning numbers in the lottery, or playing the stock market with inside information. You are building an indestructible marriage on firm foundations. When this girl comes into her millions she will throw them at your feet like so many pebbles. "Take it, my beloved! Take it Adolphe! Alfred! Take it Eugène!" she will say if Adolphe, Alfred, or Eugène have been astute enough to make sacrifices for her. What I mean by sacrifice is selling an old coat to pay for mushrooms on toast together at the Cadran Bleu before going on for the evening to the Ambigu-Comique;* it's pawning your watch to give her a shawl. Not to mention scribbling love letters or the sort of nonsense women are so keen on, like, for instance, sprinkling drops of water on the note-paper to look like tears when you are apart; it strikes me that you know the language of the heart pretty well.

'Paris, you see, is like some forest in the New World, where a score of savage tribes run about like Illinois or Huron Indians, living off the spoils of their hunt in different social circles. You are hunting for millions. To catch them you use traps, bird-limes, decoys. There are many sorts of hunting; some hunt dowries, others hunt for profit-taking on their shares; some go fishing for consciences, others sell their subscribers* all trussed up. The hunter who brings back a full bag is honoured, fêted, received in the best society. To be fair to this hospitable land, you are dealing with the most indulgent city in the world. If the proud aristocrats of every capital in Europe refuse to admit into their ranks some infamous millionaire, Paris greets him with open arms, hurries to his parties, eats his dinners and drinks toasts to his infamy...

'But where is such a girl to be found?' asked Eugène.

'She's yours, in front of you!'

'Mademoiselle Victorine?'

'That's right!'

'What do you mean?'

'She loves you already, your little Baronne de Rastignac!'

'She hasn't a penny,' Eugène replied in amazement.

'Ah! That's just the point,' said Vautrin. 'Another few words and all will become clear. Old man Taillefer is an old scoundrel who is said to have murdered one of his friends during the Revolution. He's one of those fellows with what I call opinions of his own. He is a banker, senior partner in Frédéric Taillefer and Co. He has an only son to whom he intends to leave everything, to the detriment of Victorine. I myself don't much care for that sort of injustice. I'm like Don Quixote; I like to go to the defence of the weak against the strong. If it were the will of God that Taillefer should lose his son, he would acknowledge his daughter once more; he would want an heir, whoever it might be. It's human nature to be silly like that, and I know he can't have any more children. Victorine is sweet and kind, she will soon get round her father, and will keep him spinning like a humming-top with the whip of sentiment! She will be too grateful for your love to forget you; you will marry her. As for me, I'll take on the role of Providence, I'll influence the divine will. I have a friend I've put myself out for; he's a colonel in the army of the Loire who has just been posted to the Garde Royale. He listens to my advice and has become an ultra-royalist; he's not one of those poor fools who cling to their opinions. If I have one more piece of advice for you, my pet, it is not to stick to your opinions any more firmly than to your words. When you are asked for them, sell them. A man who boasts that he never changes his opinions is a man committed always to follow a straight line, an idiot who believes in infallibility. There are no such things as principles, only events; no laws, only circumstances. Your exceptional man adjusts to events and circumstances in order to control them. If there really were fixed principles and fixed laws, nations would not keep changing them as we change our shirts. One man is not expected to be more sensible than a whole nation. The man who has rendered the least service to France has become an idol, revered because his views have always been red; he's fit at best to be put in the museum with all the machines, with a label saying *La Fayette*, while the prince* who is pilloried by all, and has such contempt for mankind that he will spit back in their faces any solemn oath they may demand, prevented France being partitioned at the Congress of Vienna. They should crown him with laurels and they pelt him with mud. Oh! I know what's what! I know the secrets of a lot of people. That's enough. I will hold an unshakable opinion the day I meet three people who agree on how to apply a principle, and I'll have a long wait! You won't find three judges in the courts with the same opinion on a point of law. To come back to my man. He would crucify Christ all over again if I told him to. Just one word from his Papa Vautrin and he'll pick a quarrel with that rascal who won't even send his poor sister five francs and ...' Vautrin stood up, took his guard and went through the motions of a fencing master lunging.

'And curtains!' he added.

'How dreadful!' Eugène said. 'You must be joking, Monsieur Vautrin?'

'Now, now, take it easy,' replied the latter. 'Don't be childish! All the same, if it gives you any pleasure, lose your temper! Rant and rave! Tell me I am a disgrace, a blackguard, a villain, a bandit, but don't call me a swindler or a spy! Go on, say it! Fire off your broadside! I'll forgive you, it's so natural at your age! Just think a moment, though. You will do worse things one day. You'll go flirting with some pretty girl and take money for it. You must have thought about it!' said Vautrin, 'for how will you ever succeed if you don't put a price on your love? Virtue, my dear student, is indivisible; it either is or is not. They talk of doing penance for our sins. Another fine system, that, allowing you to wipe out your offence with an act of contrition! Seduce a woman so that you can set your foot on a certain rung of the social ladder, sow dissension among the children in a family, doing in fact all the dirty deeds practised in secret or otherwise for one's own pleasure or personal advantage; do you regard these as acts of faith, hope, and charity? Why two months in prison for a dandy who robs a boy of half his fortune in one night, and hard labour in the galleys for a poor devil who steals a thousand-franc note "with aggravating circumstances"? That's the law for you. There's not one article that does not lead to absurdity. The smooth-tongued man in his smart yellow gloves has committed murders without bloodshed, but someone has been bled all the same; the actual murderer has jemmied open a door; two deeds of darkness! Between what I am offering now and what you will do one day the only difference is the blood shed. You believe that there is some fixed point in that sort of world? Despise mankind then, and look at how many ways there are of slipping through the net of the law. The secret of great wealth with no obvious source is some forgotten crime, forgotten because it was done neatly.'

'Stop, please, I don't want to hear any more, you will make me doubt myself. Right now my heart is all I know.'

'As you like, dear boy. I thought you were stronger than that,' said Vautrin. 'I won't tell you any more. One last word, however.' He stared at the student. 'You know my secret.'

'A young man who has turned down your offer will easily forget it.'

'Well said, I like that. Someone else, you see, would be less scrupulous. Remember what I would like to do for you. I give you two weeks. Take it or leave it.'

'There's a man as hard as iron!' Rastignac said to himself as he watched Vautrin walk away with his stick under his arm. 'He has told me bluntly what Madame de Beauséant put more delicately. He ripped my heart with claws of steel. Why do I intend to visit Madame de Nucingen? He guessed my motives as soon as they entered my head. In a word, that villain has told me more about virtue than I have ever got from men or books. If virtue admits of no compromise, does that mean that I have robbed my sisters?' he said, flinging his bag on to the table. He sat down, absorbed in a bewildering series of reflections.

'To remain faithful to virtue, martyr to a sublime cause! Bah! Everyone believes in virtue, but who is virtuous? Nations set up liberty as an idol, but what nation on earth is free? My youth is still as fair as a cloudless sky; does the desire to be great or rich not imply a decision to be a liar, bowing, crawling, springing up again, fawning, deceiving? Doesn't it mean agreeing to be the lackey of those who have already done their lying, bowing, crawling? Before becoming their accomplice you must first be their servant. Very well, I say no! I want to work with honour, with integrity! I want to work day and night, owing my success solely to my own efforts. Success will come very slowly that way, but every day I will be able to lay my head on my pillow with a clear conscience. Could anything be finer than to survey one's life and find it spotless as a lily? My life and I are like a young man and his bride-to-be. Vautrin has shown me what happens after ten years of marriage. Devil take it! My head is spinning. I wish I could stop thinking; my heart is a good guide.'

Eugène's musings were interrupted by fat Sylvie announcing

the arrival of his tailor, whom he went to meet with his two moneybags in his hand. He was not displeased by this turn of events. When he had tried on his evening dress, he put on his new daytime outfit, which completely transformed him. 'I am certainly as good as Monsieur de Trailles,' he said to himself. 'At last I look like a gentleman!'

'Monsieur,' said Père Goriot, coming into Eugène's room, 'you asked if I knew the houses Madame de Nucingen visits?'

'Yes!'

'Well, next Monday she is going to Maréchal Carigliano's ball. If you can be there, you'll be able to tell me whether my two daughters had a good time, what they were wearing, all about it.'

'How did you know that, my good Père Goriot?' asked Eugène, inviting him to sit by the fire.

'Her maid told me. I know everything they do thanks to Thérèse and Constance,' he replied cheerfully. The old man was like a lover still young enough to feel happy at devising a scheme for being in touch with his beloved without her suspecting anything. 'You will be seeing them!' he said, innocently revealing his regretful envy.

'I don't know,' Eugène replied. 'I am going to see Madame de Beauséant to ask if she can introduce me to the maréchal's wife.'

Eugène was inwardly delighted at the prospect of visiting the vicomtesse dressed as he was going to be from now on. What moralists call the depths of the human heart are merely the disappointments, the involuntary reactions of self-interest. These ups and downs so often bemoaned, these sudden reversals, are quite calculated for the enhancement of our pleasures. Seeing himself well dressed, with smart gloves, smart boots, Rastignac forgot his virtuous resolution. Young people do not dare look into the mirror of their consciences when they are being tempted to do wrong, while those of riper years have already seen themselves reflected there; therein lies the difference between these two periods of human life. In the past few days Eugène and Père Goriot had gone from being neighbours to becoming good friends. Their secret friendship derived from the same psychological causes as had engendered quite the opposite feelings between Vautrin and the student. Any philosopher bold enough to try to establish the effects of our feelings on the physical world will surely find more than one proof of their material influence in the relations they create between us and the animals. What physiognomist can interpret character more swiftly than a dog telling whether a stranger is friendly or not? *Atoms of affinity* is a proverbial expression in general use, referring to one of those facts which survive in language to disprove the philosophical inanities which engage the minds of those who enjoy winnowing the husks of basic vocabulary. You *feel* that you are loved. Feeling lays its imprint on everything and travels across space. A letter is like a soul, so faithful an echo of the speaking voice that sensitive spirits count it among love's richest treasures. Père Goriot, whose unreasoning devotion exalted him to the sublimest level of dog-like nature, had sensed the compassion, the kindly admiration, the youthful sympathy for him which had stirred in the student's heart. Yet this budding alliance had so far led to no exchange of confidences. If Eugène had revealed his intention of seeing Madame de Nucingen, it was not because he relied on the old man to effect his introduction to her, but he hoped that an indiscreet remark might indeed help him. All that Père Goriot had ever told him about his daughters arose from what Eugène had taken the liberty of saying about them in public on the day of his two visits.

'My dear sir,' he had said to him next day, 'how could you ever have imagined that Madame de Restaud would resent the fact that you mentioned my name? My two daughters are both very fond of me. I am happy to be their father. It's just that my two sons-in-law have treated me badly. I did not want these dear girls to suffer for my differences with their husbands, and I preferred seeing them in secret. This secrecy affords me countless pleasures beyond the understanding of other fathers who can see their daughters whenever they wish. But I can't do that, do you see? So when it's fine I ask their maids whether my daughters are going out, and then go along to the Champs Élysées. I wait for them to go past, my heart beats faster when their carriages come by. I admire them in all their fine clothes and the way they smile at me as they go by casts a golden glow over everything as though it were lit up by a ray of sunshine. There I stay, they are bound to come back. I see them again. The fresh air has done them good. There are roses in their cheeks. I hear people around me say: "There's a beautiful woman!" That gladdens my heart. It is my own flesh and blood, isn't it? I love the horses pulling them and would like to be the little dog they hold on their lap. I live on their pleasures. Everyone has his own way of loving, but mine does nobody any harm, so why should the world bother about me? I am happy in my own way. Am I breaking any law when I go to watch my daughters in the evening just as they are leaving to go to a ball? How disappointed I am if I arrive too late and am told "Madame has already left." One night I waited until three o'clock in the morning to see Nasie, whom I hadn't seen for two days. I nearly died of joy! I beg you not to talk about me except to say how kind my daughters are to me. They try to shower all sorts of presents on me, but I stop them and say: "Keep your money! What do you expect me to do with it? I don't need anything." In fact, my dear sir, what am I? A wretched corpse whose soul is wherever my daughters are. When you have seen Madame de Nucingen you must tell me which of the two you prefer,' said the old fellow after a moment's silence, seeing Eugène get ready to go out and stroll round the Tuileries until it was time to call on Madame de Beauséant.

That stroll had a fatal effect on the student. More than one woman noticed him. He was so handsome, so young, and dressed with such elegant good taste! When he saw that he was attracting attention and almost admiration, he stopped thinking how his sisters and his aunt had deprived themselves for his sake, and forgot his virtuous reluctance to accept their sacrifice. He had seen passing over his head that demon so easily mistaken for an angel, that Satan with glittering wings, strewing rubies, casting his golden darts at palaces, raising women to the purple, enhancing with foolish splendour the thrones which had been so simple in their origin. He had listened to the god of that flashy, tinkling vanity which seems to us a symbol of power. Vautrin's words, cynical as they were, had lodged in his heart, just as an innocent maid bears engraved on her memory the sordid features of the old bawd selling secondhand clothes who predicted for her "Riches and love in profusion." After a leisurely stroll Eugène arrived at about five o'clock at Madame de Beauséant's house, and there received one of those shattering blows against which youthful hearts are defenceless. Up till then he had always found the vicomtesse courteously affable, full of that easy grace conferred by an aristocratic upbringing, but only authentic if it comes from the heart.

When he came in Madame de Beauséant made an abrupt gesture and said curtly, 'Monsieur de Rastignac, I can't possibly see you, at least for the moment! I am very busy ...'

To an observer, and Rastignac had rapidly become one, these words, the gesture, the look, the tone of voice summed up the character and habits of her caste. He saw the iron hand in the velvet glove; the real person, the selfishness beneath the good manners; the wood beneath the varnish. He finally understood the phrase I, THE KING which extends from the plumes round the throne down to the crest of the most lowly nobleman. Eugène had too readily trusted in the woman's noble instincts, taking her at her word. Like all unfortunates he had signed in good faith the attractive compact intended to bind benefactor to beneficiary, the first article of which establishes complete equality between generous hearts. The charity which makes a single being of two individuals is a divine passion as misunderstood and as rare as true love. Both express the lavish generosity of noble souls. Rastignac wanted to attend the Duchesse de Carigliano's ball, and swallowed this snub.

'Madame,' he said, in a voice unsteady with emotion, 'I should not have come to bother you if the matter were not of importance. Be good enough to allow me to see you later, I'll wait.'

'Very well! Come and dine with me,' she said a little embarrassed at having spoken to him so harshly, for in fact this was a woman as kind as she was noble.

Although Eugène was moved by this sudden change of heart, he said to himself as he left, 'Grovel, put up with anything. What must the others be like if in a matter of moments the best of women can withdraw her promised friendship and cast you off like an old shoe? So it's every man for himself? It is true that her house is not a shop, and I'm putting myself in the wrong by needing her. As Vautrin said, one must batter down resistance like a cannon-ball.' The student's bitter thoughts were soon dispelled by the pleasure he anticipated from dining with the vicomtesse.

Thus, by some dispensation of fate, the most trivial events of his life conspired to drive him into a course of action in which, according to the observations of the fearsome sphinx of the Maison Vauquer, he must, as on the battlefield, kill or be killed, deceive or be deceived; where he must give up conscience and heart at the entrance, put on a mask, mercilessly exploit others and, as in Sparta, seize his fortune without being seen in order to earn his laurels.

When he returned to the vicomtesse he found her as kind and gracious to him as she had always been. They went together into the dining-room, where the vicomte was waiting for his wife, and where the table presented a magnificent example of that luxury which under the Restoration was carried, as everyone knows, to the ultimate degree. Like many people bored with life, almost the only pleasure left for Monsieur de Beauséant to enjoy was eating well; when it came to gluttony he belonged to the same school as Louis XVIII and the Duc d'Escars.* His table thus offered luxury in two kinds, costly vessels containing the richest food. Eugène had never

seen such a spectacular display before, for this was the first
time he had dined in one of those houses where the grand
manner is hereditary. The latest fashion had done away with
the suppers which used to come at the end of formal balls
under the Empire, when military men needed to fortify themselves in readiness for all the combats awaiting them at home
or abroad. Eugène had so far only been present at balls. The
poise which distinguished him so conspicuously later on, and
which he was beginning to acquire, saved him from gaping
inanely. But when he saw all this finely wrought silver and
the countless refinements of a sumptuous table, when for the
first time he could admire service that was discreetly silent,
it was hard for someone of such lively imagination not to
prefer this consistently elegant way of life to that of hardship
which he had been willing to embrace that morning. For
a moment his thoughts took him back to the family boarding
house. He found it so deeply repugnant that he swore to
leave in January, as much in order to move into decent lodgings as to get away from Vautrin, whose great hand he felt
on his shoulder still. Anyone of good sense who thinks of
the innumerable forms of corruption, spoken or silent, to
be found in Paris, will wonder by what aberration the State
has set up schools there, gathering young people together,
how pretty women can enjoy respect, how money-changers
can display gold without having it disappear as if by magic
from their bowls. But if one considers how few crimes, or
even misdemeanours, are committed by young people, how
deeply one should respect these patient Tantaluses who wage
an inner struggle with themselves and almost always win!
Properly depicted in his struggle with Paris, the poor student
would afford one of the most dramatic subjects in our modern
civilization. Madame de Beauséant kept looking at Eugène
in vain attempts to induce him to talk, but he would not
speak a word in the vicomte's presence.

'Are you going to take me to the Italiens this evening?'
the vicomtesse asked her husband.

'You cannot doubt the pleasure it would give me to obey

you,' he answered, with mock gallantry which deceived the student, 'but I have to meet someone at the Variétés.'*

'His mistress,' she said to herself.

'So you won't have d'Ajuda this evening?' asked the vicomte.

'No,' she replied irritably.

'Very well! If you absolutely must have an arm to lean on, take Monsieur de Rastignac.'

The vicomtesse looked at Eugène with a smile.

'That will be very compromising for you,' she said.

'*The Frenchman likes danger, because that is where he finds glory,* as Monsieur de Chateaubriand once said,' replied Rastignac, with a bow.

A few minutes later he was being swiftly conveyed in a brougham, with Madame de Beauséant by his side, to the fashionable theatre. He felt as though someone had waved a magic wand when he entered a box facing the stage, and found himself the target for all the lorgnettes, together with the vicomtesse, who was dressed quite exquisitely. He was moving from one enchantment to the next.

'You must talk to me,' said Madame de Beauséant. 'Ah, look, there is Madame de Nucingen, three boxes along from us. Her sister and Monsieur de Trailles are on the other side.'

The vicomtesse said these words looking at the box where Mademoiselle de Rochefide should be, but not seeing Monsieur d'Ajuda there, her face shone radiant with joy.

'She is charming,' said Eugène, when he had looked at Madame de Nucingen.

'Her eyelashes are too pale.'

'Yes, but what a slim and pretty figure!'

'Her hands are too big.'

'Lovely eyes!'

'Her face is too long.'

'But it's long enough for distinction.'

'How lucky for her that she has that much. Just look how she keeps picking up and putting down her opera-glasses. The Goriot likeness comes out in every movement she makes,' said the vicomtesse, to Eugène's great astonishment.

In fact Madame de Beauséant was scanning the theatre with her opera-glasses, and though apparently taking no notice of Madame de Nucingen, did not miss her slightest move. The audience was full of the most exquisite beauties. Delphine de Nucingen felt quite flattered to be the sole object of interest for Madame de Beauséant's young, handsome and elegant cousin; he had eyes for no one but her.

'If you go on staring at her you will cause a scandal, Monsieur de Rastignac. You will get nowhere by throwing yourself at people's heads like that.'

'My dear cousin,' said Eugène, 'you have already looked after me extremely well. If you would like to complete your work, all I ask of you is a favour which will cost you very little but will help me a lot. You see, I am smitten.'

'Already?'

'Yes.'

'With that woman?'

'Would my pretensions be heeded anywhere else then?' he said, looking hard at his cousin. 'Madame la duchesse de Carigliano is one of Madame la duchesse de Berry's* circle,' he continued after a pause, 'You are bound to see her. Would you be kind enough to introduce me to her and take me to the ball she is giving on Monday? I shall meet Madame de Nucingen there and embark on my first skirmish.'

'Gladly,' she said. 'If you already find her attractive your affairs of the heart are going very well. There is de Marsay in Princesse Galathionne's box. Madame de Nucingen is in torment, she is very upset. There's no better moment to approach a woman, especially a banker's wife. Those ladies of the Chaussée-d'Antin all love revenge.'

'So what would you yourself do in a case like this?'

'Personally I should suffer in silence.'

At that moment the Marquis d'Ajuda appeared in Madame de Beauséant's box.

'I have botched up my affairs so that I could come and meet you,' he said, 'and I am letting you know so that it won't be a sacrifice for nothing.'

The radiance of the vicomtesse's face showed Eugène how to recognize the signs of genuine love, and not to confuse them with the counterfeit emotions of Parisian coquetry. He found his cousin admirable, fell silent and gave up his seat to Monsieur d'Ajuda with a sigh.

'How noble and sublime is a woman who loves like this!' he said to himself. 'And this man would betray her for a doll! How could anyone betray her?' He felt a surge of childish rage. He wanted to roll at Madame de Beauséant's feet, he longed for demonic power so that he could carry her off in his heart, like an eagle bearing off to its eyrie a white sucking-kid snatched from the plain. He felt humiliated at being in this great exhibition of beauty with no picture, no mistress of his own. 'To have a mistress and rank close to royalty,' he said to himself, 'that is the sign of power!' He looked at Madame de Nucingen as a man who has been insulted looks at his opponent. The vicomtesse turned towards him and with a flicker of her eyes conveyed her heartfelt gratitude for his discretion. The first act was over.

'Do you know Madame de Nucingen well enough to introduce Monsieur de Rastignac to her?' she asked the Marquis d'Ajuda.

'She will be delighted to meet him,' said the marquis.

The handsome Portuguese rose, took the student's arm and in no time he found himself in Madame de Nucingen's presence.

'Madame la baronne,' said the marquis, 'I have the honour to present to you the Chevalier Eugène de Rastignac, the Vicomtesse de Beauséant's cousin. You have made such a deep impression on him that I wanted to make his happiness complete by bringing him closer to his idol.'

These words were spoken in somewhat ironic tones, making it easier to accept the rather crude implications, which women never take amiss if they are suitably turned. Madame de Nucingen smiled and offered Eugène the seat just vacated by her husband.

'I dare not suggest that you remain in my company, Monsieur,' she said. 'Anyone lucky enough to be with Madame de Beauséant stays there.'

'But', said Eugène in a low voice, 'it seems to me, Madame, that I can best please my cousin by remaining with you. Before Monsieur le Marquis arrived we were talking about you and your very distinguished appearance,' the last words spoken out loud.

Monsieur d'Ajuda withdrew.

'So you are really going to stay with me, Monsieur? We can become acquainted then. Madame de Restaud had already made me most eager to meet you.'

'Then she is being insincere; she has ordered her door to be closed to me.'

'How so?'

'Madame, I will be frank enough to tell you why, but I must beg all your indulgence for revealing such a secret. I am your father's neighbour. I did not know that Madame de Restaud was his daughter. I was unwise enough to mention him in all innocence and so I annoyed your sister and her husband. You would never believe how outrageous the Duchesse de Langeais and my cousin thought such filial disloyalty. I described the whole scene to them, and they couldn't stop laughing. Madame de Beauséant then compared you and your sister, and spoke of you in the warmest terms, saying how devoted you were to my neighbour, Monsieur Goriot. Indeed, how could you fail to love him? He adores you with such passion that I am already jealous of him. We talked for two hours this morning about you. Then, while I was still full of all your father had told me, over dinner with my cousin this evening I said that your beauty could not possibly equal your affection. No doubt with the intention of encouraging such ardent admiration, Madame de Beauséant brought me here, explaining with her usual kindness that I should see you here.'

'Do you mean to say, Monsieur,' said the banker's wife, 'that I already owe you a debt of gratitude? It won't be long before we are old friends.'

'Although friendship with you must be a most unusual experience,' said Rastignac, 'I would never want to be your friend.'

Such stereotyped inanities devised for the use of beginners always appeal to women, and only look trite when read in cold blood. A young man's gestures, his tone, his eyes add immeasurably to their effect. Madame de Nucingen found Rastignac charming. Then, like any woman faced with questions she cannot answer, instead of dealing directly with the one raised so bluntly by the student, answered on a quite different point:

'Yes, my sister has put herself in the wrong by treating our poor father as she does. He has really been an angel to us. It was only when Monsieur de Nucingen formally ordered me not to see my father except in the morning that I gave way on that issue. But it made me very unhappy for a long time. I used to weep about it. Such cruelty, coming on top of the harsh demands of marriage, has been one of the main reasons for our domestic discord. I must be the happiest woman in Paris in the eyes of the world, and the most unhappy in reality. You must think me crazy to talk to you like this, but you know my father and on that account I cannot look on you as a stranger.'

'No one you have ever met can have desired more ardently than I do to belong to you. What does every woman seek? Happiness,' he continued in a voice which went straight to the heart. 'Very well! If happiness means to a woman to be loved, adored, to have a friend in whom she can confide her desires, her dreams, her sorrows, her joys, to whom she can strip bare her soul, with its attractive faults and shining virtues, without fear of being betrayed, then, believe me, such devotion is only to be found in a young man, still full of illusions, ready to die at the merest sign from you, still ignorant of the world and happy to remain so, since you have come to mean the world to him. In my case, you see, you'll laugh at my *naïveté*, I have come here from a provincial backwater, absolutely green, having only known pure and upright souls, and expecting to remain untouched by love. As things turned out, I met my cousin who went too far in revealing her heart to me. She made me aware of the untold treasures of passion. Like Cherubino,* I am in love with all women, until I find one to whom I can devote myself. Seeing you as I came in I felt myself being swept towards you as if by a torrent. I had already thought so much about you! But I had never dreamed that you were as beautiful as you are in reality. Madame de Beauséant told me to stop staring at you. She does not understand how my eyes are drawn to gaze at your lovely ruby lips, your fair skin, your sweet eyes. Yes, I know that what I am saying sounds insane, but let me go on saying it!'

Women like nothing better than to hear such sweet compliments addressed to them. The most strictly devout woman will listen, even though she may not respond. Having begun like this, Rastignac continued to unburden himself in a beguilingly seductive undertone, while Madame de Nucingen gave him encouraging smiles as she periodically looked at de Marsay, who stayed where he was in Princesse Galathionne's box. Rastignac sat by Madame de Nucingen until her husband came to fetch her home.

'Madame,' Eugène said, 'I will have the pleasure of calling on you before the Duchesse de Carigliano's ball.'

'Since Matame infites you,' said the Baron, a stout Alsatian whose chubby face revealed a dangerous shrewdness, 'you can pe sure of a varm velcome.'

'I am doing very well, for she didn't take fright when she heard me ask "Could you become fond of me?" My horse has taken the bit, let's jump into the saddle and pick up the reins,' Eugène said to himself as he went to pay his respects to Madame de Beauséant, who had left her seat and was leaving with d'Ajuda. The poor student did not know that the baronne's thoughts were elsewhere, as she was waiting to receive from de Marsay one of those decisive letters which rend the heart. Highly delighted with his illusory success, Eugène accompanied the vicomtesse to where people wait for their carriages.

'Your cousin has changed completely,' said the Portuguese to the vicomtesse with a laugh once Eugène had left them. 'He is going to break the bank. He's slippery as an eel, and I think he'll go far. No one but you could have picked out a woman for him at the very moment when she needs comforting.'

'But', said Madame de Beauséant, 'we need to know whether she still loves the man who has left her.'

The student walked back from the Théâtre-Italien to the rue Neuve-Sainte-Geneviève, his head full of the most alluring plans. He had not failed to notice how closely Madame de Restaud had observed him, both in the vicomtesse's box and in that of Madame de Nucingen, and he presumed that he would no longer find the comtesse's door closed to him. He could already count on four major contacts in the most select Parisian society, for he was confident of winning the maréchale's favour. Without examining too carefully just what means to employ, he foresaw that the complex interplay of interests in that society obliged him to cling to a particular cog in order to rise to the top of the machine, and he felt strong enough to impede its progress.

'If Madame de Nucingen takes an interest in me, I will teach her how to manipulate her husband. Her husband is a very successful businessman, and he'll be able to help me make my fortune in less than no time.'

He did not say this to himself quite so plainly, he still lacked the judgement to evaluate, appreciate and estimate the potential of a situation; these ideas floated on his horizon like so many vague clouds, and although less savage than those expressed by Vautrin they would have produced nothing very pure if tested in the crucible of conscience. A succession of transactions of this kind brings men to the permissive morality commonly professed today, when it is rarer than ever before to find those four-square characters, those noble wills that never stoop to evil, for whom the least deviation from the straight and narrow path seems to be a crime; magnificent images of that probity to which we owe two masterpieces, Molière's Alceste* and, more recently, Jeanie Deans* and her father in the work of Walter Scott. Perhaps a work depicting the very opposite, the way a worldly, ambitious man contorts his conscience as he tries to skirt round evil so as to attain his ends while keeping up appearances, would be no less fine and dramatic.

By the time Rastignac arrived back at his boarding house he was quite enamoured of Madame de Nucingen, whom he had found as slim and graceful as a swallow. The intoxicating sweetness of her eyes, the silky texture of her skin, so delicately transparent that he could almost see the blood running through the veins beneath, the bewitching music of her voice, her fair hair, everything came back to him. Perhaps the walk home had contributed to this fascination by stirring up his blood. The student knocked loudly at Père Goriot's door.

'My friend,' he said, 'I have met Madame Delphine.'

'Where?'

'At the Italiens.'

'Was she enjoying herself? Do come in.' And the old fellow, who had got up in his nightshirt, opened the door and promptly returned to his bed.

'Tell me about her then,' he asked.

Eugène, who had not been in Père Goriot's room before, could not conceal his astonishment at the sight of the squalid conditions in which the father lived so soon after the daughter's finery had excited his admiration. There were no curtains at the window; the wallpaper was peeling off in several places because of the damp, and, where it curled up, revealed plaster stained yellow with smoke. The old man lay on a wretched bed covered only by a thin blanket and a patchwork quilt composed of the better scraps saved from Madame Vauquer's old dresses. The floor was damp and dusty. Facing the window stood one of those old rosewood chests of drawers with a bulging front, and brass handles shaped like vine-shoots decorated with leaves and flowers. On an ancient washstand with a wooden shelf were a water jug in its basin and a set of shaving tackle. Shoes lay in one corner, the bedside table had neither door nor marble top, in the corner of the fireplace, where there was no trace of a fire, stood the square walnut table, whose crossbar Père Goriot had used for flattening out his silver-gilt bowl. A shabby desk, with the old man's hat on it, a sagging armchair stuffed with straw and two other chairs constituted the rest of the wretched furnishings. Above the bed a shabby strip of red and white checked material hung from a rod, tied to the ceiling with a rag. The lowliest messenger could not have been worse off in his attic than Père Goriot at the Maison Vauquer. The chilling sight of this room wrung the heart; it was like the most desolate of dungeons. Fortunately Goriot could not see the expression on Eugène's face as the student set his candle down on the bedside table. The old man turned over towards him, keeping the bedclothes huddled up to his chin.

'Well now! Which do you like best? Madame de Restaud or Madame de Nucingen?'

'I prefer Madame Delphine,' answered the student, 'because she loves you more.'

At these words, so warmly uttered, the old fellow uncovered an arm and gripped Eugène by the hand.

'Thank you, thank you,' he replied with feeling. 'What did she say about me then?'

The student repeated the baronne's words with his own embellishments, and the old man listened as if he were hearing the word of the Lord.

'Dear child! Yes, yes, she is really fond of me. But you mustn't believe what she said about Anastasie. The two sisters are jealous of one another, you see. That is one more proof of their affection. Madame de Restaud is fond of me too, as I know very well. A father with his children is like God with us all; he probes their innermost hearts and can judge their intentions. They are both equally affectionate. Oh, if I had had good sons-in-law, I should have been too happy.

There is probably no such thing as perfect happiness in this world. If I could have made my home with them, just hearing their voices, knowing that they were there, seeing them come and go, as I did when they lived with me, that would have made my heart leap. Were they beautifully turned out?'

'Yes, they were,' said Eugène. 'But, Monsieur Goriot, with daughters set up as handsomely as yours, how can you live in such squalor?'

'My word,' he said with seeming indifference, 'what good would it do me to live in greater comfort? I really can't explain that sort of thing; I can't put two words together properly. That's what it's all about,' he added, striking his heart. 'My life, my own life, is all in my two daughters. If they enjoy themselves, if they are happy and finely dressed, if they have carpets to walk on, what does it matter what clothes I wear or what sort of bedroom I have? I don't feel cold it they are warm. I never feel sad if they are laughing. My only sorrows are theirs. When you become a father and say to yourself, as you hear your children babbling: "That's my doing!", when you feel these little creatures attached to you by every drop of your blood (for they were its finest flower, and that's the truth!) you will think that their skin is an inseparable part of you, your body will seem to respond to their movements. Their voice speaks to me wherever I am. One sad look from them makes my blood run cold. One day you will learn that their happiness is a greater source of joy than one's own. I can't explain it to you; something stirs inside you and fills you with contentment. In a word I live three times over. Let me tell you something strange. Well, when I became a father I understood God. His presence is everywhere, since all created things come from him. That is how I am with my daughters. Only I love my daughters more than God loves the world, because the world is not as beautiful as God, and my daughters are much more beautiful than I. I am so close to them in spirit that I had a feeling that you would see them this evening. My goodness! If any man could make my dear Delphine as happy as a woman can be when she is truly loved … I would clean his boots for him, run his errands. Her maid tells me that little Monsieur de Marsay is a mangy cur. I have often felt like wringing his neck. Imagine anyone not loving such a jewel of a woman, with her nightingale voice and perfect figure! She must have been blind to marry that great lump of an Alsatian! Both my daughters should have had really nice, handsome young men. Well, they did what they wanted!'

Père Goriot was sublime. Eugène had never before had the chance of seeing him transfigured by the ardour of paternal love. The capacity of emotions to distil a kind of energy is quite remarkable. As soon as he begins to express a strong and genuine emotion the most brutish of men gives off a special fluid which alters his features, animates his gestures, modulates his voice. Often under the stress of passion the dullest human being attains the highest degree of eloquence in concepts, if not in actual words, and seems to move in a realm of luminous brightness. At that moment the old man's voice and gestures communicated his feelings with all the intensity that marks out the great actor. But are not our finer feelings the poetry of the will?

'Very well! You may not be sorry to learn', Eugène told him, 'that she is probably going to break with that de Marsay. That young blood has given her up and formed an attachment with Princesse Galathionne. As for me, this evening I fell in love with Madame Delphine.'

'Tush!' said Père Goriot.

'Really. We got on rather well. We talked about love for an hour or so, and I am to call on her on Saturday afternoon.'

'Oh, how I should love you, my dear sir, if she took to you. You are kind-hearted, you would not cause her pain. If you ever betrayed her I should slit your throat at once. A woman does not love twice, you see. Goodness! what nonsense I am talking, Monsieur Eugène. It must be cold in here for you. Goodness! So you heard her talk; what message did she give you for me?'

'None,' Eugène said inwardly; aloud he replied, 'She sent

you a daughter's love and kisses.'

'Goodnight, neighbour, sleep well, pleasant dreams. Mine are certain to be so after that message. God be with you in all you desire! This evening you have been my good angel; you have brought me a breath of air from my daughter.'

'Poor man,' said Eugène to himself as he went to bed, 'it's enough to melt a heart of stone. His daughter no more thought of him than of the Sultan of Turkey.'

After this conversation Père Goriot saw in his neighbour an unexpected confidant and friend. The relationship established between them was the only one through which the old fellow could become attached to another man. Passions never go wrong in their calculations. Père Goriot saw himself coming a little closer to his daughter Delphine, he saw himself being welcomed more warmly if Eugène endeared himself to the baronne. Besides, he had confided to Eugène something that grieved him deeply. Madame de Nucingen, for whose happiness he prayed so constantly every day, had never known the joys of love. Eugène was indeed, to use his own expression, one of the nicest young men he had ever met, and he had a kind of presentiment that Eugène would give her all the pleasures of which she had been deprived. The old fellow thus formed an ever closer friendship with his neighbour; but for that, it would probably have been impossible to learn how this story ended.

Next morning at breakfast Père Goriot sat beside Eugène, and the affectionate way he looked at him, the brief words he addressed to him, the change in the old man's expression, usually as blank as a plaster mask, surprised the other boarders. Vautrin, who had not seen the student since their discussion, seemed to be trying to read his thoughts. During the night, before falling asleep, Eugène had surveyed the vast field opening up before him. Remembering Vautrin's scheme, he inevitably thought of Mademoiselle Taillefer's dowry, and could not help looking at Victorine as a young man of blameless virtue looks at a rich heiress. By chance their eyes met. The poor girl could not help finding Eugène attractive in his new outfit. The glance they exchanged was telling enough to leave Rastignac in no doubt that for her he represented the object of the vague desires which every young girl feels and fastens on to the first attractive person to come along. A voice cried out to him: 'Eight hundred thousand francs!' But suddenly he plunged back into memories of the previous evening, and found that his fabricated passion for Madame de Nucingen made a good antidote to the evil thoughts that came upon him involuntarily.

'They were doing Rossini's *Barber of Seville* at the Italiens yesterday. I never heard such delightful music,' he said. 'Anyone who has a box at the Italiens can count themselves lucky!'

Père Goriot caught the phrase in passing, like a dog catching a sign from his master.

'You men live like fighting cocks,' said Madame Vauquer. 'You can do whatever you like.'

'How did you come home?' asked Vautrin.

'I walked,' answered Eugène.

'Personally,' went on the tempter, 'I wouldn't enjoy doing things by halves. I should want to go there in my carriage, sit in my box and come home in comfort. All or nothing! That's my motto.'

'And a good one too,' added Madame Vauquer.

'Perhaps you will be calling on Madame de Nucingen,' Eugène said to Goriot in a low voice. 'She will certainly welcome you with open arms, she will want to know lots of little details about me. I understand that she would do anything to be received by my cousin, Madame la vicomtesse de Beauséant. Don't forget to tell her that I am too fond of her not to be thinking how I can enable her to satisfy that desire.'

Rastignac soon left for the École de Droit; he wanted to spend as little time as possible in that detestable house. He wandered about nearly all day, his thoughts racing feverishly in a way familiar to any young man suffering from excessive expectations. Vautrin's arguments had brought him to reflect on social life, just at the moment when he ran into his friend Bianchon in the Luxembourg Gardens.

'Why do you look so solemn?' asked the medical student, taking his arm as they walked in front of the palace.

'I am plagued by evil thoughts.'

'What kind? Thoughts can be cured, you know.'

'How so?'

'By giving in to them.'

'You are joking without knowing what the problem is. Have you read Rousseau?'*

'Yes.'

'Do you recall the passage where he asks what the reader would do if he could become rich by killing some old mandarin in China without stirring from Paris, simply by willing it so?'

'I do.'

'Well?'

'Bah! I am well on to my thirty-third mandarin.'

'It's no joking matter. Now if someone proved to you that such a thing is possible, and all you need to do is nod your head, what would you do?'

'Is he very old, your mandarin? But, my word, young or old, paralytic or healthy ... Devil take it! All right, no!'

'You are a good chap, Bianchon. But if you loved a woman enough to turn your soul inside out for her, and if she needed money, lots of money, for clothes, for her carriage, in a word to indulge all her whims?'

'But you are denying me the use of reason, and you expect me to argue rationally.'

'Very well! Bianchon, I am out of my mind, cure me. I have two sisters, angels of beauty and innocence, and I want them to be happy. Where can I find two hundred thousand francs for their dowry five years from now? You see, there are circumstances in life when you have to play for high stakes and not wear out your good fortune winning pennies.'

'But you are asking the question that everyone has to face

when they start out in life, and you are trying to cut the Gordian knot with a sword. You have to be Alexander, my dear fellow, to behave like that, otherwise you end up in gaol. For my part I am content with the modest living I shall make in the provinces, where I shall quite simply take over from my father. A man's desires can just as easily be satisfied in the smallest of circles as within an immense circumference. Napoleon didn't dine twice a day, and couldn't take any more mistresses than a medical student doing his house training at the Capucins. Our happiness, my friend will always lie between the soles of our feet and the crown of our head. Whether it costs a million francs a year or a hundred louis our basic perception of it is just the same within us. So I conclude that the Chinaman lives.'

'Thank you, you have done me good, Bianchon! We'll always be friends.'

'I say,' went on the medical student, 'as I came out of Cuvier's* lecture just now at the Jardin des Plantes, I noticed Michonneau and Poiret on a bench talking to a gentleman I saw last year during the disturbances round the Chambre des Députés. He looked to me then like a police spy disguised as an honest citizen of independent means. Let's keep an eye on that couple. I'll tell you why later. Goodbye for now, I am off to answer my name at the roll-call at four o'clock.'

On Eugène's return to the boarding house he found Père Goriot waiting for him.

'Here you are,' said the old man, 'here's a letter from her. Look how neatly she writes!'

Eugène broke the seal and read as follows:

Monsieur, my father tells me that you are fond of Italian music. I should be delighted if you would give me the pleasure of accepting a seat in my box. On Saturday we are to hear la Fodor and Pellegrini,* so I am sure you will not refuse my invitation. Monsieur de Nucingen joins me in requesting you to dine with us informally. If you accept, you will be pleasing him by relieving him of the tiresome conjugal duty of accompanying me. Do not answer, just come. With the compliments of D. de N.

'Let me see,' the old man said when Eugène had read the letter. 'You will go, won't you?' he added, holding the paper to his nose. 'How sweet it smells! Her fingers have touched it, of course.'

'A woman doesn't throw herself at a man's head like that,' the student said to himself. 'She is trying to use me to get de Marsay back. Only wounded pride could make anyone behave like that.'

'Well!' said Père Goriot, 'What's on your mind?'

Eugène was unaware of the feverish vanity possessing some women at that time, and did not know that a banker's wife would find any sacrifice acceptable if it would open a door to her in the Faubourg Saint-Germain. It was becoming fashionable just then to class those women who were admitted to the society of the Faubourg Saint-Germain, the so-called ladies of the Petit-Château,* as superior to all the rest; among them Madame de Beauséant, her friend the Duchesse de Langeais and the Duchesse de Maufrigneuse had pride of place. Rastignac alone did not know how frantically the women of the Chaussée-d'Antin were obsessed by the desire to ascend to the lofty heights where the constellations of their sex shone. But his natural distrust served him well by giving him a certain coolness and the unhappy power of imposing conditions rather than submitting to them.

'Yes, I'll go,' he answered.

Thus it was curiosity that brought him to Madame de Nucingen, whereas if she had scorned him he might have been led to her by passion. Nevertheless he looked forward to the next day and the hour he should set out with a certain impatience. A young man's first intrigue may well afford him as much delight as his first love. The certainty of success creates endless occasions of pleasure to which men will never admit, and which in some women is the secret of their charm. Desire can spring as much from the difficulty as from the ease of conquests. All men's passions are quite certainly aroused or sustained by one or other of these two causes, which between them divide the empire of love. This division

is perhaps a consequence of the great question of tempera-
ments, which, whatever people may say, dominates society.
If those of melancholy temperament need the stimulus of
flirtatious teasing, those of sanguine or nervous disposition
will perhaps give up if resistance is too prolonged. Put another
way, elegiac verse is in essence associated with the phlegmatic
humour, just as dithyrambic hymns go with the choleric.
As he got ready Eugène savoured to the full all the little
pleasures that young men are afraid to mention for fear of
exciting derision, but which flatter their vanity. As he
arranged his hair he imagined that an attractive woman's eyes
would soon be stealing through his dark curls. He indulged
in as many childish antics as a girl dressing up for a ball.

He felt very pleased with himself as he looked at his slim
waist and smoothed out the creases from his dress coat. 'One
could certainly find worse-looking men!' he said to himself.
Then he went downstairs just when all the regular boarders
were seated at table, and gaily acknowledged the loud applause
and silly remarks that greeted his elegant appearance. Typical
of boarding-house manners is the amazement provoked by
the sight of anyone who is well dressed. No one can appear
in new clothes without exciting comment from one and all.

'Tk, tk, tk,' went Bianchon, clicking his tongue against
his palate as though urging on a horse.

'All dressed up like a proper duke!' said Madame Vauquer.

'Monsieur Rastignac is bent on conquest?' remarked Mademoiselle Michonneau.

'Cock-a-doodle-doo!' crowed the artist.

'My compliments to your lady wife,' said the Museum assistant.

'Does Monsieur Rastignac have a wife?' asked Poiret.

'A wife, with compartments, floats in water, guaranteed
fast dye, prices range from twenty-five to forty, checkered
patterns in the latest fashion, washable, smart to wear, half-
linen, half-cotton, half-woollen, cures toothache and other
ailments approved by the Royal Academy of Medicine! Excellent too for children! Better still for headaches, feelings of

satiety and other diseases of the oesophagus, eyes and ears!'
cried Vautrin with the comic verve and emphasis of a fair-
ground quack. 'But what does this marvel cost, I hear you
ask, gentlemen? Two sous? No. Nothing at all. It's left over
from an order supplied to the Grand Mogul, and all the
crowned heads of Europe, including the Gr-r-r-rand Duke
of Baden have asked to see it! Entrance straight ahead! and
pay at the desk. Let's have some music! Booom-la-la, trinn!
la, la, boom, boom! That gentleman on the clarinet, you are
playing out of tune,' he went on in a hoarse voice, 'I'll have
to rap your knuckles!'

'My goodness! what a jolly man he is!' Madame Vauquer
said to Madame Couture, 'I could never be dull with him
around.'

Amid all the laughing and joking which this burlesque
speech precipitated, Eugène caught a furtive glance from
Mademoiselle Taillefer, who leant over to Madame Couture
and said a few words in her ear.

'Here's the cab,' said Sylvie.

'Where's he dining then?' asked Bianchon.

'At Madame la baronne de Nucingen's.'

'Monsieur Goriot's daughter,' replied the student.

At that every eye was drawn to the former vermicelli-
merchant, who was gazing almost enviously at Eugène.

Rastignac arrived at the rue Saint-Lazare, in front of one
of those insubstantial houses, with slender pillars and skimped
porticoes, which are classed as 'pretty' in Paris. It was a real
banker's house, full of expensive ostentation, stucco work,
marble mosaic floors on the landings. He found Madame de
Nucingen in a small drawing-room hung with Italian pictures,
decorated rather in the style of a café. The baronne was in
gloomy mood. She tried so hard to conceal her unhappiness
that Eugène's interest was all the more keenly aroused, since
she was clearly not play-acting. He had thought to gladden
a woman's heart by his presence, and now he found her in
despair. The disappointment stung his pride.

'I have very little claim on your confidence, Madame,' he

said, after teasing her for looking so worried, 'but if I am being a nuisance, I rely on your good faith to tell me so frankly.'

'Please stay,' she said, 'I should be all on my own if you went. Nucingen is dining out, and I don't want to be alone. I need some distraction.'

'Whatever is the matter?'

'You are the last person I would tell,' she cried.

'I should like to know; I must have something to do with this secret.'

'Perhaps! But no,' she went on, 'it is one of those quarrels between husband and wife that should stay buried in the depths of one's heart. Did I not tell you two days ago? I am not a happy woman. Chains of gold are the heaviest to bear.'

When a woman tells a young man that she is unhappy, if the young man is intelligent and well dressed, with fifteen hundred francs lying idle in his pocket, he is bound to think what Eugène thought and become conceited.

'What can you wish for?' he asked. 'You have beauty, youth, love, riches!'

'Let's not talk about me,' she said with a sorrowful shake of her head. 'We'll dine together, just the two of us, then we'll go and listen to the most delightful music. How do you like me in this?' she went on, standing up and showing off her dress of white cashmere richly decorated with Persian patterns in the most perfect taste.

'I wish you could be mine,' said Eugène, 'You are enchanting.'

'You would be making a sorry acquisition,' she said with a wry smile. 'There is nothing here to speak of misfortune, yet, despite all appearances, I am in despair. I can't sleep for worrying, I shall lose my looks.'

'Oh, that could never happen,' said the student. 'But I am curious to know about these troubles that a devoted love cannot dispel?'

'Ah! If I told you, you would run away from me,' she

said, 'In any case you only love me from a sense of gallantry which is expected of men; if you really loved me, you would be plunged into the most frightful despair. You see that I must say no more. I beg you,' she went on, 'let's talk about something else. Come and see my apartments.'

'No, let's stay here,' Eugène replied as he sat down on a love-seat in front of the fire beside Madame de Nucingen, and firmly grasped her hand.

She let him hold it and even pressed his with a concentrated intensity telling of powerful emotions.

'Listen,' Rastignac told her, 'if something is troubling you, you must tell me about it. I can prove that I love you for yourself alone. Either you must speak out and tell me what is upsetting you so that I can put it right, even if it means killing half a dozen men, or I will leave and never return.'

'All right!' she cried, so racked by despair that she struck herself on the forehead, 'I'll put you to the test right away. 'Yes,' she said to herself, it's the only way left.' She rang.

'Is the baron's carriage ready?' she asked her footman.

'Yes, Madame.'

'I'll take it. You can let him have mine and my horses. Do not serve dinner before seven o'clock.'

'Right, come along,' she said to Eugène, who thought he must be dreaming when he found himself sitting by her side in Monsieur de Nucingen's brougham.

'The Palais-Royal,' she told the coachman, 'near the Théâtre Français.'

During the journey she showed signs of agitation, and refused to answer Eugène's flow of questions. He did not know what to make of such mute, intense, stubborn resistance.

'In a moment I shall have lost her,' he said to himself.

When the carriage stopped, the baronne gave the student a look that silenced his wild outpourings, for he had quite lost his head.

'Are you really fond of me?' she asked.

'Yes,' he replied, concealing his growing uneasiness.

'You will never think ill of me whatever I may ask of you?'
'No.'
'Are you ready to obey me?'
'Blindly.'
'Have you ever been gambling?' she asked in a shaky voice.
'Never.'
'Ah! I can breathe again. You will have good luck. Here
is my purse,' she said. 'Go on, take it! There are one hundred
francs, all that this fortunate woman possesses. Go into a
gaming-house. I don't know where they are, but I know that
there are several in the Palais-Royal. Stake the hundred francs
on a game called roulette, and either lose the lot or bring
me back six thousand francs. I will tell you my troubles when
you come back.'

'The devil take it if I understand a thing about what I'm
about to do, but I'll obey you,' he said, overjoyed as he
thought, 'She is compromising herself with me, so she won't
be able to refuse me anything.'

Eugène took the dainty purse, asked an old-clothes dealer
for directions to the nearest gaming-house and hurried to
Number Nine. Going upstairs, he handed in his hat, went
in and asked for the roulette. To the amazement of the regulars
the attendant led him to a long table. Eugène, with the eyes
of all the spectators on him, quite unashamedly asked where
he should place his stake.

'If you put a louis on a single one of those thirty-six numbers
and it comes up, you'll make thirty-six louis,' he was told
by a respectable-looking old gentleman with white hair.

Eugène threw down the hundred francs on the same number
as his age, twenty-one. A cry of amazement went up before
he had had time to get his bearings. He had won without
knowing it.

'Withdraw your money now,' the old gentleman told him,
'no one ever wins twice with that system.'

Eugène took a rake proffered by the old gentleman, pulled
in his three thousand six hundred francs and, still in total
ignorance of the game, put them on red. The spectators

watched enviously when they saw that he was continuing to play. The wheel spun round, he won again, and the banker threw him another three thousand six hundred francs.

'Now you've got seven thousand two hundred francs,' the old gentleman said in his ear. 'If you take my advice you'll leave now. Red has come up eight times. If you are feeling generous you'll reward my good advice by relieving the distress of one of Napoleon's former prefects* who is now utterly destitute.'

Rastignac was so stunned that he let the white-haired gentleman take ten louis off him, and went out with his seven thousand francs, still completely ignorant of the game, but staggered by his good fortune.

'Right! Where are you taking me now?' he asked, showing Madame de Nucingen the seven thousand francs when the carriage door had closed behind him.

Delphine clasped him in a wild embrace and kissed him excitedly but without passion. 'You have saved me!' Tears of joy streamed down her cheeks. 'I'll tell you everything, my friend. You will be my friend, won't you? You see me rich, extremely wealthy, wanting for nothing or apparently wanting for nothing! Well! Let me tell you that Monsieur de Nucingen does not let me have a sou to spend freely; he pays all the household expenses, my carriages, my boxes at the theatre; he gives me a dress allowance which is never enough, he deliberately reduces me to secret penury. I am too proud to beg from him. Would I not be the lowest of the low if I bought his money at the price he demands? With my own fortune of seven hundred thousand francs how have I let myself be stripped of everything? Through pride and indignation. We are so young, so naïve when we start on married life! Asking my husband for money would have meant using words which would have choked me. I never dared to do it, I used up all my savings and the money my poor father gave me; then I fell into debt. Marriage cruelly destroyed all my illusions, I can't bring myself to talk about it. Suffice it to say that I would throw myself out of the

window if I had to live with Nucingen on any other terms
than with separate apartments for each of us. When I had
to admit to him the debts I had incurred as a young woman,
on jewels, little treats (thanks to my poor father we had grown
used to refusing ourselves nothing) I went through agonies,
but finally plucked up enough courage to tell him. I had my
own fortune after all. Nucingen was quite beside himself.
He said I would be the ruin of him, dreadful things! I wished
the earth would swallow me up. As he had taken my dowry,
he paid up, but he stipulated that in future I should have
a fixed allowance for my personal expenses, and I accepted
for the sake of peace. Since then I have tried to live up to
the self-esteem of someone you know,' she said. 'Even if he
has deceived me it's only fair to acknowledge his noble character. But in the end he left me shamefully! No man should
ever abandon a woman on whom he has showered a pile
of money when she was in the direst straits. He should always
love her! You are twenty-one, noble-hearted, young and innocent, and you will ask how a woman can take money from
a man? My goodness! Isn't it natural to share everything with
the person to whom one owes one's happiness? When you
have given yourselves completely to one another, why should
one worry about one fraction of the whole? Money only
begins to matter when feelings are dead. Isn't it a bond for
life? Which of us foresees separation while she believes herself
truly loved? You men swear that you will love us for all
eternity, how then can we have individual interests? You don't
know how I suffered today when Nucingen flatly refused
to give me six thousand francs; he gives his mistress that much
every month, that girl from the Opéra! I wanted to commit
suicide. The wildest notions passed through my mind. At
times I envied a servant's lot, even my maid's. Going to my
father would have been absurd! Anastasie and I have bled
him white. My poor father would have sold himself if it would
have brought in six thousand francs. I would just have been
driving him to despair to no purpose. You have saved me
from shame and death. I was dizzy with grief. Oh! Monsieur

Rastignac, I owed you this explanation. I treated you in the most absurdly unreasonable way. When you left me and passed out of sight, I thought of running away—where I do not know. That is how half the women in Paris live; outward luxury, within—the cruellest worries. I know poor creatures even more wretched than myself. Some women are obliged to get their tradesmen to draw up false accounts. Others are forced to cheat their husbands. Some husbands think that cashmere dresses worth two thousand francs are sold at five hundred, others that a cashmere priced at five hundred francs is worth two thousand. There are some poor women who make their children go hungry and have to scrounge to get a dress. At least I am innocent of such odious deception. This is my ultimate horror. If some women sell themselves to their husbands so that they can dominate them, at least I am free! I could get Nucingen to pour money over me, but I prefer to weep with my head resting on the heart of a man I can respect. Ah! This evening Monsieur de Marsay will not have the right to look on me as a woman to whom he once paid money.'

She buried her head in her hands to conceal her tears from Eugène, but he made her show her face so that he could gaze at her, sublime as she was in her distress.

'It's horrible to mix up money with emotions, isn't it? You will never be able to love me,' she said.

This mixture of finer feelings, which make women so noble, and moral lapses, forced on them by society as it is at present constituted, overwhelmed Eugène. He spoke gentle words of comfort, full of admiration for this beautiful woman who had been so innocently indiscreet in her cry of anguish.

'You must never use this as a weapon against me,' she said, 'Promise me that.'

'Ah! Madame, I could never do such a thing,' he said.

She took his hand and pressed it against her heart in a warm gesture of gratitude.

'Thanks to you I feel free and happy again. I was living under the weight of an iron hand, now I intend to live simply, and cheaply. You will like me as you find me, won't you, my friend? Keep this,' she said, taking only six banknotes for herself. 'In all conscience I owe you three thousand francs, because I had intended to go halves with you.' Eugène protested like a virgin defending her honour, but when the baronne said, 'I shall regard you as my enemy if you won't be my ally,' he took the money. 'I will hold it as a stake in case of emergency,' he said.

'That's what I dreaded to hear,' she cried, going pale. 'IF you want me to mean something in your life swear', she said, 'never to go gambling again. Good heavens! If you were to be corrupted through my fault I should die of grief.'

They had arrived. The contrast between her wretchedness and such opulence stunned the student, who heard Vautrin's sinister words ringing in his ear.

As they went through into her room, the baronne said 'Sit there,' indicating a love-seat by the fireside, 'I have a very difficult letter to write. I want your advice.'

'Don't write anything,' said Eugène. 'Put the banknotes in an envelope, address it and send it by hand of your maid.'

'What an adorable man you are,' she said, 'That just shows, Monsieur, what it means to have been properly brought up. That is pure Beauséant,' she said with a smile.

'She is charming,' Eugène said to himself, falling ever more deeply in love. He looked round the room whose atmosphere of sensual elegance suggested a wealthy courtesan.

'Do you like it here?' she asked, ringing for her maid.

'Thérèse, take this to Monsieur de Marsay yourself and hand it to him personally. If he is not there, bring back the letter.'

'Thérèse cast a mischievous glance at Eugène and went out. Dinner was announced. Rastignac offered his arm to Madame de Nucingen, who took him into a delightful dining-room, where he found the same luxury as he had admired at his cousin's table.

'On the days when there is something on at the Italiens,' she said, 'you can come and dine with me, and then be my escort.'

'I should get used to such a pleasant life if it were going to last, but I am a poor student with his way to make in life.'

'You will make your way all right,' she said with a laugh. 'As you see, everything has turned out for the best. I never expected to feel so happy.'

It is in woman's nature to prove the impossible from the possible, and to refute facts with intuitions. When Madame de Nucingen and Rastignac entered their box at the Bouffons her obvious happiness made her look so beautiful that everyone indulged in the kind of slanderous gossip against which a woman has no defence and which often lends credence to maliciously invented misconduct. No one who knows Paris believes a word that is said there, and not a word is said of what really goes on. Eugène took the baronne's hand, and they conversed by varying the pressure of their fingers as they shared the impressions made on them by the music. They found the whole evening intoxicating. They left the theatre together, and Madame de Nucingen insisted on taking Eugène back as far as the Pont-Neuf, arguing all the way against giving him another of those kisses which she had dispensed with such warm generosity at the Palais-Royal. Eugène reproached her for being inconsistent.

'Last time', she said, 'I was showing gratitude for a devotion I had never hoped for; now it would be a promise.'

'And you don't want to make me any promises, ungrateful woman.' He was annoyed. With one of those impatient gestures that lovers find so delightful, she offered him her hand to kiss; he took it with such bad grace that she was enchanted.

'We'll meet at the ball on Monday,' she said.

As he walked off into the beautiful moonlit night Eugène fell into serious thought. He was both happy and dissatisfied: happy at an adventure of which the likely outcome would bring him the object of his desire, one of the most attractive and elegant women in Paris; dissatisfied at seeing his plans for winning a fortune upset. Then it was that he was confronted with the reality of his half-formed musings of two days earlier. Frustration always brings home to us the intensity of our ambitions. The more Eugène enjoyed Parisian life the less ready he was to remain obscure and poor. He crumpled his thousand-franc note in his pocket as he thought of countless spurious reasons for holding on to it. Finally he reached the rue Neuve-Sainte-Geneviève. Climbing to the top of the stairs he saw a light shining. Père Goriot had left the door ajar and a candle burning so that the student would not forget to 'tell him all about his daughter' as he put it. Eugène concealed nothing from him.

'So', Père Goriot cried out in a violent fit of jealous despair, 'they think I am ruined; I still have thirteen hundred francs a year coming in! Good heavens! poor child, why didn't she come here! I would have sold my investments, we could have taken the money out of capital, and with the rest I could have purchased an annuity. Why didn't you come and tell me the fix she was in, good neighbour? How could you have had the heart to risk her pathetic little hundred francs in a gaming-house? It's enough to break your heart. That's sons-in-law for you! Oh! if I could lay my hands on them I would strangle them. Good Lord! She cried, did she?'

'With her head on my waistcoat,' said Eugène.

'Oh! do give it to me,' said Père Goriot. 'What! That's where my daughter's tears ran, my dear Delphine who never cried when she was small. Oh! I'll buy you another, don't wear it again, leave it with me. According to her marriage contract she should have the use of her own assets. Ha! I'll go and see Derville, he's a lawyer, in the morning. I'll insist that her own money is invested. I know the law, I'm an old wolf. I'm going to show that I still have sharp teeth.'

'Look, Papa, here's a thousand francs she asked me to give you out of our winnings. Keep it for her, in the waistcoat.'

Goriot looked at Eugène, and as he reached out to take his hand a teardrop fell upon it.

'You will make a success of your life,' the old man told him. 'God is just, you see. I know something about integrity, and I can assure you that there are very few men like you. So you want to be my dear child too? You must go and get some sleep. You are still able to sleep, you are not a father yet. She cried, you say, and there I was calmly eating my food like an idiot while she was suffering. I, who would gladly sell Father, Son and Holy Ghost to save either of my girls from shedding a tear!'

'Upon my word,' said Eugène to himself as he went to bed, 'I really think I shall be an honest man all my life. It feels so good to follow the promptings of conscience.'

Perhaps only those who believe in God do good in secret, and Eugène believed in God. Next day, when it was time for the ball, Rastignac went to Madame de Beauséant's house, and she took him with her to present him to the Duchesse de Carigliano. He received the most gracious welcome from the Maréchale, and found Madame de Nucingen already there. Delphine had put on all her finery with the intention of attracting general approval and thus looking all the more attractive to Eugène in particular. She waited impatiently for him to notice her, in the belief that her impatience was well concealed. Any man who knows how to read a woman's feelings will find such a moment delightful. Who has not often enjoyed delaying the expression of his opinion, teasingly concealing his pleasure, looking for telltale reactions to the disquiet he is provoking, savouring an apprehension which he can dispel with a smile? In the course of the party the student suddenly took in the implications of his position and realized that he enjoyed a certain social standing from the fact that Madame de Beauséant acknowledged him as her cousin. The conquest of Madame la baronne de Nucingen, with which he was already credited, made him so conspicuous a figure that all the young men cast envious glances in his direction. Catching some of these looks, he relished the first stirrings of conceit. Passing from one room to another, making his way through groups of people, he heard them extol his good fortune. The women all predicted that he would have further successes. Afraid of losing him, Delphine promised not to refuse him that night the kiss that she had been so loath to bestow two days earlier. At this ball Rastignac received a number of invitations. He was introduced by his cousin to several women who all aspired to elegance and whose houses were considered pleasant. He saw himself launched into the most exalted and fashionable Parisian society. The evening thus had for him all the charm of a brilliant début, and he would remember it to his dying day, as a girl remembers the ball where she scored her early triumphs. Next morning at breakfast, in front of the other boarders, he told Père Goriot all about his success. Vautrin began to smile diabolically.

'So you really think', he exclaimed with ferocious logic, 'that a fashionable young man can stay in the rue Neuve-Sainte-Geneviève, at the Maison Vauquer? An establishment of the most absolute respectability in every way, to be sure, but not exactly fashionable. It is cosy and comfortable, over-flowing with good things, proud to be the temporary seat of a Rastignac; but, when you come down to it, it is the rue Neuve-Sainte-Geneviève, a stranger to luxury because it is purely *patriarchalorama*. My young friend,' Vautrin went on with an air of paternal derision, 'If you want to cut a figure in Paris, you must have three horses and a tilbury for the daytime, and a brougham for the evening; making a total of nine thousand francs for your carriages. You would be unworthy of your destiny if you did not spend three thousand francs at your tailor's, six hundred at the perfumer's, three hundred at the bootmaker's and three hundred at the hatter's. As for your laundress, she'll cost you a thousand. Fashionable young men can't afford to be less than meticulous when it comes to linen; isn't that what people most often look at? Love and the church demand fine cloths on their altars. That comes to fourteen thousand. I'll say nothing about your gambling losses, your wagers, your presents. You can't possibly reckon with less than two thousand francs pocket-money. I have led that sort of life. I know what it costs. Add to these basic necessities six thousand francs for rations, a thousand for a billet. So, my boy, we need to raise a cool twenty-five thousand a year to meet expenses, or we land in the gutter, make ourselves a laughing-stock and find ourselves with no future, no success and no mistress! I've forgotten the valet and the groom! Do you think Christophe will carry your love letters? You might as well cut your own throat, take the word of an experienced old man for it!' he went on, making his bass voice boom even louder. 'Either move virtuously into an attic, and be wedded to your work, or choose a different path.'

With that Vautrin winked, with a leer in the direction of Mademoiselle Taillefer, recalling and resuming in that look all the tempting arguments he had planted as seeds of corruption in the student's heart. In the course of the next few days Rastignac led an extremely dissipated life. He dined almost every day with Madame de Nucingen, and went everywhere as her escort. He would come home at three or four in the morning, rise at midday to get ready to go out, and then go for a turn in the Bois when it was fine. He wasted time like this, heedless of the cost, and absorbed all the lessons and allurements of luxury with the eager ardour of the female date palm receiving the fertilizing pollen in its calyx. He played for high stakes, losing or winning a lot of money, and finally grew used to the extravagant life of the young man in Paris. From his first winnings he had sent back fifteen hundred francs to his mother and his sisters, accompanying this repayment with handsome presents. Although he had announced his intended departure from the Maison Vauquer, the end of January found him still there, and he could not see how he was going to be able to leave. Young men are almost all subject to a law which seems inexplicable but is in fact to be accounted for by their very youth and headlong pursuit of pleasure. Rich or poor, they never have enough money for the necessities of life, whereas they can always find enough for their whims. Lavish with anything that can be obtained on credit, they are miserly with anything that has to be paid for on the spot, and seem to be taking their revenge for what they do not have by wasting whatever they may possess. Thus, to state the problem simply, a student takes far more care of his hat than of his coat. The tailor's vast profits make him essentially ready to give credit, whereas the hatter's modest charges make him one of the most inflexible persons with whom the student is obliged to negotiate. If the young man in a balcony seat at the theatre displays a dazzling waistcoat to the pretty women looking at him through their opera-glasses, it is far from sure that he has any socks to wear; the hosier is yet another of the weevils eating away at his purse. Rastignac had come to that. Always empty for Madame Vauquer, always full for the demands of his vanity, his purse marked the wildest fluctuations up and down, which were always out of step with the most ordinary payments. In order to leave the vile, evil-smelling boarding house where his ambitions were regularly humiliated, he would have to pay a month's rent to his landlady and buy furniture for his fashionable apartment, would he not? That was always quite impossible. When he wanted money for gambling, Rastignac knew well enough how to buy expensive gold watches and chains from his jeweller, paid for out of his winnings, which he could then take to the pawnshop, that depressing and discreet friend of the young, but he was neither bold nor resourceful when it came to paying for his food and lodging or buying the essential equipment needed for living an elegant life. Vulgar necessity, debts incurred for needs now satisfied, no longer inspired him. Like most people who have known this haphazard sort of existence, he would wait till the last moment to pay off the debts which the solid citizen regards as sacred, just like Mirabeau,* who only paid his baker's bill when it was presented in the intimidating form of a bill of exchange.

About this time Rastignac had lost all his money and fallen into debt. The student was beginning to realize that he could not go on leading that kind of life without having fixed resources. But even while he moaned under the stinging blows inflicted by his precarious situation, he felt unable to give up the extravagant pleasures of such a life, and wanted to continue it at any price. The strokes of luck on which he had counted to make his fortune became merely chimerical, while the real obstacles loomed larger. His initiation into the domestic secrets of Monsieur and Madame de Nucingen had shown him that one can only convert love into a device for making a fortune by draining the cup of shame to the dregs and renouncing all the noble ideals which serve to absolve the faults of youth. This life of outward splendour, gnawed inwardly by all the worms of remorse whose fleeting pleasures had to be dearly atoned for by constant anguish, was what he had chosen to adopt, rolling in it, making his bed, like the Absent-minded man in La Bruyère,* in the mire of the ditch; like that character he had so far soiled only his clothes.

'So we killed the mandarin?' Bianchon said to him one day as they got up from table.

'Not yet,' he answered, 'but he's at his last gasp.'

The medical student took the last remark for a jest, but it was not. For the first time for some while Eugène had dined at the boarding house and had looked preoccupied throughout the meal. Instead of leaving when dessert was served, he stayed on in the dining-room, sitting beside Mademoiselle Taillefer and looking at her meaningfully from time to time. Some of the boarders were still at the table eating nuts, others strolled up and down, continuing earlier discussions. As on almost every evening, they went out one at a time as each one felt inclined, depending on how much interest they took in the conversation, or the degree of torpor induced by digestion. In winter the dining-room was seldom empty before eight o'clock, at which point the four women remaining there alone would take their revenge for the silence imposed on their sex for as long as the company was predominantly masculine. Struck by Eugène's obvious preoccupation, Vautrin stayed in the dining-room, although he had at first seemed to be in a hurry to leave, but took care to remain out of sight of Eugène, who probably thought he had gone. Then, instead of accompanying the last of the boarders to leave, he surreptitiously took up a position in the drawing-room. He had read the student's mind and detected signs of an impending crisis.

Rastignac was indeed in a state of perplexity which must be familiar to many young men. Whether she really loved him or was just leading him on, Madame de Nucingen had inflicted on Rastignac all the pains of a genuine passion, drawing on all the resources of feminine intrigue as practised in Paris. Having compromised herself in the public eye by being always in the company of Madame de Beauséant's cousin, she hesitated to grant him the actual rights which he appeared already to be enjoying. For the past few months she had so inflamed Eugène's senses that she finally affected his inward heart. If in the initial stages of his liaison the student had believed himself to be the master, Madame de Nucingen had now gained the upper hand, through tactics which brought into play in Eugène all the good and bad impulses of the two or three different men contained within a young Parisian. Was this a calculated action on her part? No; women are always true even when they are most deeply engaged in deception, because they are yielding to a natural impulse. Perhaps Delphine, after allowing this young man to win so much influence over her so rapidly, and after showing him too much affection, was now standing on her dignity in revoking her concessions, or suspending them for her own pleasure. A Parisian woman, at the very moment that passion begins to carry her away, finds it so natural to hesitate before she falls, and to test the heart of the man to whom she is about to surrender her future! All Madame de Nucingen's hopes had already been dashed once, and her fidelity to a self-centred young man had only recently been dismissed with contempt. She had good reason to be mistrustful. Perhaps she had observed in Eugène's attitude, since rapid success had turned his head, a certain lack of respect deriving from their peculiar situation. She no doubt wished to impress a man of that age, and stand tall before him after being made to feel small for so long by the man who had abandoned her. She did not want Eugène

to think of her as an easy conquest precisely because he knew
that she had once belonged to de Marsay. In short, after being
subjected to the degrading pleasure of a real monster, a young
libertine, she found it so sweet to roam through the flowery
fields of love, that it was no doubt a delight for her to dwell
in wonder on its every aspect, to listen to its gentle rustling
and let herself linger in the chaste embraces of its breezes.
True love was paying the price for false love. Such misunder-
standings will unfortunately continue to multiply for as long
as men fail to realize how many flowers in a young woman's
heart are trampled flat by the first onrush of betrayal. Whatever her reasons may have been, Delphine was playing with
Rastignac, and enjoyed playing with him, no doubt because
she knew he loved her and was thus confident of being able
to end her lover's woes whenever it was her sovereign pleasure
as a woman to do so.

For his own self-respect Eugène did not want his first
encounter to end in defeat, and persisted in pursuing her,
like a hunter absolutely determined to kill a partridge on
his first St Hubert's day.* His anxieties, his wounded pride,
his despair, whether true or false, bound him ever more closely
to this woman. The whole of Parisian society assumed that
Madame de Nucingen was his, when in fact he was no farther
forward with her than the day he first saw her. As yet unaware
that a woman's coquetry can sometimes offer more rewards
than her love can provide delights, he would fall into absurd
rages. If the season which finds a woman at grips with love
was bringing Rastignac the harvest of its first fruits, he was
beginning to find them as costly as they were green, acid
and delicious to taste. At times, seeing himself penniless and
without a future he thought, despite the voice of conscience,
of the chances of making his fortune by marrying Mademoiselle Taillefer, a plan which Vautrin had shown to be feasible.
He had now come to the point where his poverty protested
so loudly that he gave in almost involuntarily to the wily
schemes of the fearful sphinx whose gaze so often mesmerized
him. Just as Poiret and Mademoiselle Michonneau left to go

up to their rooms, Rastignac, thinking he was alone with Madame Vauquer and Madame Couture, who was drowsily knitting woollen sleeves for herself beside the stove, gave Mademoiselle Taillefer so tender a look that she lowered her eyes.

'Is there perhaps something troubling you, Monsieur Eugène?' asked Victorine, after a moment's silence.

'Who does not have his troubles!' replied Rastignac. 'If young men like myself could be sure of being truly loved, with a devotion so great that it would make up for the sacrifices we are always ready to offer, perhaps we should never have troubles.'

Mademoiselle Taillefer's only answer was a look which left no room for ambiguity.

'You, Mademoiselle, believe that you can be sure of your heart today, but could you answer for it never changing?'

A smile flickered over the poor girl's lips like a ray of light shooting up from her inmost soul, and so lit up her face that Eugène felt alarm at having provoked such a violent outburst of emotion.

'What! If tomorrow you were rich and happy, if a vast fortune dropped into your lap from heaven, would you still feel affection for the penniless young man whom you liked when times were hard?'

She nodded gracefully.

'A most unfortunate young man?'

Another nod.

'What nonsense are you talking over there?' cried Madame Vauquer.

'Let us be,' answered Eugène, 'we are getting on very well.'

'So there is to be a proposal of marriage between Monsieur le Chevalier de Rastignac and Mademoiselle Victorine Taillefer?' said Vautrin in his booming voice, suddenly appearing at the dining-room door.

'Oh! You frightened me!' said Madame Couture and Madame Vauquer at the same time.

'I could make a worse choice,' Eugène replied with a laugh,

more cruelly disturbed by hearing Vautrin's voice than he had ever been in his life before.

'No jokes in bad taste, gentlemen,' said Madame Couture. 'Let's go up to our room, my child.'

Madame Vauquer followed her two lodgers upstairs so that she could save her own candle and fire by spending the evening in their room. Eugène was left alone to face Vautrin.

'I knew very well that you would come round to it,' said Vautrin, imperturbably cool as ever. 'But listen! I have as much delicacy as the next man. Don't make up your mind here and now, you are not at all your usual self. You are in debt. I don't want you to be driven to me by passion or despair, but by reason. Perhaps you need three thousand francs or so? Here you are, do you want it?'

The diabolical fellow pulled a wallet out of his pocket, extracted three banknotes and fluttered them before the student's eyes. Eugène was in the cruellest predicament. He owed the Marquis d'Ajuda and the Comte de Trailles a thousand francs each as a debt of honour. He did not have the money and did not dare go to spend the evening at Madame de Restaud's, where he was expected. It was to be one of those informal evenings where people eat little cakes and drink tea, and may easily lose six thousand francs at whist.

'Monsieur,' said Eugène, barely able to conceal his convulsive trembling, 'after all you have confided in me, you must realize that I cannot put myself under any obligation to you.'

'All right! I should have been sorry if you had answered any other way,' replied the tempter. 'You are a good-looking young man with a delicate conscience, proud as a lion and gentle as a girl. You would be a fine catch for the devil. I like young men of that calibre. Two or three more high-principled remarks like that and you'll see the world as it is. If he acts out a few little scenes of virtue, the exceptional man can satisfy all his whims to the loud applause of the idiots in the pit. In a few days you will be one of us. Oh! if only you were willing to be my pupil I should ensure your success at everything. You would have only to form a wish to have it granted at once, no matter what you wish for, honours, riches, women. The whole civilized world would be reduced to celestial food for your enjoyment. You would be our spoilt child, our Benjamin, we should all gladly wipe ourselves out for your sake. Every obstacle in your path would be levelled. If you still cling to your scruples, do you then take me for a rogue? Well, a man of as much integrity as you still like to think you are, Monsieur de Turenne,* used to make little arrangements with brigands, and never thought that he was compromising his honour. You don't want to be under an obligation to me, eh? That's no problem,' Vautrin continued, not concealing a smile. 'Take these scraps of paper, and write here,' he said, pulling out a receipt form, 'there, across there: *Received the sum of 3,500 francs payable in one year's time*. And date it! The interest rate* is high enough to remove all your scruples. Call me a Jew if you like, and consider yourself clear of any debt of gratitude. I don't mind you despising me today, because I am sure that later on you will love me. You will find boundless depths in me, those vast concentrations of impulse that idiots call vices, but you will never find me cowardly or ungrateful. In a word I am neither a pawn nor a bishop, my boy, but a castle.'

'What kind of man are you then?' Eugène cried, 'created to be my tormentor!'

'Not at all. I am a good fellow, willing to get dirty so that you can be clear of mud for the rest of your days. You wonder why I am so devoted? Well! One day I'll whisper the answer, just for your ear alone. I surprised you at first when I showed you what levers have to be pulled to play tunes on the social scale. But you will get over your first alarm as the conscript does on the battlefield, and become used to the idea of regarding men as soldiers resolved to die in the service of kings who put the crown on their own heads. Times have changed indeed. Once you could say to a cut-throat, "Here's five hundred francs, go and kill Monsieur so and so for me," and carry on eating your supper after having a man put away just like that. Today I offer you a handsome fortune in return for a nod of your head which doesn't compromise you in the least, and you hesitate. This age has gone soft.'

Eugène signed the draft and exchanged it for the banknotes.

'Fine! now let's talk some sense.' Vautrin went on. 'In a few month's time I intend to leave for America, to plant my tobacco. I'll send you cigars for friendship's sake. If I become rich, I'll help you. If I don't have any children (which will probably be the case, since I am not interested in propagating myself here below with cuttings), then I'll bequeath you my fortune. Isn't that the act of a friend? But I am fond of you, and my passion is sacrificing myself for others. I have already done so. You see, my boy, I live on a loftier plane than other men. I regard actions as no more than means and look only at the end in view. What's a man to me? That!' clicking his thumbnail against his teeth. 'A man is all or nothing. He is less than nothing if his name is Poiret; you can squash him like a bug, he is flat and he stinks. But a man like you is godlike. He is no longer an automaton encased in skin, but a theatre for the finest emotions, and I only live on emotions. An emotion is the world contained in an idea, do you see? Look at Père Goriot; his two daughters make up his whole universe, the thread that guides him through the maze of creation. Well! I've looked deeply into life, and for me there's only one real emotion: the friendship of one man for another. Pierre and Jaffier, there's my passion! I know *Venice Preserv'd* off by heart.* Have you met many men stout-hearted enough to go off without a murmur or tiresome moralizing and just do it when a comrade says "Come and bury a body"? Well, I am one who's done it. I wouldn't talk like that to everyone, but in your case, you are an exceptional man, one can say anything to you and you understand. You won't squelch about for long in the swamps that are home to the little toads who are all round us here. Right! That's all I have to say. You will get married. Let's both press our points! Mine is cold steel, and never bends, ha, ha!'

Vautrin went out without waiting to hear the student's

objections, to put him at his ease. He seemed to know the secret of the token resistance, the struggles which men stage for their own benefit, and then use to justify themselves for blameworthy actions.

'He can do what he likes. I shall certainly never marry Mademoiselle Taillefer!' said Eugène to himself.

At the idea of making a pact with this man whom he found so repellent, but whose stature grew in his eyes because of the very cynicism of his ideas and his ruthless stranglehold on society, Rastignac's head swam with an inner fever. He dressed, ordered a cab and drove to Madame de Restaud's. For the past few days she had been increasingly attentive to this young man who advanced closer to the heart of fashionable society with every step he took, and who seemed destined one day to exert a formidable influence. He paid his debt to Monsieur de Trailles and Monsieur d'Ajuda, played whist for part of the evening and won back what he had lost. Superstitious like most men who still have their own way to make and are more or less fatalistic, he chose to interpret his good fortune as a reward sent from above for staying on the right path. Next morning he lost no time before asking Vautrin if he still had the bill of exchange. When Vautrin replied that he had, Eugène gave him back the three thousand francs with every sign of quite understandable satisfaction.

'Everything is going nicely,' said Vautrin.

'But I am not your accomplice,' said Eugène.

'I know, I know,' Vautrin broke in, 'You are still playing childish games. You balk at the mere idea of making a pass.'

3

Death-Dodger

Two days later Poiret and Mademoiselle Michonneau were sitting on a bench in the sun, by a secluded path in the Jardin des Plantes, talking to the gentleman about whom the medical student entertained quite justifiable suspicions.

'Mademoiselle,' Monsieur Gondureau was saying, 'I cannot see why you should have such scruples. His Excellency Monseigneur the Minister of Police for the whole Kingdom of France ...'

'Ah! His Excellency Monseigneur the Minister of Police for the whole Kingdom ...' Poiret repeated.

'Yes. His Excellency is dealing with the matter.'

It may seem most unlikely that Poiret, a retired clerk, no doubt endowed with solid middle-class virtues, though without an idea in his head, should go on listening to the self-styled man of independent means from the rue de Buffon once mention of the word 'police' had revealed the true face of an agent from the rue de Jérusalem* beneath his mask of ordinary respectability. Yet nothing could be more natural. One can better understand the particular species to which Poiret belonged within the large family of fools in the light of a point already noted by certain observers, though hitherto unpublished. There is a *plumigerous** race, whose habitat in the budget is concentrated between the first degree of latitude, comprising salaries of twelve hundred francs, a sort of administrative Greenland, and the third, where slightly more generous salaries of three to six thousand begin, a temperate region where the bonus has been acclimatized and flourishes in spite of difficulties of cultivation. One of the characteristics which most clearly reveals the feeble narrow-mindedness of this inferior breed is a sort of involuntary, automatic, instinctive respect for the Grand Lama of any ministry, known to the clerk by an illegible signature and the title HIS EXCELLENCY MONSEIGNEUR THE MINISTER, five words corresponding to *Il Bondo Cani* in the *Caliph of Baghdad*,* and which, in the eyes of this grovelling people, stands for a sacred power from which there is no appeal. Like the Pope for Catholics, Monseigneur is administratively infallible in the eyes of the ministry clerks; his personal lustre extends to his acts, his words and those uttered in his name; his gold braid provides a universal cover and any action ordered by him is thereby legalized. His title of 'Excellency', attesting the purity of his intentions and the sanctity of his wishes, serves as passport for the most unacceptable ideas. Actions which these poor people would never take in their own interests, they hasten to perform as soon as the words 'His Excellency' are pronounced. Government offices have their own system of passive obedience, just like the army: a system that stifles conscience, destroys the individual, and in time ends up by moulding him like a screw or a nut to fit the machinery of government. Thus Monsieur Gondureau, who seemed to be a good judge of men, quickly identified Poiret as one of these bureaucratic fools and produced his *deus ex machina*, the magic words 'His Excellency', at the crucial moment for unmasking his batteries and dazzling Poiret, who seemed to him the male version of Michonneau, as Michonneau seemed like the female of Poiret.

'Seeing that His Excellency in person, His Excellency Monseigneur the ...! Oh, that is quite a different matter,' said Poiret.

'You hear what this gentleman says, and you seem to trust his judgement,' the false man of means went on, addressing Mademoiselle Michonneau, 'Well! His Excellency is now absolutely certain that the so-called Vautrin, residing at the Maison Vauquer, is an escaped convict from the prison at Toulon, where he is known as *Death-Dodger*.'

'Ha! Death-Dodger,' said Poiret, 'he must be a lucky man

if he has earned that name.'

'Yes, indeed,' the agent replied. 'The nickname comes from the fact that he has been fortunate enough to escape with his life from all the extremely risky exploits he has carried out. This man is dangerous, you see! He has certain qualities which put him in a class of his own. The very fact of his conviction brought him the most enormous honour among his own sort ...'

'So he is a man of honour?' asked Poiret.

'In his own way. He agreed to take the blame for another man's crime; a forgery committed by a very good-looking young man whom he was very fond of, a young Italian rather keen on gambling, who has since joined the army, where in fact his conduct has been exemplary.'

'But if His Excellency the Minister of Police is so sure that Monsieur Vautrin is Death-Dodger, why should he need my help?' asked Mademoiselle Michonneau.

'Ah yes!' said Poiret, 'if indeed the Minister, as you have done us the honour of informing us, is at all certain ...'

'Certain is not the word; there are grounds for suspicion. You will understand the problem. Jacques Collin, nicknamed Death-Dodger, enjoys the full trust of the inmates of three prisons, and they have chosen him as their agent and banker. He makes a good living from this sort of business, which naturally requires a man of mark.'

'Ha! ha! do you understand the pun, Mademoiselle,' said Poiret, 'The gentleman calls him a man of mark because he has been marked by a branding iron.'

'The false Vautrin', the agent continued, 'receives funds from the convicts, invests and looks after the money, makes it available to any of them who escape, or to their families when they leave it in their wills, or their mistresses, when they draw on him on their behalf.'

'Their mistresses! You mean their wives,' Poiret remarked.

'No, sir. In general convicts only go in for unofficial wives; we call them concubines.'

'You mean they all live in a state of concubinage?'

'That follows.'

'Well!' said Poiret, ' that is quite shocking, and Monseigneur ought never to allow it. Since you have the honour of seeing His Excellency, it is up to you, with the philanthropic views you appear to hold, to enlighten him regarding the immoral conduct of these people, who set a very bad example to the rest of society.'

'But the government doesn't put them where they are, sir, to be a model of all the virtues.'

'That's quite true. However, allow me, sir ...'

'But let the gentleman speak, my pet,' said Mademoiselle Michonneau.

'You realize, Mademoiselle,' Gondureau went on, 'the government may be very interested in laying hands on illicit funds, reputedly amounting to a tidy sum. Death-Dodger has collected considerable amounts by harbouring not only the money belonging to some of his comrades, but also some emanating from the Society of Ten Thousand ...'

'Ten thousand thieves!' cried Poiret in alarm.

'No, the Society of Ten Thousand is an association of top thieves, men who only go for the big money, and won't get involved in any job where there is less than ten thousand francs to be made. This society consists of all the most distinguished of our customers who are sent directly to the assizes. They know the Code, and never risk incurring the death sentence when they are caught. Collin is their confidential agent, their expert adviser. Thanks to his vast resources this man has been able to build up a network of his own, with the most extensive contacts, all under a veil of secrecy no one has been able to penetrate. Although we have had spies watching him everywhere for the past year, we haven't yet been able to find out just what he is up to. So his cash resources and his ability are always available to pay for wrongdoing, to provide the funds for crime and to support a standing army of villains permanently at war with society. Arresting Death-Dodger and seizing his funds would mean cutting off the evil at source. That is why this mission has become a matter of the highest importance to the State, and those who contribute to its success are likely to win honours. You yourself, Monsieur, might find yourself employed in the administration again, perhaps become secretary to a Police Commissioner. Such a post would not disqualify you from drawing your retirement pension.'

'But', said Mademoiselle Michonneau, 'why doesn't Death-Dodger simply bolt with the cash?'

'Oh!' said the agent, 'wherever he went he would be followed by someone with orders to kill him, if he did steal from the convicts. And then it's not as easy to run off with a pile of money as with a young lady of good family. Besides Collin is not the sort of fellow who could ever play such a trick; he would think it dishonoured him.'

'Monsieur,' said Poiret, 'you are right. It would utterly dishonour him.'

'All that doesn't explain why you don't simply go in and capture him,' said Mademoiselle Michonneau.

'Well, Mademoiselle, my answer to that is . . . But', he whispered in her ear, 'do stop your gentleman friend interrupting me or we'll never have done. He'll have to be very lucky to get anyone to listen to him, that old chap. When Death-Dodger came here he slipped into the skin of an honest man, he turned himself into a solid citizen of Paris, he took up lodgings in an unassuming boarding house. He's a smart one, right enough, you'll never catch him napping. So Monsieur Vautrin is a respected person who handles a respectable amount of business.'

'Of course,' Poiret said to himself.

'The Minister doesn't want to risk having the business world in Paris, or public opinion, turn against him in case they arrested a genuine Vautrin by mistake. Monsieur the Prefect of Police is in a shaky position; he has enemies. If there were any mistake the ones who would like to take his place would make the most of the yapping and screeching of the liberals to get him sacked. The thing here is to proceed just as in the Cogniard affair,* that bogus Comte de Sainte-Hélène. If he had been a real Comte de Sainte-Hélène we shouldn't have come out of it looking too good. So we've go to check our facts.'

'Yes, but what you need is a pretty woman,' said Mademoiselle Michonneau eagerly.

'Death-Dodger would never let a woman get near him,' said the agent. 'Let me tell you a secret: he doesn't like women.'*

'But then I don't understand what use I would be for making that sort of check, always supposing I agreed to do it for two thousand francs.'

'Nothing easier,' said the stranger, 'I will give you a phial containing a dose of a liquid which makes the blood rush to your head and looks like apoplexy, but without the slightest danger. The drug can be mixed equally well in wine or coffee. You have your man carried to a bed straight away, and you undress him to find out if he is dying. As soon as you're alone with him you clap him on the shoulder, bam!, and you'll see the brand appear.'

'There's nothing to it,' said Poiret.

'Well, do you agree?' Gondureau asked the old maid.

'But my dear sir,' said Mademoiselle Michonneau, 'If there did not happen to be any letters there, would I still get the two thousand francs?'

'No!'

'What reward would there be then?'

'Five hundred francs.'

'Think of doing such a thing for so little. One's conscience feels the same guilt, and it's my conscience I have to pacify, Monsieur.'

'I can assure you', Poiret said, 'that Mademoiselle has a very sensitive conscience, apart from the fact that she is a most able and helpful person.'

'All right!' went on Mademoiselle Michonneau, 'give me three thousand francs if he is Death-Dodger, and nothing if he is an ordinary man.'

'Agreed,' said Gondureau, 'but on condition that the job

is done tomorrow.'

'Not so soon, my dear sir, I need to consult my confessor.'

'There's a crafty one!' said the agent as he stood up. 'Until tomorrow then. And if you need to speak to me urgently, come to the petite rue Sainte-Anne, at the end of the cour de la Sainte-Chapelle.* There's only one door under the archway. Ask for Monsieur Gondureau.'

The rather unusual name Death-Dodger caught Bianchon's ear as he made his way back from Cuvier's lecture, and then he heard the 'Agreed' from the celebrated head of the Sûreté.

'Why not conclude the deal now, it would mean an annuity of three hundred francs?' Poiret said to Mademoiselle Michonneau.

'Why?' she asked. 'Because I need to think about it. If Monsieur Vautrin really was this Death-Dodger, it might be more profitable to come to some arrangement with him. All the same, if I asked him for money, he would be forewarned, and he's the sort of man who would disappear without paying a penny. That would be the most awful disaster.'

'Even if he did have warning,' Poiret went on, 'didn't this gentleman tell us that he was under surveillance? But you, you would lose the lot.'

'Besides', thought Mademoiselle Michonneau, 'I don't really like the man. He can never speak to me without being unpleasant.'

'But', said Poiret, 'you could do still better. As the gentleman said, and he looks most respectable to me, aside from the fact that he is acting under the most proper authority, one is simply obeying the law in ridding society of a criminal, whatever virtues he may have. Once a thief, always a thief. Suppose he took it into his head to murder us all? Devil take it! we should be guilty of those murders, not to mention being the first victims.'

Mademoiselle Michonneau was so preoccupied that she did not listen to the remarks falling from Poiret's lips one after another like drops of water dripping from a leaky tap. Once the old man had begun his series of remarks, if Mademoiselle

Michonneau did not stop him he would go on talking as though wound up like clockwork. He began by launching into one subject, was then led by his digressions into something completely different, and never came to any conclusions. By the time they reached the Maison Vauquer he had wriggled his way through a whole sequence of transitional passages and quotations, which had brought him to describe the statement he had made in the case of Monsieur Ragoulleau and Madame Morin,* in which he had been called as a defence witness. As they went in, his companion did not fail to notice Eugène de Rastignac and Mademoiselle Taillefer engaged in intimate conversation of such thrilling interest that neither paid any attention to the two elderly boarders as they passed through the dining-room.

'It was bound to come to that,' Mademoiselle Michonneau said to Poiret. 'They have been exchanging such heart-rending looks for the past week.'

'Yes,' he said, 'So she was convicted.'

'Who?'

'Madame Morin.'

'I talk to you about Mademoiselle Victorine', said Michonneau, going into Poiret's room without noticing, 'and you come back with something about a Madame Morin. Who on earth is she?'

'What is Mademoiselle Victorine guilty of then?' asked Poiret.

'She is guilty of loving Monsieur Eugène de Rastignac, and she is pressing on with no idea where that will take her, poor innocent!'

In the course of the morning Eugène had been reduced to despair by Madame de Nucingen. In his inmost heart he had completely surrendered to Vautrin, but he was unwilling to probe too deeply the reasons for that extraordinary man's friendship for him, or the future of such a partnership. Only a miracle could pull him back from the abyss towards which he had already stepped an hour before, when he had exchanged the tenderest promises with Mademoiselle Taillefer. For

Victorine it was like hearing the voice of an angel, the heavens opened for her, the Maison Vauquer took on the strange, dreamlike colours which scene-painters give to palaces in the theatre: she was in love, she was loved in return, or at least so she thought! And what woman would not have thought like her, seeing and hearing Rastignac during that hour stolen from all the watchful eyes in the house? As he struggled with his conscience, aware that he was doing wrong and intending to do it, telling himself that he would redeem this venial sin by making a woman happy, his despair made him still more handsome and he shone with all the splendour of the fires of hell burning in his heart. Fortunately for him the miracle happened. Vautrin came in full of joy, and read the feelings of the young couple whom he had joined together through the scheming of his diabolical genius. Suddenly, though, he disturbed their bliss by singing in his deep, mock-ing voice:

> 'My Fanchette is charming
> In her simplicity ...'

Victorine promptly fled, but she took with her as much happiness as there had so far been unhappiness in her life. Poor girl! Her hand clasped in his, her cheek brushed by Rastignac's hair, words spoken so closely in her ear that she had felt the warmth of the student's lips, her waist encircled by a trembling arm, a stolen kiss on her neck; with such rites did she plight her troth, and the threat of Sylvie, so near at hand, liable at any moment to come into this radiant dining-room, made them more ardent, more eager, more enchanting than the finest tokens of devotion recounted in the most famous love stories. These 'small favours', to use the charming phrase of our forebears, felt quite criminal to a pious girl who went to confession every fortnight! During that hour she had more lavishly poured out the treasures of her heart than when in later years, rich and happy, she surrendered herself completely.

'It's all fixed up,' Vautrin told Eugène. 'Our two dandies

have come to blows. It all went off very correctly. A difference of opinion. Our dove insulted my hawk. Tomorrow in the redoubt at Clignancourt.* At half-past eight Mademoiselle Taillefer will become heir to her father's love and wealth while she sits calmly dipping her fingers of bread and butter in her coffee. Isn't it funny to be able to tell oneself such a thing? Young Taillefer is very handy with a sword, he's as sure of himself as if he had been dealt four aces, but there's a stroke I invented, a way of lifting the sword and pinking your man in the forehead, that will bleed him. I will show you how to do that thrust, it comes in devilish useful.'

Rastignac listened like a man in a daze, quite unable to respond. At that moment Père Goriot, Bianchon and some of the others came in.

'That's how I wanted to see you,' Vautrin said to him, 'You know what you're doing. Right, my little eaglet! You will be a ruler of men. You are strong, forthright and stout-hearted, and I have a lot of respect for you.'

He put out his hand, but Rastignac hastily withdrew his, and went pale as he slumped on to a chair; he had a vision of a pool of blood on the ground in front of him.

'Ah! so we still have some baby clothes stained with virtue,' Vautrin said in a low voice. 'Papa d'Oliban* has three millions, I know what he's worth. The dowry will wash you as white as a bridal dress, and in your own eyes too.'

Rastignac hesitated no longer. He resolved to go that evening to warn the Taillefers, father and son. At that moment, after Vautrin had gone, Père Goriot said in his ear, 'You look unhappy, my boy! I'll cheer you up. Come along!' And the old vermicelli-merchant lit his wax taper from one of the lamps. Eugène followed him, full of curiosity.

'Let's go into your room,' said the old fellow, who had got the student's key from Sylvie. 'This morning you thought she didn't love you, eh?' he went on. 'She sent you packing, and you went off angry and downcast. Silly billy! She was waiting for me. Do you understand? We had arranged to go and finish setting up a really lovely apartment for you

to move into in three days from now. Don't give me away.
She wants to give you a surprise, but I don't feel like keeping
it secret from you any longer. You will be in the rue d'Artois,*
a couple of steps from the rue Saint-Lazare. You will live
there like a prince. We've furnished it for you fit for a bride.
We have done a lot in the past month, without saying a word
to you about it. My lawyer got busy, my daughter will have
her thirty-six thousand francs a year interest on her dowry,
and I'm going to insist in having her eight hundred thousand
francs invested in some good real estate.'

Eugène did not say a word, but paced up and down with
arms folded in his wretched, untidy room. Père Goriot
grasped the opportunity while the student's back was turned
to put on the mantelpiece a red morocco box with the Rastignac arms stamped on it in gold.

'My dear boy,' the poor old fellow said, 'I am in this up
to my neck. But, you see, a lot of it was selfishness on my
part, I have a personal interest in your change of quarters.
You won't turn me down if I ask something of you, eh?'

'What is it you want?'

'On the fifth floor, above your apartment, there's a room
which goes with it; I can live there, can't I? I am getting
old, I live too far from my daughters. I won't bother you,
I'll just be there. You can talk to me about her every evening.
That won't be a nuisance, will it? When you come home
and I'm already in bed, I'll hear you and say to myself: "He
has been seeing my little Delphine. He took her to the ball.
She is happy, thanks to him." If I were ill it would hearten
me to listen to you coming and going, moving about. There
will be so much of my daughter in you! It will only take
me a few steps to the Champs Élysées where they go by
every day. I will always be there to see them; now I sometimes
arrive too late. And maybe she'll come to visit you! I'll hear
her, I'll see her in her quilted morning-gown coming and
going as daintily as a little cat. In the past few months she
has gone back to being the cheerful, sprightly girl she used
to be. Her spirits are on the mend, she owes her happiness

to you. Oh! I would do anything for you. Just now, when she came in, she said to me, "Papa, I am so happy!" When they are formal and call me "Father" it chills my heart, but when they call me "Papa" it's as though I can still see them as little girls, they bring back all my memories. I feel more like their father. I can imagine them not yet belonging to anyone else!'

The old fellow wiped his eyes, he was in tears.

'It was so long since I had heard those words, since she had offered me her arm. Oh! yes, it's ten years since I walked beside one of my daughters. What delight to feel her dress brushing against me, to walk in step with her, to share her warmth! This morning I took Delphine everywhere. I went shopping with her, and saw her home. Oh! please let me stay with you! You will sometimes need someone to do you some service, and I'll be there. Oh! if only that great lump of an Alsatian would die, if only his gout had the sense to move up into his guts, how happy my poor daughter would be! You would be my son-in-law, you could openly be her husband. Bah! She is so unhappy at being denied all the pleasures of this world that I can forgive her anything. God must be on the side of loving fathers. She is so fond of you!' he said, nodding his head after a pause. 'As we walked along she talked to me about you. "Don't you agree, Father, he is good-looking! and kind-hearted! Does he talk about me?" Bah! she talked and talked, from the rue d'Artois to the passage des Panoramas,* enough to fill volumes! She really poured her heart out into mine. All that lovely morning I was no longer an old man, I felt light as a feather. I told her that you had given me the thousand-franc note. Oh! that moved my darling to tears! But what's that on your mantelpiece?' Père Goriot asked at last, dying with impatience as he saw Rastignac still making no move.

Eugène, quite dumbfounded, was looking at his neighbour in a daze. The duel which Vautrin had told him was due to take place next day was in such violent contrast to the realization of his most cherished hopes that he was going through all the sensations of a nightmare. He turned towards the mantelpiece, saw the little square box, opened it, and found inside a paper wrapped round a Bréguet watch. On the paper these words were written: 'I want you to think of me every hour of the day *because* ... DELPHINE.'

The last word no doubt referred to something that had passed between them. Eugène was deeply touched. His coat-of-arms was enamelled on the inside of the gold case. This jewel which he had coveted for so long, the chain, the key, the workmanship, the design, fulfilled all his wishes. Père Goriot was radiant. He had no doubt promised to report to his daughter in minutest detail just how Eugène reacted to the surprise of her present, for he was a third party to these youthful emotions and did not seem to be the one least happy. He was already fond of Rastignac both for the sake of his daughter and for his own sake.

'You must go and see her this evening, she is expecting you. The great lump of an Alsatian is having supper with his dancer. Ha! ha! he looked very foolish when my lawyer told him a few home truths. And he claims to adore my daughter! Let him just touch her and I'll kill him. The mere thought that my Delphine belongs to ...' (he sighed) 'would drive me to commit a crime, but it would not be homicide, for he's a calf's head on a pig's body. You'll take me with you, won't you?'

'Yes, my dear Père Goriot, you know very well that I am fond of you ...'

'I can see that, at any rate you are not ashamed of me! Let me embrace you.' And he hugged the student in his arms. 'You'll make her really happy, promise! You will go this evening, won't you?'

'Oh yes! I have to go out on some business that can't be put off.'

'Can I help in any way?'

'My word, yes, you can! While I go round to Madame de Nucingen, will you go to Monsieur Taillefer, the father, and ask him to name a time this evening when I can come and talk to him about a matter of the greatest urgency?'

'So the rumour is true, young man!' said Père Goriot, his expression changing, 'you are courting his daughter, as those imbeciles downstairs are saying. Damn and blast! You don't know what a Goriot punch means. If you were deceiving us you would feel my fist. Oh! it can't be so.'

'I swear to you that I love only one woman in the world,' the student said, 'It's something I realized only a moment ago.'

'How happy I am!' said Père Goriot.

'But', the student went on, 'young Taillefer is to fight a duel tomorrow, and I have heard that he will be killed.'

'How does that concern you?' asked Goriot.

'The old man must be told to prevent his son going ...' Eugène cried.

At that moment he was interrupted by the voice of Vautrin standing in the doorway of his room singing:

> "O Richard, oh my king!
> The whole world abandons you ..."*

Broom! brooom! brooom! brooom! brooom!

> 'I've roamed the world for many a year,
> And I've been seen ...

Tra la, tra la, tra la!'

'Gentlemen,' shouted Christophe, 'the soup is ready waiting, and everyone else has sat down to table.'

'Here,' said Vautrin, 'come and take down a bottle of my Bordeaux.'

'Don't you think the watch is lovely?' said Père Goriot, 'She has good taste, eh?'

Vautrin, Père Goriot and Rastignac went down together, and as a result of being late found themselves sitting side by side at table. During dinner Eugène treated Vautrin with chilly aloofness, although the latter, so popular with Madame Vauquer, had never given a more entertaining performance.

His sparkling sallies put everyone in high spirits. Such cool self-confidence dismayed Eugène.

'Whatever has got into you today?' Madame Vauquer asked Vautrin. 'You're happy as a lark.'

'I'm always happy when I've brought off a good deal.'

'Deal?' asked Eugène.

'Yes, that's right. I've delivered a batch of goods which will bring me in a handsome commission. Mademoiselle Michonneau,' he said, becoming conscious of the old maid's scrutiny, 'is there something you don't like about my face that makes you look at me so keenly? You've only got to say! I'll gladly change it if that will make you happy. Poiret, we won't let that upset us, will we?' he said, leering at the old clerk.

'Egad! you ought to pose as jesting Hercules,' the young artist said to Vautrin.

'My word, so I will, if Mademoiselle Michonneau will pose as the Venus of the Père Lachaise,' replied Vautrin.

'And Poiret?' asked Bianchon.

'Oh, Poiret can pose as Poiret. He can be the god of gardens!' cried Vautrin. 'The name comes from pear...'

'A mushy one!' Bianchon chimed in, 'So you would come between the pear and the cheese, rounding off the meal, so to speak.'

'What a lot of nonsense you're talking,' said Madame Vauquer, 'You'd do better to pour us out some of that Bordeaux from that bottle I can see poking its nose out there! That will keep our spirits up, apart from the fact that it's good for the *digestives*.'

'Gentlemen,' said Vautrin, 'Madame chairman is calling us to order. Madame Couture and Mademoiselle Victorine will not take offence at your light-hearted banter, but do respect Père Goriot's innocence. I propose a little *bottleorama* of Bordeaux, made doubly illustrious by the name Laffitte,* no political reference intended. Come on, Chinaman!' he said, looking at Christophe, who did not stir, 'Don't you know your own name? Chinaman, bring on the liquor!'

'Here you are, Monsieur,' said Christophe, presenting the bottle to him.

He poured out a full glass each for Eugène and Père Goriot, and then slowly poured himself a few drops which he tasted, while his two neighbours drank, and suddenly he pulled a face.

'Devil take it! It's corked. Keep that one for yourself, Christophe, and go and get us some more; on the right, you know? There are sixteen of us, bring down eight bottles.'

'As you are lashing out,' said the artist, 'I'll pay for a hundred chestnuts.'

'Oh! oh!'—'Booohouh!'—'Prrr!'

Everyone joined in with exclamations which went off like rockets in a firework display.

'Come on, Ma Vauquer, let's have a couple of bottles of champagne,' cried Vautrin.

'How's that? You'll ask for the whole house next! Two bottles of champagne! That's twelve francs! I don't make that much, I can tell you. But if Monsieur Eugène would like to pay for that, you can have some cassis on the house.'

'That blackcurrant of hers is as good a purge as the stuff made from manna,' the medical student murmured.

'Will you shut up, Bianchon!' cried Rastignac, 'I can't hear anyone mention manna without feeling sick ... All right, I'll pay for the champagne,' the student added.

'Sylvie,' said Madame Vauquer, 'put out the biscuits and little cakes.'

'Your little cakes are too grown up,' said Vautrin, 'they've got whiskers. But let's have the biscuits.'

The Bordeaux was soon going round, the guests grew livelier, the merriment increased. Peals of raucous laughter were interspersed with various animal imitations. When the Museum attendant took it into his head to reproduce a Paris street cry not unlike the wailing of a lovesick tomcat, straight away eight voices bellowed, all at the same time, such phrases as: 'Knives to grind!—Birdseed for the little birdies!—Cream puffs here, ladies, cream puffs!—China to mend!—All aboard, all aboard!—Beat your wives, beat your clothes!—Any old clothes, any old braid, any old hats for sale!—Cherries, sweet cherries!—' The palm went to Bianchon for his nasal rendering of the cry 'Umbrella man!'

In a few moments there was an earsplitting din, conversation full of inconsequential nonsense, a real opera with Vautrin conducting, while he kept an eye on Eugène and Père Goriot, who looked already quite drunk. Leaning back in their chairs, they were both solemnly contemplating the unusually riotous behaviour and hardly touching their drink. They were both concerned about what they had to do in the course of the evening, but none the less felt quite unable to rise to their feet. Vautrin, who was following the changes in their expressions with sidelong glances, took the opportunity when their eyelids began to flutter and seemed about to close, to lean over to Rastignac and say in his ear,

'My little lad, we are not wily enough to tangle with our Papa Vautrin, and he's too fond of you to let you do anything silly. Once I've made up my mind about something, God alone is powerful enough to bar my way. Ah! So we thought of going to warn old Taillefer; just the sort of elementary mistake a schoolboy might make! The oven is hot, the dough is kneaded, the bread is on the shovel; tomorrow we'll bite into it and send crumbs flying everywhere; and we thought we'd prevent it getting into the oven? Oh no, it's all going to be baked! If we feel a twinge or two of remorse, digestion will soon cure that. While we are having our little snooze, Colonel Comte Franchessini will be seeing Michel Taillefer's succession through probate for you with the point of his sword. When she comes into her brother's inheritance Victorine will have a cool little income of fifteen thousand francs a year. I've already made enquiries, and I know that her mother's estate amounts to more than three hundred thousand ...'

Eugène heard these words, but was incapable of reply. He felt his tongue cleave to his palate, and an irresistible desire for sleep overcame him. The table and the faces of those round it were already mere blurs in a luminous haze. Soon the noise died down, and the boarders left one by one. Then, when only Madame Vauquer, Madame Couture, Mademoiselle Victorine, Vautrin and Père Goriot remained, Rastignac saw, as if in a dream, Madame Vauquer busily emptying bottles and filling up others with the dregs.

'Ah! how wild they are! how young!' the widow was saying. This was the last phrase that Eugène was able to take in.

'There's no one like Monsieur Vautrin for starting a bit of fun,' said Sylvie. 'Just look at Christophe over there, snoring like a top.'

'Goodnight, Ma,' said Vautrin, 'I'm off to the boulevard to admire Monsieur Marty in the *Mont Sauvage*,* a splendid play taken from *Le Solitaire*. If you like, I'll take you and these other ladies as well.'

'No, thank you very much,' said Madame Couture.

'What, neighbour,' exclaimed Madame Vauquer, 'you refuse to see a play taken from *Le Solitaire*, a work of Atala de Chateaubriand,* which we so much enjoyed reading, and so lovely that we cried our eyes out over Élodie under the *loime-trees* last summer? In fact it's the sort of moral work that could be most instructive for your young lady.'

'We're not allowed to go to the theatre,' Victorine answered.

'Look, they are well away, those two,' said Vautrin, making Eugène and Père Goriot wag their heads comically.

As he settled the student's head against the chair so that he could sleep comfortably, he kissed him warmly on the forehead and sang:

> 'Sleep, my dearest loves
> I will always be watching over you.'*

'I'm afraid he may be unwell,' said Victorine.

'Stay and look after him then,' Vautrin replied, then whispered in her ear, 'It's your duty as an obedient wife. That young man adores you, and you will become his little wife, that's my prediction.' He went on aloud, '"In the end they were esteemed throughout the land, lived happily ever after and had lots of children." That's how all the love stories end. Come on, Ma,' he said, turning to Madame Vauquer and hugging her, 'put on your hat, your nice floral dress, the comtesse's scarf. I'll go and fetch you a cab, in person.'

And he went off singing:

> Sun, sun, O sun divine,
> The pumpkins ripen when you shine...'*

'Goodness! I can tell you, Madame Couture, that man would make me happy to live on the rooftops. Well now,' turning towards the vermicelli-merchant, 'Père Goriot is well away. That old skinflint never thought of taking me nowhere. But my word, he'll fall on to the floor! It's downright indecent for a man of his age to take leave of his senses like that! You'll say that no one can lose what they haven't got. Sylvie, get him up to his room now.'

Sylvie grasped the old man under the arms, got him moving upstairs, and threw him fully dressed on to his bed like a parcel.

'Poor young man,' said Madame Couture, pushing Eugène's hair away from his eyes, 'he is like a girl, he doesn't know what it is to overdo things.'

'Ah! I can tell you that I have been running my boarding house for the past thirty-one years,' said Madame Vauquer, 'and a lot of young men have passed through my hands, as they say, but I have never seen one so nice and distinguished as Monsieur Eugène. How handsome he looks when he's asleep! Prop his head on your shoulder, will you, Madame Couture. Ha! he's falling over on to Mademoiselle Victorine's shoulder. There's a god looks after young people, a bit further and he would have cracked his head against the knob of his chair. What a lovely couple those two would make.'

'Do be quiet, dear neighbour,' cried Madame Couture, 'the things you say!'

'Bah!' said Madame Vauquer, 'He can't hear. Come along, Sylvie, help me dress. I'll be putting on my big stays.'

'Will you now! Your big stays after you've eaten your

dinner, Madame,' said Sylvie. 'No, you'll have to get someone
else to lace you up, I'm not going to be the one to murder
you. You would be most unwise to do any such thing, enough
to cause your death.'

'I don't care, I must do Monsieur Vautrin credit.'

'You must be very fond of your heirs then!'

'Come on, Sylvie, stop arguing,' said the widow as she went
out.

'At her age!' said the cook, to Victorine, with a nod towards
her mistress.

Madame Couture and her ward, with Eugène asleep on her
shoulder, stayed alone in the dining-room. Christophe's
snores resounded through the silent house, contrasting with
the peaceful slumbers of Eugène, who slept as winsomely
as a child. Victorine, happy that she could allow herself one
of those acts of kindness through which a woman's emotions
can be fully expressed, and which permitted her in all innocence to feel the young man's heart beating against her own,
wore a maternally protective expression on her face which
lent her a certain nobility. Amid the countless thoughts stirring in her heart, a turmoil of delight broke through at this
exchange of innocent and youthful warmth.

'Poor dear girl!' said Madame Couture, squeezing her hand.

The old lady looked admiringly at this artless face marked
by suffering on which a halo of happiness had fallen. Victorine
resembled one of those naïve medieval paintings in which
the artist ignores all accessories, reserving the calm, noble
strokes of his brush for the almost sallow face to which heaven
seems to impart a reflected sheen of gold.

'Yet he only drank two glasses, Mama,' said Victorine, running her fingers through Eugène's hair.

'But if he were used to debauches, dear girl, he would have
carried his drink like all the others. The fact that he is so
drunk is all to his credit.'

The noise of carriage wheels echoed from the street.

'Mama,' said the girl, 'that's Monsieur Vautrin. You take
Monsieur Eugène. I don't want that man to see me like this.

He uses expressions which make you feel dirty inside, and the way he looks at women makes you feel as uncomfortable as if you were undressed.'

'No,' said Madame Couture, 'you are mistaken. Monsieur Vautrin is a fine man, a bit like the late Monsieur Couture, bluff but good-hearted, and kindly for all his gruff manners.'

At that moment Vautrin came in very quietly, and looked at the picture of these two young people in the lamplight, which seemed to play on them caressingly.

'Well now!' he said, crossing his arms, 'there's a scene which would have inspired some fine pages from the good Bernardin de Saint-Pierre, author of *Paul and Virginie.** Youth is a lovely thing, Madame Couture. Poor boy, sleep sound,' he said as he gazed at Eugène, 'things sometimes turn out well while we sleep. Madame,' he went on, addressing the widow, 'what I find so attractive in this young man, so moving, is knowing that the beauty of his soul matches that of his features. Look, wouldn't you say that is a cherub leaning on an angel's shoulder? That boy is worthy to be loved! If I were a woman I'd want to die, no that's stupid!, to live for him. As I look on them in wonder, Madame,' he said in a low voice, leaning over to speak in the widow's ear, 'I can't help thinking that God created them for each other. The ways of divine providence are hidden, he searches the reins and the hearts,' he cried loudly. 'Seeing you together, my children, united by the same innocence, by every human emotion, I tell myself that it would be impossible for you ever to be parted in the future. God is just. But', he said to the girl, 'I seem to remember seeing lines of prosperity in your hand; may I look, Mademoiselle Victorine? I know something about palmistry. I have often told fortunes. Come on, don't be afraid. Oh! What do I see? Upon my word as an honest man, before very long you will be one of the wealthiest heiresses in Paris. You bring the greatest happiness to the one who loves you. Your father calls you to his side. You marry a young, handsome, titled gentleman who worships you.'

Just then the heavy tread of the widow coming downstairs

interrupted Vautrin's prophecies.

'Here's Ma Vauquer, radiant as a star, dressed up to kill. Doesn't it feel a tiny bit too tight?' he said, laying his hand on the upper part of the whalebone stays. 'There's not much room to breathe up there in front, Ma. If we start weeping there'll be an explosion, but I'll gather up all the bits as carefully as any antiquary.'

'There's a man who knows the language of true French gallantry!' said the widow, bending over to speak in Madame Couture's ear.

'Goodbye, children,' Vautrin went on, turning towards Eugène and Victorine. 'I give you my blessing,' he said, laying his hands on their heads. 'Believe me, Mademoiselle, the prayers of an honest man count for something, they are bound to bring good fortune, for God hears them.'

'Goodbye, my dear friend,' said Madame Vauquer to her boarder, adding in a low voice, 'Do you think Monsieur Vautrin has designs on my person?'

'Hm! hm!'

'Ah! my dear mother,' Victorine sighed, looking at her hands when the two women were alone, 'if only that good Monsieur Vautrin were right in what he said!'

'But it would take only one thing to make it so,' the old lady answered, 'your monster of a brother would only have to fall off his horse.'

'Ah, Mama!'

'My goodness, perhaps it is a sin to wish ill of an enemy,' the widow went on, 'Very well! I'll do penance for it. To tell the truth I should be quite happy to put flowers on his grave. Wicked-hearted fellow! He hasn't the courage to speak up for his mother, and he does you out of her inheritance by underhand tricks. My cousin had a handsome fortune, but unluckily for you the marriage contract never mentioned her own contribution.'

'I should often find my good fortune too heavy a burden if it had cost someone's life,' said Victorine, 'and if my happiness meant that my brother had to die, I would rather stay here for the rest of my life.'

'My goodness, as the good Monsieur Vautrin says—and as you see, he is truly religious,' went on Madame Couture, 'I was very glad to learn that he is not an unbeliever like the others who show less respect when they talk of God than of the devil—Well! who can know the ways in which it pleases Providence to lead us?'

With Sylvie's help the two women finally managed to carry Eugène to his room, and laid him on his bed. The cook loosened his clothes so that he would be more comfortable. Before leaving the room, while her guardian's back was turned, Victorine planted a kiss on Eugène's forehead with all the rapture that so stealthy a crime could be expected to excite. She looked round the room, gathered up into a single thought, as it were, the countless joys of that day, composed them into a picture which she contemplated at length, and went to sleep the happiest person in Paris.

The revelry which Vautrin had used as a cover for getting Eugène and Père Goriot to drink drugged wine sealed his doom. Bianchon, half tipsy, forgot to ask Mademoiselle Michonneau about Death-Dodger. If he had pronounced that name he would certainly have put Vautrin on his guard, or rather, to give him his real name, Jacques Collin, that convict celebrity. Then the use of the nickname Venus of the Père Lachaise made Mademoiselle Michonneau decide to betray the convict, just when she was calculating, confident of Collin's generosity, whether it might not be better to warn him and let him escape during the night.

She had gone out, accompanied by Poiret, to call on the famous chief of the Sûreté, in the petite rue Sainte-Anne, still under the impression that she was dealing with a senior official by the name of Gondureau. The director of the detective branch received her courteously. Then, after talking over all the details, Mademoiselle Michonneau asked for the potion by means of which she was to verify the existence of the brand. The great man of the petite rue Sainte-Anne evinced such satisfaction as he looked for a phial in his desk drawer that Mademoiselle Michonneau realized that there was something more important at stake in this capture than the arrest of an ordinary convict. After much racking of brains, she suspected that the police, relying on information supplied by traitors in the prison, were hoping to arrive in time to seize a substantial amount of loot. When she voiced her conjectures to the old fox, he began to smile and tried to divert her suspicions.

'You are mistaken,' he answered. 'Collin is the most dangerous *Sorbonne* there has ever been among the thieves. That's all. The rascals know that very well: he is their flag, their mainstay, in fact their Bonaparte; they all love him. That joker will never leave his *tronche* in the place de Grève.'

As Mademoiselle Michonneau did not understand the two slang words he had used, Gondureau explained them to her. *Sorbonne* and *tronche* are two forceful expressions in thieves' slang; they were the first to feel the need to consider the human head from two points of view. The *Sorbonne* is the head of the living man, his judgement and his intelligence. The *tronche* is a word of contempt to express how worthless the head becomes after it has been severed.

'Collin is playing games with us,' he went on. 'When we meet such men, tough as bars of English tempered steel, we can kill them as a last resort if they take it into their heads to offer the least resistance while being arrested. We are counting on some physical violence tomorrow morning so that we can kill Collin. That way we can avoid a trial, the expense of food and custody, and society is rid of him. Legal proceedings, summoning witnesses, paying them compensation, the actual execution, all that is laid down by due process of law for getting rid of such rascals, costs a lot more than the three thousand francs you will get. And it saves time. One good bayonet thrust in Death-Dodger's guts and we'll prevent a hundred and fifty bad lads being led astray; instead they'll behave well enough to keep out of the courts. That's good policing for you. According to the real philanthropists, that's the best way to prevent crime.'

'In the service of your country too,' said Poiret.

'Well now!' the chief replied, 'you are talking some sense this evening. Yes, indeed, we do serve our country. People are most unfair to us. We render the greatest services to society, and they are ignored. Well, a superior man must be above prejudice and a Christian must accept the misfortunes entailed by doing good along unconventional lines. Paris is Paris, you see. That phrase explains my life. I have the honour to bid you goodbye, Mademoiselle. I shall be at the Jardin du Roi tomorrow with my men. Send Christophe round to Monsieur Gondureau's in the rue de Buffon, to the house where I was staying. Monsieur, I am obliged. If you ever have anything stolen, apply to me to get it back; I am at your service.'

'Well!' Poiret said to Mademoiselle Michonneau, 'Some people are foolish enough to get into a real state when they hear the word police. That is a most affable gentleman, and what he is asking you to do is as easy as falling off a log.'

The next day was to figure among the most extraordinary in the history of the Maison Vauquer. Up till then the most notable event in its peaceful life had been the meteoric appearance of the bogus Comtesse d'Ambermesnil. But everything else paled in comparison with the happenings of that great day, which were to provide Madame Vauquer with an endless topic of conversation. First Goriot and Eugène de Rastignac slept on until eleven o'clock. Madame Vauquer, who had returned at midnight from the Gaîté, stayed in bed until half-past ten. The fact that Christophe overslept after finishing the wine provided by Vautrin delayed the service of breakfast. Poiret and Mademoiselle Michonneau had no complaints about the postponement. As for Victorine and Madame Couture, they slept on late. Vautrin went out before eight, and came back just as breakfast was served. There were no complaints, then, when at about quarter-past eleven Sylvie and Christophe went round knocking at all the doors to announce that breakfast was ready. While Sylvie and the servant were out of the way, Mademoiselle Michonneau, who was the first down, poured the liquid into Vautrin's silver cup, in which the cream for his coffee was being warmed up in the bain-marie with all the others. The old maid had relied on this particular custom of the house to accomplish her task. It was only with some difficulty that the seven boarders were finally assembled. Just as Eugène, who was the last of all to come down, arrived, yawning and stretching his arms, a messenger handed him a letter from Madame de Nucingen, which ran as follows:

With you, my friend, I feel no false pride or anger. I waited for you until two in the morning. What it is to wait for a loved one! Anyone who has known such torment would never inflict it on another. I can see very well that this is the first time you have been in love. Whatever happened? I am so worried. If I had not been afraid of betraying the secrets of my heart I should have gone to find out what had happened to you, be it for good or ill. But going out at that time of night, on foot or in a carriage, would have been disastrous, would it not? I realized how unfortunate it is to be a woman. Reassure me, explain why you did not come after what my father told you. I shall be annoyed, but I will forgive you. Are you ill? Why do you live so far away? Send me word, I beg you, and soon, won't you? One word will suffice if you are busy. Say 'I am on my way' or 'I am sick'. But if you were unwell, my father would have come to tell me! Whatever has happened? . . .

'Yes, whatever has happened?' cried Eugène, rushing into the dining-room, crumpling the letter without reading it through to the end. 'What time is it?'

'Half-past eleven,' said Vautrin, putting sugar into his coffee.

The escaped convict gave Eugène one of those coldly compelling looks for which certain exceptionally magnetic individuals have a gift and which, it is said, can even calm raving lunatics in asylums. Eugène trembled in every limb. A cab could be heard out in the street, and a servant in Monsieur Taillefer's livery, recognized at once by Madame Couture, rushed in in great alarm.

'Mademoiselle,' he cried, 'your father is asking for you.

Monsieur Frédéric has fought a duel. He's been wounded in the forehead, and the doctors see no hope of saving him. You will barely have time to bid him farewell; he is unconscious.'

'Poor young man!' cried Vautrin. 'How can someone with a solid thirty thousand livres income get into a quarrel? The young certainly have no idea how to behave.'

'Monsieur!' Eugène shouted at him.

'Yes, what is it, my big boy?' Vautrin said, calmly drinking up his coffee, a process too closely observed by Mademoiselle Michonneau for her to feel any emotion at the extraordinary event that had stunned everyone else. 'Aren't there duels every day in Paris?'

'I'll come with you, Victorine,' said Madame Couture.

And the two women flew out without shawls or hats. Before going, Victorine looked at Eugène with tears in her eyes, as if to say, 'I never thought that our happiness would bring me to tears!'

'My! So you are a prophet, Monsieur Vautrin,' said Madame Vauquer.

'I am everything,' said Jacques Collin.

'Isn't it strange!' Madame Vauquer went on, offering a succession of pointless comments on the event. 'Death takes us away without consulting us. The young often go before the old. We women are fortunate in not having duels to fight, but we have other disabilities that men don't have. We produce children, and a mother's pain lasts a long time! What a stroke of luck for Victorine! Her father will be forced to accept her now!'

'Just so!' Vautrin said, looking at Eugène. 'Penniless yesterday, this morning she is a rich woman worth several millions.'

'Well now, Monsieur Eugène,' cried Madame Vauquer, 'you picked a winning number there.'

At this remark, Père Goriot looked at the student, and saw the letter crumpled in his hand.

'Didn't you finish reading it? What does that mean? Are you just like all the others?' he asked.

'Madame, I shall never marry Mademoiselle Victorine,' said Eugène, addressing Madame Vauquer in a tone of appalled revulsion that surprised his audience.

Père Goriot seized the student's hand and grasped it tightly. He would have liked to kiss it.

'Oho!' said Vautrin, 'the Italians have a saying, *col tempo*.'*

'I am to wait for an answer,' Madame de Nucingen's messenger said to Rastignac.

'Say that I'm coming.'

The man left. Eugène was so furiously angry that he had no time for caution. 'Whatever shall I do!' he said aloud, but to himself. 'There's no evidence!'

Vautrin began to smile. At that moment the potion he had absorbed into his stomach began to take effect. Nevertheless the convict was so robust that he rose, looked at Rastignac and said in hollow tones: 'Young man, things turn out well for us while we sleep.'

And fell down like a log.

'So there is such a thing as divine justice,' Eugène said.

'Well now! Whatever can have come over poor dear Monsieur Vautrin?'

'A stroke!' cried Mademoiselle Michonneau.

'Sylvie, my girl, go on, go and fetch the doctor,' said the widow. 'Oh, Monsieur Rastignac, run as quick as you can to Monsieur Bianchon; Sylvie may not be able to find Monsieur Grimprel, our doctor.'

Rastignac, happy at having an excuse to leave that chamber of horrors, ran off.

'Christophe, come on, hurry round to the chemist and get something for a stroke.'

Christophe went out.

'Now, Père Goriot, do give us a hand getting him upstairs to his room.'

Vautrin was lifted up, manœuvred up the stairs and laid on his bed.

'I am no use to you, I'm going to see my daughter,' said Monsieur Goriot.

'Selfish old man!' cried Madame Vauquer, 'go then. I hope you die like a dog.'

'Go and see if you have any ether,' Mademoiselle Michonneau said to Madame Vauquer, when, with Poiret's assistance, she had loosened Vautrin's clothes.

Madame Vauquer went down to her room, leaving Mademoiselle Michonneau mistress of the field.

'Come on, off with his shirt then and turn him over quickly! Make yourself useful, and save me the sight of a man without his clothes on. You are just standing there like a dummy!'

Vautrin was turned over, and Mademoiselle Michonneau slapped the patient's shoulder smartly: the two fateful letters stood out white against the reddened patch of skin.

'Goodness, you earned your three thousand francs reward pretty sharply,' cried Poiret, holding Vautrin up while Mademoiselle Michonneau put his shirt back on him. 'Oof! he's heavy,' he added, laying him down.

'Shut up! Supposing there's a money-box?' the old maid said avidly, her eyes scanning every stick of furniture in the room so keenly that they seemed to bore through the walls. 'What about opening this desk on some pretext or other?' she went on.

'That might be wrong,' Poiret replied.

'No, stolen money, taken from all kinds of people, doesn't belong to anyone any more. But time's running out,' she answered, 'I can hear that Vauquer woman coming.'

'Here's some ether,' said Madame Vauquer. 'My word, this day is one excitement after another ... Goodness! that man can't be ill, he's as white as a chicken.'

'A chicken?' Poiret repeated.

'His heartbeat is quite regular,' said the widow, putting her hand on his chest.

'Regular?' said Poiret in amazement.

'He's perfectly healthy.'

'You think so?' asked Poiret.

'Why! he looks as if he's asleep. Sylvie has gone for the doctor. Look, Mademoiselle Michonneau, he's sniffing the ether. Bah! it's only a *spassmum*. His pulse is strong. He's as strong as an ox. Look, Mademoiselle, at that fur pelt on his chest! His wig hasn't come off anyhow. Look, it is stuck on, he's wearing false hair, seeing as his own is red. They say that redheads are very good or very bad! So he's a good one, I suppose?'

'Good for hanging,' said Poiret.

'You mean round a pretty woman's neck,' Mademoiselle Michonneau hastily exclaimed. 'Off you go then, Monsieur Poiret. It's up to us women to look after you men when you are ill. Besides, for all the help you are, you might as well clear off,' she added, 'Madame Vauquer and I will take good care of dear Monsieur Vautrin.'

Poiret went off quietly without a murmur, like a dog kicked by his master. Rastignac had gone out for a walk, to get some fresh air; he was stifling. The night before he had tried to prevent the crime which had been committed at the appointed hour. What had happened? What should he do? He trembled to think he had been an accomplice. Vautrin's cold-bloodedness appalled him still more.

'If only Vautrin could die without talking,' Rastignac said to himself.

He went up and down the paths in the Luxembourg as if pursued by a pack of hounds, and he seemed to hear them barking.

'Well!' Bianchon called out, 'have you seen the *Pilote*?'

The *Pilote* was a radical paper edited by Monsieur Tissot; some hours after the morning papers it published a provincial edition with the day's news, which thus reached the provinces twenty-four hours earlier than the other papers.

'There's a remarkable story in it,' said the houseman from the Cochin hospital. 'Young Taillefer fought a duel with Comte Franchessini, of the old Guards, who stuck two inches of cold steel into his forehead. So now little Victorine is one of the wealthiest matches in Paris. Eh! if we had only known! What a lottery death is! Is it true that Victorine looked on you with a certain favour?'

'That's enough, Bianchon, I'll never marry her. I am in love with a charming woman, who loves me in return, and ...'

'You say that as if staying faithful to her was like flogging a dead horse. Just show me a woman worth sacrificing old Taillefer's fortune for.'

'Are all the devils in hell after me then?' cried Rastignac.

'What devils are you talking about? Are you crazy? Give me your hand, then,' said Bianchon, 'let me take your pulse. You're feverish.'

'Run along then to Ma Vauquer's,' Eugène told him, 'that scoundrel Vautrin has just dropped down like a dead man.'

'Ah!' said Bianchon, leaving Rastignac once more alone, 'You confirm my suspicions and now I am going to make sure.'

The law student walked about for a long time in solemn mood. He inspected his conscience from every angle. If there were moments of indecision, of closer scrutiny, of hesitation, at least his integrity emerged from this harsh and terrible inner dialogue fully proven, like an iron bar that has come through every test. He remembered the secrets Père Goriot had confided in him the day before, he recalled the apartment chosen for him in the rue d'Artois, near Delphine; he took out her letter again, read it once more, kissed it.

'Such a love is my sheet anchor,' he said to himself. 'The poor old man has surely had much to suffer in his heart. He never mentioned his own troubles, but anyone could guess! Very well! I will care for him as if he were my real father. I will bring him abundant happiness. If she loves me she will often come to spend the day in my apartment near him. The great Comtesse de Restaud is quite disgraceful; she would make a doorman of her own father. Dear Delphine! She treats the old fellow more kindly, she is worthy to be loved. Ah! so this evening I shall find happiness.'

He pulled out his watch and admired it.

'Everything has turned out well for me! When people love each other for always it's all right for them to help each other, and it's all right for me to accept this. In any case I shall certainly succeed and be able to repay everything a hundredfold. There's nothing sinful in this liaison, nothing to bring a frown to the strictest upholder of virtue. How many respectable people contract similar unions! We are not deceiving anyone, and it is lies that are so degrading. Lying amounts to betraying oneself, surely? She and her husband have lived separate lives for a long time. Besides, I'll tell that Alsatian he must give up his wife to me since he finds it impossible to make her happy.'

Rastignac's struggle lasted a long time. Although final victory had to go to youthful virtues, yet irresistible curiosity brought him back, at about half-past four, as dusk was falling, to the Maison Vauquer, which he vowed to himself he would leave for ever. He wanted to know whether Vautrin was dead. Bianchon had conceived the idea of giving Vautrin an emetic, and had then despatched the matter vomited up to his hospital for chemical analysis. When he saw how Mademoiselle Michonneau insisted that it should be thrown away, his suspicions were reinforced. Besides, Vautrin's recovery was so rapid that Bianchon inevitably suspected some plot against the jovial life and soul of the boarding house. By the time Rastignac came back, therefore, Vautrin was standing by the stove in the dining-room. The news of young Taillefer's duel had brought down all the lodgers, except for Père Goriot, earlier than usual. Curious to know the details of the affair and how it affected Victorine's destiny, they were discussing the incident. When Eugène came in, his eyes met Vautrin's, which were imperturbable as ever. Vautrin's gaze went so deep into his heart and struck such evil chords that he shuddered.

'Well! dear boy,' said the escaped convict, 'the grim reaper will have a long, hard job with me. According to these ladies, I've come through with flying colours from a stroke that would have killed an ox.'

'Ah! you might even say a bull,' cried Madame Vauquer.

'Are you sorry to see me still alive, then?' Vautrin said in Rastignac's ear, believing he could read his thoughts, 'It would take a devilish strong man!'

'Ah, my word,' said Bianchon, 'the day before yesterday Mademoiselle Michonneau was talking about some gentleman nick named Death-Dodger; there's a name that would just suit you.'

This remark left Vautrin thunderstruck; he went pale and staggered, his magnetic gaze fell like a ray of bright sunlight on Mademoiselle Michonneau, whose legs buckled under her at such a projection of will-power. The old maid collapsed on to a chair. Poiret quickly interposed himself between her and Vautrin, realizing that she was in danger, for the convict had discarded the genial mask which concealed his true nature to reveal an expression of naked ferocity. As yet completely mystified by this dramatic scene, all the boarders watched dumbfounded. At that moment the tread of marching men was heard from the street, and the noise of rifle butts ringing on the cobbles as the soldiers halted. Just as Collin had automatically begun to check the walls and windows for some way out, four men appeared at the door of the drawing-room. The chief of the Sûreté came first, followed by three police officers.

'In the name of the law and the King,' said one of the officers, his words drowned in a murmur of astonishment.

Silence soon reigned in the dining-room, the boarders moved aside to let through three of the men, each with his hand in his side pocket holding a loaded pistol. Two gendarmes behind the detectives blocked the drawing-room door, and two more appeared at the door leading out to the stairs. From the path running along the front of the house a number of soldiers could be heard patrolling, their rifles ringing against the stones. All hope of flight was thus denied to Death-Dodger, on whom all eyes were irresistibly fastened. The chief went straight up to him, and began by hitting him on the head so violently that the wig came off and revealed Collin's head in all its true horror. The cropped brick-red hair conferred a terrifying quality of strength and cunning on the head and face, which matched the powerful torso, and shone with a

baleful intelligence as if lit up by the fires of hell. Everyone
now fully understood Vautrin, his past, present and future,
his ruthless doctrines, his religion of indulging his own good
pleasure, his regal authority, deriving from the cynicism of
his thoughts and deeds and a power of organization applied
to everything. The blood rushed to his face, his eyes glittered
like those of a wildcat. He bounded up and down with such
ferocious energy, he roared so fiercely, that he wrung cries
of terror from all the boarders. At this gesture of a lion at
bay, and justified by the general uproar, the agents drew their
pistols. Collin realized the danger as soon as he saw the ham-
mer of each weapon gleaming and suddenly proved himself
supremely endowed with human strength. Terrible and majestic sight! The phenomenon to be read in his face can only
be compared to that of a boiler full of steam with the power
to lift mountains, and which a drop of cold water dissolves
in the twinkling of an eye. The drop of water which cooled
his rage was a thought that occurred to him with lightning
speed. He began to smile, and looked at his wig.

'It's not one of your polite days,' he said to the chief of
the Sûreté. Then he held out his hands to the gendarmes,
summoning them with a jerk of his head. 'Officers, you may
put the cuffs on my wrists or my thumbs. I call those present
to witness that I offer no resistance.' A murmur of reluctant
admiration ran through the room as they saw how swiftly
the lava and flames erupted and then withdrew into this
human volcano.

'That's taken the wind out of your sails, my old crime-
buster,' the convict went on, looking at the famous director
of the detective branch.

'Come along, off with your clothes,' the man from the
petite rue Sainte-Anne ordered in contemptuous tones.

'Why?' said Collin, 'There are ladies present. I am not denying anything and I am giving myself up.'

He paused and looked round his audience like an orator
about to say something surprising.

'Write this down, Papa Lachapelle,' he said, addressing a

little old white-haired man who had sat down at the end of the table with the official record of arrest, which he had taken out of a portfolio. 'I acknowledge that I am Jacques Collin, also known as Death-Dodger, sentenced to twenty years in irons; and I have just proved my nickname well earned. I had only to raise my hand', he told the boarders, 'and these three ferrets would have spilled my claret all over Ma Vauquer's house and home. These jokers make a business out of setting up ambushes!'

Madame Vauquer felt quite faint when she heard these words.

'Gracious! I'm in a real state. And I went to the Gaîté with him last night, I did,' she said to Sylvie.

'Try and be philosophical, Ma,' Collin went on. 'Did it do you any harm being in my box at the Gaîté last night?' he exclaimed. 'Are you any better than us? The brand we bear on our shoulders is not as shameful as what you have in your hearts, flabby members of a putrid society. The best among you could not stand up to me!' His eyes fastened on Rastignac; the kindly smile he gave him contrasted strangely with the harsh expression on his face.

'Our deal is still on, my pet, provided you accept, of course! You know?' He sang:

'My Fanchette is charming,
In her simplicity.'

'Don't worry,' he went on, 'I know how to collect payment. People are too afraid of me to diddle me!'

The prison world with its own code of behaviour and speech, its abrupt transitions from the humorous to the horrible, its fearful grandeur, its disrespect, its vileness, was all at once embodied in this challenging speech and in this man, no longer an individual but the very type of a whole degenerate race, a people at once savage and logical, brutal and adaptable. In a moment Collin became a poetic creation out of hell, depicting every human emotion but one: repentance. He had the look of the fallen archangel whose eternal desire is for war. Rastignac lowered his eyes, accepting his relationship to this criminal in expiation for his evil thoughts.

'Who betrayed me?' asked Collin, sweeping them with his terrible gaze, then fixing Mademoiselle Michonneau. 'It was you,' he said, 'you old bitch, you brought on that bogus stroke, always snooping around! It would take only a couple of words from me to have your head cut off before the week's out. I'll forgive you, Christian that I am. Besides you weren't the one that sold me. But who was it? Ah! ah! so you are searching my room,' he cried, as he heard the policemen opening his cupboards and seizing his belongings. 'The birds have flown, they left the nest yesterday. And you will never know a thing. My business records are all in there,' tapping his forehead. 'Now I know who sold me. It can only be that blackguard Silk-Threads. Isn't that right, my old copper?' he said to the police chief. 'That fits in only too well with the time our banknotes were stashed up there. Nothing left, my little ferrets! As for Silk-Threads, he'll be food for worms in a fortnight, even if you set your whole police force to guard him.—What did you give that Michonnette?' he asked the policeman, 'Three thousand francs or so? I was worth more than that, you decaying Ninon, you ragged Pompadour,* you Venus of the Père Lachaise. If you had warned me, you would have had six thousand. Ah! you had no idea, you old flesh-peddler, otherwise I should have had preference. Yes, I would have paid that to avoid an unwelcome journey that will make me lose money,' he said as they handcuffed him.

'Those fellows are going to have fun dragging things out endlessly so as to drive me crazy. If they sent me straight back to gaol, I would soon be back in business, in spite of our little ninnies from the quai des Orfèvres.* There in prison they would all put their heart and soul into helping their general to escape, good old Death-Dodger! Is there one of you who can claim, like me, to have more than ten thousand brothers ready to do anything for you?' he proudly asked. 'There's good stuff there,' he said, striking his heart, 'I have never betrayed anyone! Just look at them, you old bitch,' he said, addressing the old maid. 'They look at me in terror, but you make them sick with disgust. Collect your winnings.' He paused while he stared at the boarders.

'How stupid you are, you lot. Haven't you ever seen a convict before? A convict of Collin's calibre, and here I am, is not such a coward as other men; he is protesting against the monstrous betrayals of the Social Contract, to use the words of Jean-Jacques,* whose disciple I am proud to be. In a word, I stand alone against the government, with its pile of courts, policemen and civil budgets, and I get the better of them.'

'Gad!' said the artist, 'he'd make a damn fine subject for a picture.'

'Tell me, gentlemen-in-waiting to the Lord High Executioner, governor of the Widow' (the gruesomely poetic name which convicts give the guillotine) he added, turning to the chief of the Sûreté, 'be a good chap, tell me if it was Silk-Threads who sold me! I wouldn't like him to pay for someone else, that wouldn't be fair.'

Just then the agents who had opened up and listed everything in his room came in and spoke in undertones to the leader of the expedition. The record of arrest was finished.

'Gentlemen,' said Collin, addressing the boarders, 'they are going to take me away. You have all been very kind to me during my stay here, and I shall always be grateful. I bid you goodbye. Allow me to send you some figs from Provence.' He took a few steps, then turned back to look at Rastignac. 'Goodbye, Eugène,' he said in a sad, gentle voice, contrasting strangely with the rough tone of his earlier words. 'In case you have any trouble, I have left you a devoted friend.' In spite of his handcuffs, he managed to take guard as if with a sword, called 'One, two!' like a fencing master and lunged. 'In case of emergency that's the address. Man and money are all at your disposal.'

This extraordinary character put so much buffoonery into these last words that they were intelligible only to Rastignac and himself. When the gendarmes, the soldiers and the detectives had all left the house, Sylvie, who was rubbing her mistress's temples with vinegar, looked at the astonished boarders.

'Oh well!' she said, 'He was a real man for all that.'

The flood of contrasting emotions aroused by this scene had held them all spellbound, until this comment broke the spell. At that moment the boarders, who had been studying one another, all at once saw Mademoiselle Michonneau, lanky, dessicated and cold as a mummy, huddled by the stove with eyes downcast, as if afraid that her eyeshade did not cast enough shadow to conceal the expression in her eyes. This face, which had for so long aroused their antipathy, was suddenly explained. A low murmur arose from them all in perfect unison, expressing their unanimous disgust. Mademoiselle Michonneau heard and understood, but stayed where she was. Bianchon was the first to turn to his neighbour, and said in a low voice,

'I'm leaving if that creature is to go on eating with us.'

In a flash everyone save Poiret approved the medical student's proposal, and reinforced by general support he approached the elderly boarder.

'As you are a special friend of Mademoiselle Michonneau,' he said, 'you should speak to her and make her see that she must leave this very minute.'

'This very minute?' Poiret repeated in amazement.

Then he went up to the old maid and said something in her ear.

'But I've paid my rent, I want my money's worth like everyone else,' she said, looking viperishly at the boarders.

'No matter, we'll pass the hat round to make it up for you.'

'Monsieur Rastignac supports Collin,' she replied, giving the student a venomous and challenging look, 'it's not hard to guess why.'

At that Eugène sprang as if to hurl himself at the old maid and strangle her. He understood the treachery behind that look, which had just made him see things with appalling clarity.

'Leave her alone!' cried the others.

Rastignac folded his arms and stood without a word.

'Let's have done with Mademoiselle Judas,' said the artist, addressing Madame Vauquer. 'Madame if you don't show that Michonneau woman the door, we'll all leave this dump of yours, and tell everyone that the place is full of spies and convicts. On the other hand, if you do, we'll all keep quiet about this incident. When all's said and done, it's the sort of thing that could happen in the best of societies, until such time as convicts are branded on the forehead, forbidden to disguise themselves as respectable Parisians and to play the fool as they all do.'

At these words Madame Vauquer was miraculously restored to health, sat up, folded her arms, and opened eyes which were clear and showed no sign of tears.

'But, my dear sir, do you want my house to be ruined then? Here's Monsieur Vautrin ... Oh, my goodness,' she said, interrupting herself, 'I can't help calling him by the name he used to pass as an honest man! Here', she went on, 'is one apartment vacant, and you want me to be landed with two more to let at a time of year when everyone is fixed up with lodgings.'

'Gentlemen, let's take our hats and go and dine in the place de la Sorbonne at Flicoteaux's,'* said Bianchon.

It took Madame Vauquer only a moment to work out her most profitable course of action. She waddled across to Mademoiselle Michonneau.

'Come now, my dear little friend, you don't want to kill off my establishment, do you? You can see what a pretty pickle these gentlemen have put me in; just go up to your room for this evening.'

'No, no,' cried the boarders, 'we want her out this very minute!'

'But she hasn't had any dinner, poor lady,' said Poiret in piteous tones.

'She can go and dine anywhere she likes,' cried several

voices.

'Out with her! Out with the stool pigeon!'

'Out with both stool pigeons!'

'Gentlemen!' cried Poiret, suddenly rising to the level of courage of an amorous ram, 'have some respect for the weaker sex!'

'Stool pigeons don't have a sex,' said the artist.

'Some *sexorama*!'

'*Outorama*!'

'Gentlemen, this is most improper. When people are sent packing, it must be done correctly. We have paid the rent, we're staying,' said Poiret, putting on his cap, and taking a seat beside Mademoiselle Michonneau, while Madame Vauquer harangued her.

'Naughty!' the artist said to him, putting on a comic tone. 'Off with you, naughty boy!'

'All right, if you won't go, we shall,' said Bianchon.

And the boarders moved in a body to the drawing-room.

'Mademoiselle, what are you trying to do?' cried Madame Vauquer, 'I shall be ruined. You can't stay, they will end up being violent.'

Mademoiselle Michonneau rose.

'She's going!'—'She's not going!'—'She's going!'—'She's not going!' These alternate cries and counter-cries and the hostile remarks they were beginning to make about her forced Mademoiselle Michonneau to leave, after making some points in a low voice to her hostess.

'I'm going to Madame Buneaud's,' she said threateningly.

'Go where you please, Mademoiselle,' said Madame Vauquer, who took it as a deadly insult that she should choose a boarding house which competed with her own and was therefore quite detestable in her eyes. 'Go to that Buneaud woman; you'll get wine there that would set goats dancing, and food off the bargain barrow.'

The boarders formed two ranks in total silence. Poiret looked so tenderly at Mademoiselle Michonneau, betrayed such patent uncertainty as to whether he should follow her or stay, that the boarders, delighted at Mademoiselle Michonneau's departure, began to laugh as they looked at one another.

'Gee up, gee up, Poiret,' cried the artist, 'Come on, oop-la, giddy-oop!'

The Museum attendant began to sing in a comic voice the opening lines of the well-known ballad:

> 'Leaving for Syria,
> Handsome young Dunois . . .'

'All right, go then, you are dying to go, *trahit sua quemque voluptas*,' said Bianchon.

'*Everyone follows his own bent*, free translation of Virgil,' said the tutor.

Mademoiselle Michonneau looked at Poiret and made as if to take his arm; he could not resist her appeal, and went to offer his support to the old maid. There was a burst of applause, an explosion of mirth. 'Bravo, Poiret!'—'Good old Poiret!'—'Apollo-Poiret!'—'Intrepid Poiret!'

Just then a messenger came in and handed a letter to Madame Vauquer, who read it and collapsed on to her chair.

'All we need now is for the house to burn down; thunderbolts are just raining down. Young Taillefer died at three o'clock. It serves me right for wishing those ladies well at his expense. Poor young man. Madame Couture and Victorine ask me to send on their effects. They are going to live with her father, and Monsieur Taillefer is letting his daughter keep on the widow Couture as her companion. Four apartments vacant, five boarders lost!' She sat down and seemed on the verge of tears. 'Disaster has fallen on my house!' she cried.

A carriage was suddenly heard rumbling outside, and then stopping.

'Here's another windfall,' said Sylvie.

Goriot suddenly appeared, his face flushed and shining with joy, so that he looked like a man reborn.

'Goriot in a cab,' the boarders said, 'The end of the world is at hand!'

The old fellow went straight up to Eugène, who stood pen-

sive in a corner, and took him by the arm. 'Come on,' he
said to him in joyful tones.

'Don't you know what's going on?' Eugène said to him.
'Vautrin was a convict and they have just arrested him; young
Taillefer is dead.'

'Oh yes? What does that matter to us?' Père Goriot
answered. 'I am dining with my daughter, in your apartment,
do you hear? She is waiting for you, come along!'

He tugged at Rastignac's arm so violently that he forced
him to move, and he looked like a man abducting his mistress.

'Let's have dinner!' cried the artist.

In a moment they had all taken their places and sat down
to table.

'Well I never!' said fat Sylvie, 'everything's going wrong
today, my mutton stew has caught. Oh well, you'll have to
eat it burnt, it's just too bad.'

Madame Vauquer was too upset to say a word as she saw
only ten people round the table instead of eighteen, but they
all tried to cheer her up and make her feel better. If the outside
boarders started by discussing Vautrin and the events of the
day, they soon fell in with the rambling course of the conversation and began talking about duels, penal servitude, justice,
laws needing revision, prisons. By then they were miles away
from Jacques Collin, Victorine and her brother. Although
there were only ten of them, they made enough noise for
twenty, and seemed to be more numerous than usual; that
was the only difference between that dinner and the one the
evening before. The habitual unconcern of that self-centred
world, which would next day find fresh grist for its mill in
the daily events of Paris, reasserted itself, and Madame
Vauquer herself calmed down as she lent an ear to hope,
speaking through the voice of fat Sylvie.

That whole day was for Eugène a phatasmagoria, right on
into the evening. Despite his strength of character and sound
sense, he was quite unable to put his thoughts in order when
he found himself sitting in the cab beside Père Goriot, whose
conversation revealed a mood of unwonted joy but sounded

to Eugène, reeling from so many different emotions, like words heard in a dream.

'It was finished this morning. The three of us are dining together! Do you realize? It's four years since I dined with my Delphine, my little Delphine. I shall have her for a whole evening. We have been in your apartment since morning. I've been toiling like a workman, with my coat off. I helped carry in the furniture. Ah! ah! You don't know how sweet she is at table, she'll look after me: "Here, Papa, have a bit of that, it's good." And then I can't eat it. Oh! it's a long time since I've been able to enjoy her company in peace as we are going to!'

'Does that mean,' said Eugène, 'that the world is turned upside down today?'

'Upside down?' said Père Goriot. 'But there's never been a time when things have been better. I see nothing in the street but cheerful faces, people shaking hands and embracing one another; people looking happy as if they were all going to dine with their daughters, and scoff a nice little dinner I heard her order from the chef at the Café des Anglais.* But gall and wormwood would taste as sweet as honey in her company.'

'I feel as if I am coming back to life,' said Eugène.

'But get a move on there, driver,' Père Goriot cried, opening the front window. 'Go faster; I'll give you five francs tip if you get me you know where in ten minutes!' When he heard that promise the driver shot through Paris fast as lightning.

'This driver's not moving,' said Père Goriot.

'But wherever are you taking me?' asked Rastignac.

The cab stopped in the rue d'Artois. The old man got out first, and threw the cabby ten francs with the extravagance of a widower who is having such a good time that he does not care what he does.

'Right, let's go up then,' he said to Rastignac, leading him across a courtyard and up to the door of an apartment on the third floor, at the back of a newly built house of fine appearance. Père Goriot did not need to ring. Thérèse, Madame de Nucingen's maid, opened the door to them. Eugène found himself in a delightful bachelor apartment, consisting of anteroom, a small drawing-room, a bedroom and a study, looking out on to a garden. In the small drawing-room, furnished and decorated to stand comparison with the prettiest and most tasteful examples to be found anywhere, he saw Delphine in the candlelight, rising from a love-seat by the fireside. She put her screen on the mantelpiece, and said to him in a voice full of affection, 'So we had to go and fetch you, Monsieur, the man who never understands.'

Thérèse went out. The student took Delphine in his arms, hugged her eagerly and wept for joy. This latest contrast between what he saw and what he had just been seeing in the course of a day when his heart and mind had been exhausted by the demands of so much excitement, finally caused Rastignac's nerves to crack and for a moment he broke down.

'I knew very well that he loved you,' Père Goriot said in an undertone to his daughter as Eugène lay prostrate on the love-seat, unable to utter a word or as yet to take in how the magic wand had been waved to produce this latest effect.

'But come and see,' Madame de Nucingen said, taking him by the hand and showing him into a room whose carpets, furnishings and smallest detail reminded him, on a smaller scale, of Delphine's own.

'There's no bed,' said Rastignac.

'No, Monsieur,' she said, blushing and pressing his hand.

Eugène looked at her, and young as he still was, understood how much true modesty there is in the heart of a woman in love.

'You are one of those beings who must be adored for ever,' he said in her ear. 'Yes, I dare to tell you, since we understand each other so well: the more eager and sincere love is, the more it should be veiled, mysterious. Don't let's give away our secret to anyone.'

'Oh, I'm not going to be just anyone,' said Père Goriot

grumpily.

'You know very well that you are part of *us*, you . . .'

'Ah! that's just what I wanted. Take no notice of me, will you? I'll come and go like a good spirit who is everywhere, and whose presence you know but never see. Well! Delphinette, Ninette, Dedel! Wasn't I right when I told you: "There's a nice apartment in the rue d'Artois, let's furnish it for him!" You didn't want to. Ha! I'm the one responsible for your joy, as I am the one responsible for giving you life. Fathers must always be giving to be happy, to be always giving is what makes one a father.'

'What did you say?' asked Eugène.

'No she didn't want to; she was afraid of foolish gossip, as if people's opinions mattered as much as happiness! But every woman dreams of doing what she is doing . . .'

Père Goriot was talking to himself, for Madame de Nucingen had taken Rastignac into the study, from where came the sound of a kiss, lightly though it was taken. The room matched the elegance of the rest of the apartment, in which moreover provision had been made for everything.

'Did we rightly guess your wishes?' she said, coming back in to the drawing-room to sit down to dinner.

'Yes,' he said, 'only too well. Alas! such utter luxury, the fulfilment of such perfect dreams, all the romantic fancies of a young, fashionable life, I appreciate them all too much to be undeserving, but I cannot accept them from you, and I am still too poor to . . .'

'Aha! so you are resisting me already!' she said with a little air of mock authority, pouting prettily as women do when they are trying to make light of some scruple the better to dispose of it.

Eugène had asked himself too many serious questions in the course of that day, and Vautrin's arrest, by showing him the depths of the abyss from which he had only just been saved, had too effectively confirmed his instinctive feelings of honour and delicacy for him now to yield to this tempting denial of his generous ideals. A deep sadness came over him.

'What!' said Madame de Nucingen, 'you can't be refusing? Do you know what such a refusal implies? You are doubtful about the future, you do not dare bind yourself to me. Are you afraid then of betraying my affection? If you love me, if I ... love you, why do you shrink from such trivial obligations? If you knew how much I've enjoyed arranging this whole bachelor apartment, you wouldn't hesitate, and you would beg my forgiveness. I had some money that belonged to you and I put it to good use, that's all. You think you are being noble, when you are just petty. You ask for much more ... ah!' she said, catching Eugène's passionate look, 'and you are making a fuss about a lot of silly nonsense. If you don't love me, all right, don't accept. My fate hangs on a word. Speak up! But, Father, can't you talk some sense into him?' she added, turning to her father after a pause. 'Does he think I'm less sensitive about our honour than he is?'

Père Goriot wore the fixed smile of a drugged man as he watched and listened to this pretty squabble.

'Child that you are! You stand on life's threshold,' she went on, seizing Eugène's hand, 'you come upon a barrier that a lot of people could never pass, a woman's hand opens it up for you, and you hesitate! But you will succeed, your career will be brilliant, success is written on your handsome brow. And then you'll be able to pay me back what I am lending you today. Wasn't it the custom in olden days for ladies to give their knights armour, swords, helmets, coats of mail, horses, so that they could fight tournaments in their ladies' name? Well! Eugène, what I am offering you are the weapons of our day, the necessary tools for anyone who wants to get somewhere. The attic where you live must be lovely if it is anything like papa's room. Look here, aren't we going to have dinner after all? Do you want to upset me? But answer something!' she said, giving his hand a violent shake. 'My goodness, Papa, get him to make his mind up or I'll go out and never see him again.'

'I'll make up your mind for you,' said Père Goriot, coming out of his ecstasy. 'Dear Monsieur Eugène, you are going to borrow money from the Jews, aren't you?'

'I've no choice,' he said.

'Good, now I've got you,' went on the old man, pulling out a worn, shabby old leather wallet. 'I've become your Jew. I have paid all the bills; here they are. You don't owe a penny on anything here. It's not a vast sum, five thousand francs at most. I'll lend it to you myself! You can't refuse me, I'm not a woman. Just acknowledge receipt on a bit of paper, and pay me back later.'

Eugène and Delphine looked at each other in surprise and both at the same time felt tears start. Rastignac reached out to the old fellow and clasped him by the hand.

'All right, then! Aren't you my children?' said Goriot.

'But my poor father,' said Madame de Nucingen, 'how ever did you manage it?'

'Ah! that's just the point,' he answered. 'When I finally persuaded you to set him up near you, and saw you buying things, as you would for a bride, I said to myself, "She's going to find herself in trouble!" According to the lawyer, proceedings to make your husband return your fortune to you will take six months and more. Right. I sold the capital that gave me my thirteen hundred and fifty livres for life: I used fifteen thousand of it to buy well-secured annuities of twelve hundred francs, and I paid off your tradesmen with the rest of the capital, children. For myself, I have a room upstairs for a hundred and fifty francs a year, I can live like a prince on two francs a day, and I'll still have something over. I never wear anything out, so I hardly need any clothes. For the past fortnight I've been laughing up my sleeve as I said to myself, "How happy they are going to be!" Well, aren't you happy?'

'Oh! Papa, Papa!' said Madame de Nucingen, flinging herself at her father, who took her on his knee. She smothered him with kisses, her fair hair caressing his cheeks, and shed tears on his radiant, beaming old face. 'Dear Father, what a father you are! No, there isn't another father like you on the face of the earth. Eugène loved you so much before, what will it be like now?'

'Come, children,' said Père Goriot, who had not felt his daughter's heart beating against his own for the past ten years, 'but, Delphinette, do you want to make me die of joy? My poor heart is breaking. Come now, Monsieur Eugène, we're already quits!' The old man hugged his daughter in such a wild frenzied embrace that she cried, 'Oh! you're hurting me!'

'I've hurt you!' he said, going pale. He looked at her with an expression of more than human grief. One could only paint a faithful portrait of this suffering Christ of Fatherhood by drawing comparisons with pictures created by princes of the palette to represent the suffering endured for the sake of the world by the Saviour of mankind. Père Goriot very gently kissed the waist that his fingers had clutched too roughly. 'No, no. I haven't hurt you. No,' he went on, challenging her with a smile, 'you are the one who hurt me with your cry. It cost more than that,' he said in his daughter's ear, as he cautiously kissed it, 'but I had to make sure of hooking him, or he would have been upset.'

Eugène was awestruck by the old man's boundless devotion, and gazed at him with the innocent admiration which in the young accompanies religious faith.

'I will be worthy of all this!' he cried.

'Oh, my dear Eugène, what noble words!' and Madame de Nucingen kissed the student on the forehead.

'It was for your sake he refused Mademoiselle Taillefer and her millions,' said Père Goriot. 'Oh yes, that little girl loved you; and now her brother is dead she's as rich as Croesus.'

'Oh! Why did you have to say that?' cried Rastignac.

'Eugène,' Delphine said in his ear, 'now I have one regret about this evening. Ah! I too will love you truly, and for always!'

'This is the loveliest day I have had since my two daughters got married,' exclaimed Père Goriot. 'The good Lord can make me suffer as much as he likes, so long as it is not on your account, and I'll say to myself: in February of this year

I knew more happiness in a few minutes than other men in the whole of their lives. Look at me, Fifine!' he said to his daughter. 'She's very beautiful, isn't she? Have you met many women with her pretty colouring and her little dimple? You haven't, have you? Well, I'm the one who made this adorable woman. From now on, with you making her happy, she'll become infinitely more beautiful. I don't mind going to hell, neighbour,' he said, 'if you need my share of heaven you can have it. Let's eat, let's eat,' he went on, no longer aware of what he was saying, 'it's all ours.'

'Poor Father!'

'If only you knew, my child,' he said, standing up and going over to her, taking her head and kissing it in the middle of her plaits of hair, 'how little it costs to make me happy! Come and see me sometimes, I'll be up there, it's no distance for you to go. Promise me, do!'

'Yes, dear Father.'

'Say it again!'

'Yes, kind Father.'

'That will do now. I'd make you say it a hundred times over if I listened to my own wishes. Let's have dinner.'

The whole evening was spent in childish behaviour, and Père Goriot was not the least foolish of the three. He lay down at his daughter's feet and kissed them; he gazed into her eyes for ages; he rubbed his head against her dress; in a word he behaved as foolishly as the most tender young lover.

'You see?' Delphine said to Eugène, 'when my father is with us, he demands all my attention. That could sometimes be very awkward.'

Eugène, who had already more than once felt twinges of jealousy, could not dissent from that remark, which contained the basic principle of all ingratitude.

'And when will the apartment be finished?' asked Eugène, looking round the bedroom. 'We shan't be able to stay together this evening, I suppose?'

'That's right, but tomorrow you will be coming to dinner

with me,' she said with a shrewd look, 'Tomorrow is one of the days for the Italiens.'

'I'll go in the pit,' said Père Goriot.

It was midnight. Madame de Nucingen's carriage was waiting. Père Goriot and the student returned to the Maison Vauquer talking about Delphine with increasing fervour, each trying to outdo the other, expressing the strength of his passion in curious contention. Eugène could not deny that the father's love, unblemished by any selfish interest, left his own far behind in scope and persistence. For the father, his idol was always pure and beautiful, and his worship was intensified by all that lay in the past as well as in the future.

They found Madame Vauquer alone beside the stove with Sylvie and Christophe. Their old hostess remained there like Marius amid the ruins of Carthage. She was waiting for the only two boarders who remained to her, sharing her sorrow with Sylvie. Although Lord Byron has put some fine lamentations into Tasso's mouth, they fall far short of the profound sincerity of those which Madame Vauquer could not hold back.

'So there'll only be three cups of coffee to make tomorrow morning, Sylvie! Oh! seeing my house deserted like this is enough to break your heart! What is life without my boarders? Just nothing. It was the men that made this house feel furnished, and now it's stripped bare. It's the furniture that makes a house feel lived in. What's heaven got against me to bring all these disasters on my head? We've laid in enough beans and potatoes for twenty. Police in my house! So we'll have to eat nothing but potatoes! I'll have to give Christophe the sack!'

The Savoyard suddenly woke up from his sleep and said:

'Madame?'

'Poor lad! he's like a big dog,' said Sylvie.

'It's the dead season, everyone is fixed up with lodgings. Where on earth are boarders going to come from? I'll go out of my mind. And that old witch Michonneau taking Poiret away with her! Whatever did she do to that fellow to get him to follow her like a poodle on a lead?'

'Ah! blow me!' said Sylvie, nodding her head, 'Those old maids, they knows a trick or two!'

'That poor Monsieur Vautrin, making out he was a convict,' went on the widow. 'Well! Sylvie, I can't help it, I still don't believe it. Such a jolly man; always a tot with his coffee, at fifteen francs a month, and paid cash on the nail!'

'And so generous!' said Christophe.

'There must be some mistake,' said Sylvie.

'Oh no, he admitted it himself,' replied Madame Vauquer. 'And just think, all this happened in my house, in a neighbourhood where nobody ever stirs! Upon my word as a respectable woman, I must be dreaming. Look at it like this; we've seen Louis XVI have his accident, we've seen the Emperor fall, we've seen him return and fall again, all that was in the nature of things liable to happen, but there aren't any odds against family boarding houses. You can do without a king, but you've always got to eat; and when a respectable woman, née de Conflans, serves up all kinds of good things for dinner, well, unless it's the end of the world ... But that's just it, this is the end of the world.'

'And just think that Mademoiselle Michonneau, who's caused you all this harm, is going to get three thousand francs a year for it, so they say!' cried Sylvie.

'Don't mention her to me, she's nothing but an evil wretch!' said Madame Vauquer. 'And she's moving to that Buneaud woman's house, on top of everything else! But she'd stop at nothing. She must have done some frightful things, killed and stolen in her time, for sure. She ought to have gone to gaol instead of that poor dear man ...'

At that moment Eugène and Père Goriot rang the bell.

'Ah! that's my two faithful friends,' the widow said with a sigh.

The two faithful friends, who only dimly remembered the disasters which had befallen the boarding house, informed their hostess without ceremony that they were going to live in the Chaussée-d'Antin.

'Oh, Sylvie!' said the widow, 'there goes my last card. You have struck me a mortal blow, gentlemen! You've stabbed me in the vitals. That's finished me off. This day has put ten years on my life. I'm going out of my mind, on my word of honour. What am I going to do with the beans? All right, if I am going to be left all alone here, you can be off tomorrow, Christophe. Goodbye, gentlemen, good-night.'

'What on earth is the matter with her?' Eugène asked Sylvie.

'Goodness gracious! Everyone's left on account of all the goings-on. She's gone off her head. Hark! I can hear her crying. It'll do her good to have a bit of a weep. That's the first time she's had a good cry since I've been in service with her.'

Next day Madame Vauquer had, in her own words, 'made herself see reason'. While she appeared as distressed as any woman who has lost all her boarders and whose life has been turned upside down, she was now completely lucid, and showed the real, root cause of her grief, the damage to her own interests and disruption of her habits. Certainly no departing lover could look back more sadly at his mistress's dwelling than Madame Vauquer at her empty table. Eugène tried to console her by saying that Bianchon, whose spell as houseman would be over in a few days, would no doubt take his place; that the Museum assistant had often expressed a wish to have Madame Couture's apartment; and that in quite a short time she would have filled up the number of boarders again.

'May God grant it so, my dear sir! But there's a curse on this place. Before ten days are out there'll be a death here, you'll see,' she said, with a mournful glance at the dining-room. 'Who will be taken?'

'It's a good thing we're moving out,' Eugène said very quietly to Père Goriot.

'Madame!' said Sylvie, running up in a fright, 'I haven't seen Mistigris for three days!'

'Ah! Well, if my cat is dead, if he has left us, I . . .'

The poor widow did not finish her sentence, but clasped her hands together and slumped back in her chair, overcome by this fearful portent.

At about noon, the usual time for postmen to reach the Panthéon district, Eugène received a letter in an elegant envelope, sealed with the Beauséant arms. It contained an invitation, addressed to Monsieur and Madame de Nucingen, to the grand ball announced a month earlier, which was to take place in the vicomtesse's house. Enclosed was a brief note for Eugène:

I thought, Monsieur, that you would be glad to accept responsibility for conveying my sentiments to Madame de Nucingen; I am sending you the invitation you requested, and shall be delighted to make the acquaintance of Madame de Restaud's sister. Bring that charming person to meet me then, but see to it that she does not take up all your affection, for you owe me much of it in return for that which I have for you. Vicomtesse de BEAUSÉANT

'Well,' said Eugène to himself, rereading this note, 'Madame de Beauséant is quite clearly telling me that she doesn't want anything to do with Baron de Nucingen.' He went quickly round to Delphine, happy at having obtained for her a pleasure for which he would no doubt be rewarded. Madame de Nucingen was in her bath. Rastignac waited in the boudoir, feeling all the natural impatience of an eager young man in a hurry to possess a mistress who for two years had been the object of his desires. Such emotions do not occur twice in young men's lives. The first woman, real woman, to whom a man becomes attached, that is, the one who appears to him in all the dazzling splendour of the setting required by Parisian society, will never have a rival. Love in Paris is totally unlike all other kinds of love. In Paris neither men nor women are taken in by the ostentatious parade of commonplaces with which everyone cloaks supposedly disinterested emotions for the sake of decency. In that society a woman has to satisfy not only her heart and senses, she is perfectly well aware that she is under still greater obligations to the countless vanities of which life there is composed.

There above all love is essentially a boastful, brazen, wasteful, ostentatious charlatan. If all the women at the Court of Louis XIV envied Mademoiselle de La Vallière* the passionate impulse which made the great prince forget that his lace cuffs had cost three thousand francs each when he ripped them helping the Duc de Vermandois into the world, what then can one expect of the rest of humanity? Be young, rich, titled, do better still if you can; the more incense you burn before the idol, the more favour she will show you, always supposing you have an idol. Love is a religion, and its cult must cost more than that of all other religions. Love soon passes, but like a mischievous urchin, likes to leave a trail of devastation to mark its passing. A wealth of sentiment is the poetry that goes with life in a garret; without such riches, what would become of love there?

If there are some exceptions to these draconian laws of the Parisian Code, they are to be found living in solitude, in spirits who have refused to be carried away by the doctrines of society, who dwell beside some source of limpid water, ever fleeting, ever flowing; spirits faithful to the greenery that shades them, listening happily to the language of the infinite, which they find written in every created thing, and also within themselves, waiting in patience for wings to fly away and full of pity for those bound to the earth. But Rastignac, like most young men who have had a foretaste of greatness, wanted to appear fully armed in the lists of the world. He had caught its feverish excitement, and felt perhaps strong enough to become its master, while still unaware of the means or the goal of such an ambition. For want of a pure and sacred love to fill one's life, such a thirst for power can become a fine thing; it is enough to renounce all personal interest and set up as a goal the greatness of one's country. But the student had not yet reached the point from which a man can examine the course of his life and judge it. So far he had not even completely shaken off the spell of those ideas sweet and fresh as greenery which hedge round the early years of children brought up in the country. He had continually hesitated to cross the Parisian Rubicon. Despite a consuming curiosity, he had always felt a lingering attraction for the contented life of the true nobleman in his castle. However, his remaining scruples had disappeared the previous evening, when he found himself in his new apartment. By enjoying the material advantages of wealth, as he had so long enjoyed the moral advantages of noble birth, he had sloughed off his skin as a provincial, and smoothly moved into a position from which he could look forward to a fine future. So, as he waited for Delphine, seated comfortably in this charming boudoir, which he was beginning to regard as almost his own, he saw himself so far removed from the Rastignac who had come to Paris the year before, that, looking closely at that person through some trick of mental vision, he asked himself if at that moment there was any resemblance between his two selves.

'Madame is in her room,' Thérèse announced, startling him.

He found Delphine reclining on the love-seat by the fireside, refreshed and rested. Seeing her like that, spread out amid cascades of muslin, he could not help comparing her to those beautiful Indian plants whose fruit appears within the flower.

'Oh, here you are!' she said with feeling.

'Guess what I've brought you,' Eugène said, sitting down beside her and raising her arm to kiss her hand.

Madame de Nucingen made a gesture of delight as she read the invitation. She looked at Eugène with tears in her eyes, threw her arms round his neck and pulled him close in a frenzy of satisfied vanity.

'And it is to you, Monsieur ('my dear one,' she whispered in his ear, 'But Thérèse is in the dressing-room and we must be careful!') that I owe this joy? Yes, I dare call it joy. As it is something that you have obtained for me, isn't it more than a triumph for my self-esteem? You may perhaps think of me at this moment as small-minded, frivolous, empty-headed as any woman in Paris; but just think, my friend, I am ready to make any sacrifice for you, and if I am longing more fervently than ever to gain admission to the Faubourg Saint-Germain it is because you are already there.'

'Don't you think', said Eugène, 'that Madame de Beauséant seems to be saying that she doesn't expect to see Baron de Nucingen at her ball?'

'Yes, indeed,' said the baronne, handing the letter back to Eugène, 'Those women have a genius for rudeness. No matter, I'll go. My sister intends to be there, I know she is having a lovely dress made. Eugène,' she went on in a low voice, 'she is going there to allay the most dreadful suspicions about her. You don't know the rumours that are going around? Nucingen came to tell me this morning that they were talking about it yesterday at the Club quite freely. My goodness, what does the honour of women and families depend on? I felt as though it were an attack on me, as if I were being wounded in the person of my poor sister. According to certain people, Monsieur de Trailles signed bills of exchange amounting to a hundred thousand francs, almost all now overdue, and he is going to be sued for recovery of the money. In this emergency my sister is supposed to have sold her diamonds to a Jew, those beautiful diamonds which you may have seen her wearing; they came from Madame de Restaud, her mother-in-law. Well, for the past two days everyone has been talking about it, so I can understand why Anastasie is having a lamé dress made, and wants to be the centre of attention at Madame de Beauséant's ball by appearing there in all her splendour and wearing her diamonds. But I don't want to be outdone by her. She has always tried to squash me, she has never been kind to me, though I have done so much for her and have always had money for her when she had none. But let's forget the outside world. Today I want to be happy.'

Rastignac was still with Madame de Nucingen at one in the morning. As she spun out the lovers' leave-taking, a farewell full of promised joys to come, she said to him with a mournful air, 'I am so apprehensive, so superstitious, call my premonitions whatever you like, that I am terrified of having to pay for my happiness with some appalling catastrophe.'

'Child!' said Eugène.

'Ah! so this evening I am the child!' she said with a laugh.

Eugène returned to the Maison Vauquer certain that he would leave there next day, and so as he walked back he gave himself up to the pleasant dreams of all young men who still have the taste of happiness on their lips.

'Well!' said Père Goriot as Rastignac passed his door.

'Well!' answered Eugène, 'I'll tell you everything tomorrow.'

'Everything, mind!' cried the old fellow. 'Go to bed now. Tomorrow we begin our life of happiness.'

4

The Father's Death

NEXT day Goriot and Rastignac were all ready to move out of the boarding house and waited only on the pleasure of a removal man, when at about noon the rue Neuve-Sainte-Geneviève echoed with the sound of a carriage drawing up at the door of the Maison Vauquer. Madame de Nucingen stepped out and asked if her father was still there. When Sylvie replied that he was, she slowly climbed the stairs. Eugène was in his room, though his neighbour did not know that. In the course of breakfast he had asked Père Goriot to see to the removal of his effects, and said that they would meet again at the rue d'Artois at four o'clock. But while the old fellow had gone out to find porters, Eugène, after punctually answering his name at roll-call in the Law School, had come back, without anyone noticing, to settle up with Madame Vauquer. He did not want to leave this task to Goriot, who was no doubt fanatical enough to have paid for him as well. Their hostess had gone out, so Eugène went up to his room to see whether he had forgotten anything, and congratulated himself for thinking of it on finding in his table drawer the blank bill made out to Vautrin, which he had heedlessly tossed there the day he had paid off the debt. As his fire was unlit, he was about to tear the paper into shreds when he recognized Delphine's voice. He did not want to make a sound, and stopped to listen, never thinking she might have any secrets to hide from him. Then from the first words of the conversation between father and daughter he found himself too interested not to go on listening.

'Ah! Father,' she said, 'Please God that your idea of asking

for an account of my money has come in time to save me
from ruin! Can I talk?'

'Yes, there's no one in the house,' said Père Goriot in a
broken voice.

'But what is the matter with you, father?' Madame de
Nucingen went on.

'You have just dealt me a crushing blow,' answered the
old man. 'God forgive you, my child! You don't know how
much I love you. If you did, you wouldn't suddenly say such
things to me, especially if the situation is not desperate. What
has happened then that is so urgent that you came here to
find me when we were going to be at the rue d'Artois in
a few minutes' time?'

'Oh, Father, can we always control our first reactions to
a catastrophe? I am going mad! Your lawyer has given us
a little advance notice of a disaster which will surely break
into the open later on. We are going to need your long business
experience, and I rushed to find you like a drowning man
clutching at a branch. When Monsieur Derville saw Monsieur
de Nucingen putting up his endless quibbling objections, he
threatened to take him to court, and told him that the author-
ization of the president of the court would be readily forth-
coming. Nucingen came in to see me this morning to ask
if I was intent on ruining him, and myself too. I replied that
I knew nothing at all about that, I had money of my own,
I ought to be in possession of that money, anything relevant
to this dispute concerned my lawyer, I was totally ignorant
on the subject and quite unable to understand it. Wasn't that
what you advised me to say?'

'That's right,' answered Père Goriot.

'Well!' Delphine went on, 'he informed me as to the true
state of his affairs. He has thrown all his capital, as well as
mine, into projects which are barely under way and which
have required considerable further investment. If I forced him
to return my dowry, he would be obliged to declare bankruptcy, whereas, if I am willing to wait a year, he promises
on his honour to bring me in a fortune worth two or three

times what I have now by investing my capital in building development, which, once completed, would leave me mistress of all the property. Dear Father, he was so sincere, he frightened me. He begged forgiveness for his past behaviour, he gave me back my freedom, with permission to behave as I wanted, on condition that I allow him absolute freedom to manage business affairs in my name. As proof of his good faith he has promised to call on Monsieur Derville whenever I wish to judge whether my title deeds to the property are properly drawn up. In a word he has put himself at my mercy, tied hand and foot. He asks to have the running of the house for another two years, and begged me to spend no more on myself than what he allows me. He convinced me that the most he can do is keep up appearances. He's sent his dancer packing, and is going to practise the strictest economy, but in absolute secrecy, if he is to see his speculations reach maturity without spoiling his credit. I gave him a very hard time, and queried everything, driving him to despair so that I could learn more. He showed me his books. Finally he burst into tears. I have never seen a man in such a state. He lost his head, talked about suicide, raved. I felt sorry for him.'

'And you believe all that twaddle!' exclaimed Père Goriot. 'He's putting on an act! I have met Germans in business; they are almost all men of good faith, open and honest, but when they become wily and deceitful behind their frank and jovial manners, then they are worse than anyone else. Your husband is fooling you. He feels hard pressed, he's lying low, he wants to retain more control under your name than he can under his own. He's going to exploit this situation to cover himself against any risk of his business going wrong. He's as cunning as he is treacherous; he's a bad lot. No, no, I won't go to my grave at the Père Lachaise with my daughters left destitute. I still know a bit about business. He has, so he says, committed his capital to particular ventures. All right! His interests are represented by securities, receipts, contracts! Let him show them, and settle with you. We'll choose the best speculations and accept the risks, and have them registered in our name as *Delphine Goriot, married to Baron de Nucingen with separate ownership of property*. But does that fellow take us for fools? Does he suppose that I could stand the idea of leaving you penniless, hungry, for two days? I couldn't stand it for one day, one night, not for two hours! If such an idea came true I couldn't go on living. What! Spend forty years of my life toiling, carrying sacks on my back, sweating blood, going without things all my life for your sakes, my angels, for you who eased my toil and lightened my burdens, just to see all my fortune, my very life go up in smoke today! That would drive me raving mad to my death. By all that is most sacred in heaven and earth, we'll get this straight, check the books, the funds, the projects! I won't sleep, I won't rest, I won't eat until I have proof that your fortune is intact. Thank heavens the marriage settlement was for separate ownership of property; you'll have Maître Derville as your lawyer, and fortunately he is an honest man. By God! you'll keep your tidy little million, your fifty thousand a year, to the end of your days or I'll make such an unholy row in Paris ... I'd appeal to Parliament if the courts did us down. The knowledge that you were comfortable and happy as far as money was concerned relieved all my pains and soothed my woes. Money is life. Cash can do anything. What sort of tale is he spinning, then, that great lump of an Alsatian? Delphine, don't hand over a farthing to that great brute who put you on a leash and made you so wretched. If he needs you, we'll make him dance to our tune and see he goes straight. Goodness, my brain is boiling, I can feel something burning inside my skull. My Delphine penniless! Oh! my Fifine, my dear! Good grief, where are my gloves? Come on! Let's be off, I want to go and see the lot, books, dealings, cash, correspondence, and at once. I won't calm down until I have proof that your fortune is no longer at risk, and can see it with my own eyes.'

'My dear Father! Do take care! If you gave the slightest hint that you were seeking revenge in this matter and betrayed hostile intentions I should be lost. He knows you, and found it quite natural that I should be concerned about my fortune at your instigation; but I swear he has the money in his own hands, and has always intended that. He is quite capable of absconding with all the capital and leaving us behind, the scoundrel! He knows full well that I would never dishonour the name I bear myself by proceeding against him. He is strong and weak at the same time. I have looked into it very closely. If we push him to the limit I shall be ruined.'

'But is he just a rogue then?'

'Well, yes, Father,' she said, throwing herself into a chair and weeping. 'I didn't want to admit it to you, so as to spare you the grief of having let me marry a man of that sort! Private conduct and conscience, body and soul, he's all of a piece! It's horrible, I hate and despise him. Yes, I can't respect that vile Nucingen any more after all he's told me. Anyone capable of entering into the sort of shady dealings he talked about must be quite unscrupulous, and what makes me so afraid is what I have so clearly read in his heart. My own husband proposed outright that I should have my freedom. You know what that means? If I were willing, in the event of disaster, to be a tool in his hands, that is if I were willing to let him use my name as a cover.'

'But there are laws! There is a place de Grève for sons-in-law like that!' cried Père Goriot. 'I would guillotine him myself if there were no public executioner to do it!'

'No, Father, there aren't any laws against him. Listen to what he says in a nutshell and without all his fancy trimmings: "Either all is lost, you are left without a farthing, you are ruined, for I would never find anyone else to be my accomplice; or you leave me to carry through my ventures to a successful conclusion." Is that clear enough? He still depends on me. He is reassured by having so honest a wife, he knows that I would let him keep his money and be content with my own. I have to agree to be associated with dishonesty and theft for fear of facing ruin. He is buying my conscience at the price of letting me carry on as I like with Eugène. "I am allowing you to commit sins, let me commit crimes by ruining poor people." Is that also clear enough? Do you know what he calls business deals? He buys plots of land in his own name, then gets men of straw to put up houses on the land. These men agree terms for the buildings with the contractors, whom they pay in long-dated bills, and agree, in return for some small sum, to give my husband clearance, so that he is then owner of the houses, while the men of straw get out of their debt to the duped contractors by going bankrupt. The name of the firm of Nucingen was used to bedazzle the poor builders. I can understand all that. I also understood that in case he needed proof that vast sums had been paid, Nucingen has sent bills for considerable amounts to London, Naples and Vienna. How could we ever get hold of them?'

Eugène heard a dull thud as Père Goriot fell on his knees upon the floor of his room.

'My God, what have I done? My daughter delivered up to this wretch. He will demand anything he chooses from her. Forgive me, dear daughter!' cried the old man.

'Yes, if I am in the direst straits, you may be partly to blame. We are not very sensible when we get married! What do we know about the world, about business, about men or the facts of life? Our fathers ought to do our thinking for us. Dear Father, I am not blaming you, forgive me for what I said. The fault is entirely mine. No, don't cry, Papa,' she said, kissing her father on the forehead.

'Don't you cry either, my little Delphine. Come closer so that I can kiss the tears away from your eyes. There! I'll get my old brain working again and unravel all the threads of this business that your husband has put in such a tangle.'

'No, leave it to me; I know how to handle him. He loves me, all right, I'll exploit the power I have over him to make him invest some of my capital in property right away. Perhaps I'll get him to buy back Nucingen in Alsace under my name; he is keen on that. Only come tomorrow to go through his books and his business deals. Monsieur Derville doesn't know anything about money matters. No, don't come tomorrow,

I don't want to be upset. Madame de Beauséant's ball is the day after tomorrow, and I want to make sure I look lovely and relaxed there, and do honour to my dear Eugène! Let's go then and have a look at his room.'

At that moment a carriage stopped in the rue Neuve-Sainte-Geneviève, and Madame de Restaud's voice could be heard from the stairs, saying to Sylvie:

'Is my father in?' Her arrival came as a stroke of luck to save Eugène, who was already planning to fling himself on his bed and pretend to be asleep.

'Oh! Father, has anyone said anything to you about Anastasie?' said Delphine, recognizing her sister's voice. 'Apparently there are some queer things going on in her home too.'

'Whatever next!' said Père Goriot, 'that would finish me off. My poor head would never stand a double disaster.'

'Good morning, Father,' said the comtesse as she came in. 'Oh! so you're here, Delphine!'

Madame de Restaud seemed embarrassed at meeting her sister.

'Good morning, Nasie,' said the baronne. 'Do you find it strange then that I should be here? *I* see my father every day.'

'Since when?'

'If you ever came you would know.'

'Don't tease me, Delphine,' said the comtesse in a piteous voice. 'I am really unhappy, I am ruined, my poor father! Really ruined this time!'

'What's wrong, Nasie?' cried Père Goriot. 'Tell me all about it, my child.' She went pale. 'Delphine, come on, help her, be kind to her, it will make me love you all the more, if that is possible.'

'My poor Nasie,' said Madame de Nucingen, helping her sister into a chair. 'Tell us all about it. In us you see the only two people who will always love you enough to forgive you anything. You see, the ties of family affection are the strongest.'

She pressed smelling-salts on her, and the comtesse

recovered.

'This will be the death of me,' said Père Goriot. 'There now,' he went on, poking his peat fire, 'come closer, both of you. I am cold. What is wrong, Nasie? Hurry up and tell me, you are killing me.'

'Very well,' said the poor woman, 'My husband knows everything. Just imagine, Father, do you remember that bill of exchange of Maxime's? Well, it was not the first, I had already paid off a number of others. About the beginning of January Monsieur de Trailles seemed very despondent. He didn't say anything, but it's so easy to read the feelings of those you love. The least thing is enough, and then one has premonitions. In fact he was more loving, more tender than I have ever known him, and I felt happier and happier. Poor Maxime! In his mind he was saying goodbye to me, he told me; he was intending to blow his brains out. Finally I went on at him so much, begged him so often—I once clung to his knees for two hours—that he told me he owed a hundred thousand francs! Oh, Papa, a hundred thousand francs! I went out of my mind. You didn't have that much, I had devoured all ...'

'No,' said Père Goriot, 'I couldn't have managed that much, short of stealing it. But I would have gone that far, Nasie! I'll do it!'

The mournful cadence of these words, sounding like the last gasp of a dying man, expressed the agony of a devoted father seeing himself powerless to meet his children's need, and gave the two sisters pause. How could anyone remain indifferent to such a cry, plumbing such depths of despair, like a falling stone echoing from the bottom of an abyss?

'I found the amount by disposing of something that did not belong to me, Father,' said the comtesse, bursting into tears.

Delphine was touched by this and wept too, with her head on her sister's shoulder.

'So it is all true,' she said.

Anastasie bowed her head. Madame de Nucingen clasped

her round the waist, kissed her tenderly, and said, pressing
her to her heart: 'Here you will always find love, not
judgement.'

'My angels,' said Goriot feebly, 'why does it take disaster
to bring you together?'

'To save Maxime's life, indeed to save all my happiness,'
the comtesse went on, encouraged by such manifestations
of warm, vibrant affection, 'I went to the moneylender you
know, a man created in hell, incapable of pity, that Monsieur
Gobseck, with the family diamonds Monsieur de Restaud is
so attached to, his, mine, the lot, and sold them. Sold, do
you understand! It saved Maxime, but it destroyed me. Restaud got to know everything.'

'Who told him? How? Let me kill the man!' cried Père
Goriot.

'Yesterday he summoned me to his room. I went ... "Anastasie," he said in a voice ... oh! his voice was enough, I guessed
everything. "Where are your diamonds?"—"In my room."—
"No," he said, looking right at me, "there they are, on my
chest of drawers."—and he showed me the jewel case which
he had covered over with a handkerchief. "Do you know
where they have come from?" he said. I fell at his feet ...
I wept, I asked him what death he would have me die.'

'You said that!' cried Père Goriot, 'By all that is holy,
anyone who harms either of you while I am alive can be
quite sure that I will kill him by inches! Yes, I'll tear him
to shreds like ...'

Père Goriot stopped. The words died in his throat.

'At length, my dear sister, he asked me to do something
worse than dying. Heaven preserve any woman from hearing
what I heard!'

'I'll murder that man,' said Père Goriot quite calmly, 'but
he has only one life and he owes me two. Well, what was
it?' he continued, looking at Anastasie.

'Very well!' the comtesse went on, after a pause, 'he looked
at me and said, "Anastasie, I'll draw a veil of silence over
all this, we'll stay together, we have children. I won't shoot

Monsieur de Trailles, I might miss him, and if I tried to get rid of him any other way I might come up against human justice. Killing him in your arms would bring dishonour on the children. But if you don't want to see your children, their father or me perish, I lay down two conditions. Answer me: are any of the children mine?" I said yes.—"Which?" he asked.—"Ernest, the eldest."—"Good," he said, "Now swear that you will obey me from now on on just one point." I swore. "You will give me signed authority to sell your property whenever I ask you to do so."'

'Don't sign!' cried Père Goriot. 'Don't ever sign such a thing. Ah! ah! Monsieur de Restaud, you don't know how to make a woman happy, so she goes looking for happiness where she can find it, and you punish her for your own silly incapacity! But I am there, telling you to stop just where you are! He'll find me blocking his way. Don't worry, Nasie. So he is fond of his heir, is he? Good, good. I'll grab his son from him, damn and blast, he's my grandson! I suppose I can see the kid? I'll put him in my village, I'll take good care of him, rest assured. I'll make that monster capitulate when I say to him: "It's between the two of us! If you want your son, return my daughter's property and let her live as she chooses."'

'Father!'

'Yes, father! Oh, I am a real father. That scoundrel of a nobleman had better not harm my daughters. Blast! I don't know what runs in my veins; it must be tiger's blood. I'd like to eat those two men alive! Oh my children! So that is your life? But it is death to me. What will happen to you when I am no longer there? Fathers ought to live as long as their children. Oh God, how badly your world is arranged! Yet you have a son, so we are told. You ought to prevent us suffering through our children. My dearest angels, why, I have only your sorrows to thank for your presence here. You only let me see your tears. All right, yes, you love me, I can see. Yes, come here with your grief! My heart is big enough, it can find room for all of it. Yes, even if you rend it, each shred will form a father's heart. I wish I could take your troubles on myself, suffer for you. Ah! when you were little, you were so happy ...'

'That's the only good time we ever had,' said Delphine. 'What happened to all those hours we spent tumbling down the sacks in the great loft?'

'Father! that's not all,' Anastasie said in Goriot's ear, making him start. 'The sale of the diamonds didn't make a hundred thousand francs. They are taking Maxime to court. We have only twelve thousand francs still to pay. He promised to be sensible, to stop gambling. His love is all I have left in the world, and I have paid so dearly for it that losing it would kill me. For his sake I have sacrificed my fortune, my honour, my peace of mind, my children. Oh! at least do something so that Maxime does not lose his freedom or his honour, so that he can remain a member of society and make a position for himself. Now it's not only my happiness he owes me, but our children, who would be penniless. All is lost if they put him in Sainte-Pélagie.'*

'I haven't got that much, Nasie. I've nothing left, nothing, nothing! It's the end of the world. Oh! the world is falling apart, that's certain. Off you go, save yourselves before it happens! Ah! I still have my silver buckles, six table settings, the first that I ever had in my life. Then all I have left is my annuity of twelve hundred francs ...'

'What did you do then with your securities?'

'I sold them, and just kept that bit of income for my own needs. It cost me twelve thousand francs to fix up the apartment for Fifine.'

'In your house, Delphine?' Madame de Restaud asked her sister.

'Oh! what does that matter!' went on Père Goriot, 'The twelve thousand francs have been spent.'

'I can guess,' said the comtesse, 'on Monsieur de Rastignac. Ah! My poor Delphine, don't go on; look what I've come to.'

'My dear, Monsieur de Rastignac is not the sort of young

man who would ever ruin his mistress.'

'Thank you, Delphine. In my desperate situation I expected something better from you, but you have never had any love for me.'

'But she does love you, Nasie,' cried Père Goriot, 'she told me so just a moment ago. We were talking about you, and she herself claimed that you were beautiful while she was only pretty!'

'Her, pretty!' repeated the comtesse. 'Cold as marble, she is.'

'Even if I were,' said Delphine, flushing with anger, 'what about your behaviour towards me? You rejected me, you saw to it that I would find the door closed to me in every house where I wanted to gain entry, in fact you never missed the smallest opportunity of hurting me. And did I ever come, as you did, to squeeze every last penny out of our poor father, a thousand francs at a time, and reduce him to the state he is in now? That's your doing, dear sister. For my part, I saw my father as often as I could, I didn't show him the door, I didn't come fawning over him when I needed him. I simply didn't know that he had spent the twelve thousand francs on me. I like to keep things under my control, as you know. Besides, whenever papa gave me presents, I had never come begging for them.'

'You were better off than I. Monsieur de Marsay was rich, as you should know. You have always been mean about money. Goodbye, I don't have a sister now, nor . . .'

'Be quiet, Nasie!' cried Père Goriot.

'It takes a sister like you to repeat what no one else believes any more. You are a monster,' said Delphine.

'Children, children, stop it, or I'll kill myself in front of you.'

'Come now, Nasie, I forgive you,' went on Madame de Nucingen, 'you are unhappy. But I'm kinder than you. To say that to me just when I was ready to do anything to help you, even to sharing my husband's bedroom, something I wouldn't do for my own sake or for . . . That's up to the standard of all the harm you have done me in the past nine years.'

'Children, children, kiss and make up!' said their father. 'You are a pair of angels.'

'No, leave me alone,' cried the comtesse, shaking her father's hand off her arm. 'She is less sorry for me than my husband would be. Anyone would think she was a model of all the virtues.'

'I would rather people believed I owed money to Monsieur de Marsay than to admit that Monsieur de Trailles has cost me over two hundred thousand francs,' replied Madame de Nucingen.

'Delphine!' cried the comtesse, taking a step towards her.

'I am simply answering your lying slanders with truth,' the baronne coldly retorted.

'Delphine, you are a . . .'

Père Goriot moved swiftly to restrain the comtesse, and put a hand over her mouth to prevent her speaking.

'Goodness! Whatever have you been handling this morning, Father?' asked Anastasie.

'All right, I shouldn't have done that,' said their poor father, wiping his hand on his trousers, 'but I didn't know you were coming. I'm moving out.'

He was happy to have earned a rebuke from his daughter, and thus divert her anger on to himself.

'Ah!' he went on, sitting down, 'you've broken my heart. I am dying, children! My head is burning inside as though it were on fire. Won't you be nice and loving to each other? You'll kill me. Delphine, Nasie, there are rights and wrongs on both sides. Look, Dedel,' he went on, looking at the baronne through his tears, 'she needs twelve thousand francs, let's try and find it. Don't look at each other like that.' He knelt down in front of Delphine. 'Ask her forgiveness, just to please me,' he whispered in her ear, 'she is in a worse plight than you, don't you see?'

'My poor Nasie,' said Delphine, appalled at the wild, demented expression of grief on her father's face, 'I've done you wrong, kiss me . . .'

'Ah! that's balm to my soul,' cried Père Goriot. 'But where can we find twelve thousand francs? Suppose I offered myself as a substitute to do someone's military service?'

'Oh Father!' his two daughters said, embracing him, 'No! No!'

'God will reward you for that suggestion, our lives would not suffice! Isn't that so, Nasie?' Delphine went on.

'And anyhow, poor Father, it would be only a drop in the ocean,' remarked the comtesse.

'Is there no way then to use one's life-blood?' the old man cried in despair. 'I promise myself heart and soul to the man who can save you, Nasie! I am ready to commit murder for him. I'll do what Vautrin did, I'll go to gaol! . . .' He stopped short, as if struck by a thunderbolt. 'Nothing left!' he said, tearing his hair. 'If I only knew where to steal it, but it's hard enough to think of a place to rob. And in any case I would need a lot of other people and time to rob the Bank. Well, then, I'll have to die. There's nothing more for me but to die. No, I'm no use to anyone any more! No, I'm not. She asks for my help, she needs me, and, wretch that I am, I have nothing to offer. Ah! you bought yourself annuities, you old villain, and you had daughters! So you don't really love them? Die, then, die like the dog you are! Oh yes, I'm lower than a dog, a dog wouldn't behave like that! Oh, my head! It's bursting!'

'But, Papa!' cried the two young women, holding him tight to stop him banging his head against the wall, 'do be reasonable.'

He sobbed. Eugène, appalled, took the bill of exchange made out to Vautrin, which bore a stamp valid for a larger amount. He altered the figure and made it into a proper bill of exchange for twelve thousand francs to Goriot's order, and walked in.

'Here is the whole sum you need, Madame,' he said, handing her the paper. 'I was asleep, your conversation woke me up, and that is how I learned what I owe Monsieur Goriot. Here is my security for it. You can cash it in, I'll pay it off faithfully.'

The comtesse stood motionless, the paper in her hand.

'Delphine,' she said, pale and trembling with anger, fury, rage, 'I was prepared to forgive you anything, as God is my witness, but this! This gentleman was here, and you knew it! You were petty enough to get your revenge by making me reveal my secrets to him, my life, my children's life, my shame, my honour! Now you mean nothing to me any more, I hate you, I will hurt you in every possible way, I ...'. Anger prevented her from saying more, and her throat went dry.

'But he is my son, our child, your brother, your saviour,' cried Père Goriot. 'Kiss him then, Nasie! There, I'll kiss him,' he went on, hugging Eugène in a kind of frenzy. 'Oh, my boy! I'll be more than a father to you, I'll try to be a family. I'd like to be God and cast the whole universe at your feet. But go on, give him a kiss, Nasie! He is not a mere man, but an angel, a real angel!'

'Leave her alone, Father, she's quite crazy just now,' said Delphine.

'Crazy, crazy! And what about you, what are you?' asked Madame de Restaud.

'Children, I'll die if you go on,' cried the old man, dropping on to his bed as if hit by a bullet. 'Those girls are killing me!' he said to himself.

The comtesse looked at Eugène, who stood stock still, bewildered by the violence of the scene. 'Monsieur,' she said, with a query in her gesture, her voice, her look, paying no attention to her father, whose waistcoat Delphine had rapidly undone.

'Madame, I'll pay and say nothing,' he answered without waiting for her question.

'You've killed our father, Nasie!' said Delphine, showing the unconscious old man to her sister, who fled.

'I readily forgive her,' said the old fellow, opening his eyes, 'She is in a dreadful situation, and it would turn a stronger head than hers. Comfort Nasie, be gentle with her, promise your poor father, who is dying,' he begged Delphine, as he squeezed her hand.

'But what's come over you?' she said in alarm.

'Nothing, nothing,' answered her father, 'it will pass. There's something pressing on my forehead, a migraine. Poor Nasie, what a future!'

At that moment the comtesse came back, flung herself at her father's knees and cried, 'Forgive me!'

'Come, come,' said Père Goriot, 'now you are making me feel even worse.'

'Monsieur,' the comtesse said to Rastignac, her eyes brimming with tears, 'sorrow made me unjust. Will you be a brother to me?' she went on, holding out her hand.

'Nasie,' Delphine said, hugging her, 'little Nasie, let's forget all about it.'

'No,' she said, 'I shall always remember!'

'You angels,' exclaimed Père Goriot, 'you have lifted the veil from my eyes, your voices are bringing me back to life. Embrace one another again. Well now! Nasie, will this bill of exchange save you?'

'I hope so. Look, Papa, will you add your signature?'

'There. How stupid of me to forget that! But I wasn't feeling well. Nasie, don't hold it against me. Send me word when you are in the clear. No, I'll go. No I won't. I can't see your husband again or I'll kill him there and then. As for making over your property, I'll be there. Go quickly, my child, and make Maxime behave more sensibly.'

Eugène was astounded.

'Poor Anastasie has always been a violent person,' said Madame de Nucingen, 'but she has a kind heart.'

'She came back for the endorsement,' Eugène said for Delphine's ear alone.

'Do you think so?'

'I wish I didn't. Be wary of her,' he replied, looking upwards as though confiding to heaven thoughts he did not dare utter.

'Yes, she has always been inclined to play-acting, and my poor father lets himself be taken in by her pretence.'

'How do you feel, my good Père Goriot?' Rastignac asked the old man.

'I need some sleep,' he answered.

Eugène helped Goriot to bed. Then, when the old fellow had fallen asleep holding Delphine's hand, his daughter withdrew.

'I'll see you this evening at the Italiens,' she said to Eugène, 'and you can tell me how he is. Tomorrow you'll be moving out, Monsieur. Let's have a look at your room. Oh! how awful!' she said as she went in. 'But you were worse off than my father. Eugène, you have behaved well. I would love you even more for it if that were possible; but, my boy, if you want to make your fortune, you must not throw twelve thousand francs out of the window like that. The Comte de Trailles is a gambler. My sister chooses not to see that. He would have gone looking for his twelve thousand francs in the same place where he manages to win or lose piles of money.'

A groan brought them back to Goriot's room. They found him apparently asleep, but when the two lovers came near they heard the words, 'They are not happy!' Whether he was asleep or awake, he uttered the words in a tone which touched his daughter's heart so deeply that she went over to the wretched bed where her father lay and kissed him on the forehead. He opened his eyes and said: 'It's Delphine!'

'Well, how are you?' she asked.

'Fine,' he said, 'Don't worry, I'll be going out, be off with you children, have a good time.'

Eugène saw Delphine home, but worried by the state in which he had left Goriot, he declined dinner with her and returned to the Maison Vauquer. He found Père Goriot out of bed and about to sit down at table. Bianchon had placed himself so as to have a good view of the old vermicelli-merchant's face. When he saw Goriot pick up his bread and sniff it to identify the flour from which it was made, the student, noting in the automatic gesture no evidence of conscious awareness, indicated that he feared the worst.

'Come and sit by me, Monsieur, our medical expert from Cochin,' said Eugène.

Bianchon changed places all the more readily because he

thus came closer to the old boarder.

'What's wrong with him?' Rastignac asked.

'Unless I'm mistaken, it's all up with him! Something quite extraordinary must have happened to him. It looks to me as though he's on the point of an apoplexy from cerebral oedema.* Although the lower part of his face is fairly calm, the upper part is drawn and pulled up taut towards the forehead, do you see? Then the condition of his eyes is a specific symptom of exudate leaking in the brain. Don't they look as if they were full of fine specks of dust? Tomorrow morning I'll know more.'

'Is there any cure?'

'None. It might be possible to delay his death if there were some way of drawing off the pressure towards his extremities,* his legs, but if the symptoms haven't stopped by tomorrow evening the old fellow is doomed. Do you know what happened to cause his illness? He must have had a violent shock which caused a breakdown.'

'Yes,' said Rastignac, recalling how the two daughters had relentlessly battered away at their father's heart.

That evening at the Italiens Rastignac took some pains to avoid causing Madame de Nucingen undue alarm.

'Don't worry,' she replied, when he began to speak, 'my father is tough. Only, this morning we upset him a bit. Our fortunes are at stake, can you imagine what a total disaster that would be? I couldn't go on living but for the fact that your affection has made me indifferent to what I should once have considered an anguish too dreadful to survive. Today I have only one fear, I can imagine only one disaster, and that would be to lose the love which has made me glad to be alive. Apart from that love, nothing matters, nothing else in the world means anything to me. You are everything to me. If I enjoy being rich, it is to enable me to give you more pleasure. I am, to my shame, more lover than daughter. Why? I don't know. My whole life is in you. My father gave me a heart, but you made it beat. The whole world may condemn me, what do I care? So long as you, who have no right to

hold it against me, acquit me of the crimes to which an irresistible passion condemns me. Do you think I am an unnatural
daughter? Oh no. It's impossible not to love a father as good
as ours. Could I help it if he finally saw the natural conse-
quences of our deplorable marriages? Wasn't it up to him
to think it out for us? Today, I know, he is suffering as much
as we are, but what could we do about it? Console him! we
could never give him any consolation. Our resignation grieved
him more than our reproaches and complaints would have
hurt him. There are some situations in life in which there
is nothing but bitterness.'

Eugène remained silent, moved to tenderness by this
ingenuous expression of a genuine emotion. Parisian women
may often be false, drunk with vanity, selfish, flirtatious, cold,
yet it is certain that when they are really in love they sacrifice
more feelings than other women to their passion. They grow
out of all their pettiness and become sublime. Eugène was
struck too by the profound and judicious intelligence which
women bring to bear in judging the most natural feelings
once a privileged emotion has made them detached and objec-
tive observers. Madame de Nucingen was disturbed by
Eugène's continuing silence.

'What are you thinking about?' she asked.

'I am still hearing what you just said to me. Up till now
I believed that I loved you more than you loved me.'

She smiled and resisted the pleasure she felt, so that their
conversation should remain within the limits imposed by con-
vention. She had never before heard young love expressed
with such vibrant sincerity. A few more words, and she would
have been unable to restrain herself.

'Eugène,' she said, changing the subject, 'I suppose you don't
know what is going on? All Paris will be at Madame de Beauséant's tomorrow. The Rochefides and the Marquis d'Ajuda
have agreed to keep it dark, but the king is to sign the marriage
contract tomorrow, and your poor cousin still knows nothing
about it. She won't be able to cancel her reception, and the
marquis will not be present at her ball. Everyone is talking

of nothing else but this affair.'

'And the world is amused at such infamous behaviour and connives at it! Don't you realize that Madame de Beauséant will never survive it?'

'Oh no!' said Delphine with a smile, 'you don't know women of her sort. But all Paris will be at her house, and so shall I! I owe that good fortune to you, all the same.'

'But', said Rastignac, 'couldn't it be one of those absurd rumours that are always circulating in Paris?'

'We'll know the truth tomorrow.'

Eugène did not go back to the Maison Vauquer. He was too impatient to enjoy his new apartment. Whereas the night before he had been obliged to leave Delphine at one in the morning, now it was Delphine who left him at about two o'clock to go home. He slept in quite late next day and waited for Madame de Nucingen, who came about midday to have breakfast with him. Young people are so greedy for such delightful pleasures that he had almost forgotten Père Goriot. It was one long treat for him to get used to each elegant thing that now belonged to him, and Madame de Nucingen was there giving it all a new value. However, at about four o'clock the loving couple thought of Père Goriot as they recalled the happiness he promised himself in coming to live in their house. Eugène remarked that the old fellow must be brought there at once if he was going to be ill, and left Delphine while he hurried to the Maison Vauquer. Neither Père Goriot nor Bianchon were at table.

'Well!' the artist said to him, 'Père Goriot is out of action. Bianchon is up there with him. The old fellow saw one of his daughters, the Comtesse de *Restaurama*. Then he decided to go out and his condition got worse. Society is about to be deprived of one of its finest ornaments.'

Rastignac rushed towards the stairs.

'Hey! Monsieur Eugène!'

'Monsieur Eugène! Madame is calling you,' cried Sylvie.

'Monsieur,' the widow said, 'Monsieur Goriot and you were supposed to be out by the 15th February. It's now three days past the 15th; it's the 18th today. You'll have to pay me a month's rent for the two of you, but if you are willing to guarantee Père Goriot, your word will be enough for me.'

'Why? Don't you trust him?'

'Trust! If the old fellow went off his head and died his daughters wouldn't give me a farthing, and all his things aren't worth ten francs. This morning he took away his last bits of silver, I don't know why. He had got himself up like a young man. God forgive me, I think he was wearing rouge. He looked quite young again.'

'I'll take responsibility for everything,' said Eugène, with a shiver of horror, fearful of some disaster.

He went up to Père Goriot's room. The old man lay in bed, with Bianchon by his side.

'Good afternoon, Father,' said Eugène.

The old man gave him a sweet smile, and looking at him with glassy eyes replied, 'How is she?'

'Fine. And you?'

'Not so bad.'

'Don't tire him,' said Bianchon, leading Eugène into a corner of the room.

'Well?' said Rastignac.

'Only a miracle can save him. The cerebral oedema has developed. We have applied mustard plasters. Fortunately he can feel them; they are working.'

'Can he be moved?'

'Quite impossible. He must be left where he is; any physical movement and any excitement must be avoided.'

'My good Bianchon,' said Eugène, 'we'll look after him between us.'

'I have already sent for a senior doctor from my hospital.'

'And?'

'He'll deliver his verdict tomorrow evening. He promised to come after his tour of duty. Unfortunately this confounded old fellow did something most unwise this morning and won't give me an explanation. He is as stubborn as a mule. When I speak to him he pretends not to hear, and falls asleep so that he doesn't have to answer; or, if his eyes are open, he begins groaning. He went out early this morning, and has been walking about Paris, but no one knows where. He took with him everything he owned of any value. He went out to do some blasted deal and overdid things. One of his daughters has been.'

'The comtesse?' asked Eugène. 'A tall brunette, bright, pretty eyes, dainty feet, slender figure?'

'Yes.'

'Leave me alone with him for a moment,' said Rastignac, 'I'll get him to confess. He'll tell me everything.'

'I'll go and have my dinner in the meantime. Only try not to excite him too much; there's still some hope.'

'Don't worry.'

'They will have a fine time tomorrow,' Père Goriot said to Eugène once they were alone. 'They are going to a grand ball.'

'Whatever did you do this morning, Papa, to make you so ill this evening that you have to stay in bed?'

'Nothing.'

'Has Anastasie been?' asked Rastignac.

'Yes,' answered Père Goriot.

'Very well! Don't keep anything from me. What did she want this time?'

'Ah!' he replied, summoning up all his strength to speak, 'She was very unhappy, you see, my boy! Nasie hasn't a penny of her own since that business with the diamonds. She had ordered a gold lamé gown for the ball; it must look as dazzling on her as a jewel. Her dressmaker, wretched creature, would not allow her credit, and her maid paid out a thousand francs on account for the gown. Poor Nasie, to be reduced to that! It made my heart bleed. But the maid, seeing that Restaud had lost all faith in Nasie, was afraid of losing her money, and came to an agreement with the dressmaker that the gown would only be delivered when the thousand francs was repaid. The ball is tomorrow, the dress is ready, Nasie is in despair. She wanted to borrow my silver place settings to pawn them.

Her husband wants her to go to the ball to show off the diamonds she is supposed to have sold for the whole of Paris society to see. Could she tell that monster, "I owe a thousand francs, will you pay it?" Of course not. I quite understood that. Her sister Delphine will go dressed superbly. Anastasie mustn't be outdone by her younger sister. And then she is crying her eyes out, my poor daughter! I felt so humiliated at not having the twelve thousand francs yesterday that I would have given the rest of my miserable life to make up for that failure. Do you see? I was strong enough to bear anything, but being short of money that last time broke my heart. Oh! oh! I made up my mind like a shot, patched myself up, smartened up a bit. I got six hundred francs for my silverware and some buckles, then I pledged a year's annuity to Papa Gobseck in return for four hundred francs cash down. Bah! I'll just eat bread! That was enough for me when I was young, and it will be enough again now. At least she'll have a lovely evening, my Nasie. She'll be smartly turned out. I have the thousand-franc note there under my pillow. It gives me a warm glow to have something under my head that will bring poor Nasie some pleasure! She'll be able to sack that worthless Victoire of hers. Did you ever hear of such a thing, servants not trusting their masters? I'll be all right tomorrow, Nasie is coming at ten o'clock. I don't want them to think I'm ill; they wouldn't go to the ball, they'd be looking after me. Tomorrow Nasie will kiss me like her own child, and a hug from her will cure me. In fact wouldn't I have spent a thousand francs at the apothecary? I'd rather give the money to my Cure-all, my Nasie. At least I'll be giving her some comfort in her misery. That'll make up for the wrong I did in buying myself an annuity. She has sunk to the bottom of the pit, and I don't have the strength any more to pull her out. Oh! I'll go back into business. I'll go to Odessa to buy grain. Wheat there costs a third of what we have to pay here. Importing raw cereals may be forbidden, but the fine folk who make the laws didn't think of prohibiting products made from grain. Ha, ha! I thought that one up this morning! There are some good deals to be made in starches.'

'He's demented,' Eugène told himself as he looked at the old man. 'Come now, you must rest, don't talk ...'

Eugène went down to dinner when Bianchon came back. Then the two of them spent the night taking turns to watch over the patient, one reading his medical books, the other writing to his mother and sisters. Next day the patient's symptoms seemed, according to Bianchon, to give grounds for some hope, but they were such as to demand continuous care, which only the two students were able to provide and which cannot be described here without offending against the prudish phraseology of our times. The leeches applied to the old man's wasted body were accompanied by poultices, foot baths and medical operations requiring furthermore the strength and devotion of the two young men. Madame de Restaud never came; she sent a messenger to collect her money.

'I thought she would have come herself. But it's no bad thing, she would have been worried,' said the father, apparently quite happy at the way things had turned out.

At seven o'clock that evening Thérèse came with a letter from Delphine:

What are you doing then, my friend? I have hardly had time to know your love; am I already to be neglected? In the confidences we exchanged, pouring out our hearts to each other, you showed me so noble a soul that you must be one of those who remain ever faithful once they have seen how many and varied are the tones of love. As you said when you heard Moses' prayer:* 'For some people it is all on the same note, for others it is the infinite in music!' Remember that I am expecting you this evening to take me to Madame de Beauséant's ball. Monsieur d'Ajuda's marriage contract was definitely signed this morning at Court, and the poor vicomtesse only learned of it at two o'clock. All Paris will flock to her house, just as the crowd fills the place de Grève when there is to be an execution. Isn't it horrible to go and see whether this woman will hide her grief, whether she will die bravely? I should certainly not be going, my dear, if I had ever been to her house before; but she will certainly give no more receptions and all my efforts would have been wasted. Besides I am going for your sake too. I am awaiting you. If you are not with me in two hours' time I do not know if I could ever forgive you such disloyalty.

Rastignac took up a pen and replied as follows:

I am awaiting the doctor to tell me whether your father has any longer to live. He is a dying man. I will come and bring you the verdict, and I fear it will be a death sentence. You will see then whether you can go to the ball. With all my love.

The doctor came at half-past eight, and without expressing a favourable opinion, did not think that the end was imminent. He forecast alternating ups and downs, on which the life and sanity of the old man would depend.

'It would be better for him to die quickly,' was the doctor's last word.

Eugène left Père Goriot in Bianchon's care and went to take Madame de Nucingen the sad news, which, to his mind, imbued still with a sense of family duty, must check all feelings of joy.

'Tell her to enjoy herself despite all,' cried Père Goriot, who had seemed to be dozing, but sat up as Rastignac left.

The young man was grief-stricken when he arrived at Delphine's, to find her with her hair already done, her shoes on and ready except for putting on her ball-gown. But, like the last brush-strokes with which an artist completes his picture, the final touches required more time than the actual groundwork.

'Why, you are not dressed!' she said.

'But, Madame, your father ...'

'Always on about my father!' she exclaimed, cutting him short. 'But I don't need you to teach me my duty to my father. I have known my father a long time. Not a word, Eugène. I won't listen to you until you are dressed for the ball. Thérèse has put out all your things ready in your apartment. My carriage is ready, take it, then come back here. We'll talk about my father on the way to the ball. We must set off in good time. If we get caught in the line of carriages we'll be lucky to arrive at eleven o'clock.'

'Madame!'

'Off you go! Not a word,' she said, hurrying to her boudoir to fetch a necklace.

'Do go, then, Monsieur Eugène, you will make Madame angry,' said Thérèse, giving the young man a push, while he stood horrified that anyone could commit parricide with such elegance.

He went to dress, full of the most gloomy and depressing reflections. He saw society as an ocean of mire into which one had only to dip a toe to be buried in it up to the neck. 'The only crimes committed there are petty ones!' he said to himself. 'Vautrin was a bigger man than that.' He had seen the three major manifestations of society: Obedience, Struggle, and Revolt; Family, the World, and Vautrin, and he was afraid to choose. Obedience was tedious, Revolt impossible, Struggle uncertain. In his thoughts he returned to the bosom of his family. He remembered the pure emotions of that tranquil life, he recalled days spent among those who held him dear. By following the natural laws of hearth and home, those dear creatures found complete, unbroken, untroubled happiness. Despite such worthy thoughts, he did not feel bold enough to go to Delphine and confess the faith of pure souls by bidding her follow Virtue in the name of Love. The education on which he had embarked had already borne fruit. He already loved selfishly. An innate sense had enabled him to recognize the nature of Delphine's heart. He knew intuitively that she was quite capable of treading on her father's body in order to go to the ball; he was not forceful enough to make her listen to reason, not brave enough to displease her, not principled enough to leave her. 'She would never forgive me if I put her in the wrong in this situation,' he said to himself. Then he analysed the doctor's words, readily accepted the idea that Père Goriot was not as dangerously ill as he had thought. In a word he accumulated deadly arguments to justify Delphine. She did not realize her father's condition. The old man would send her off to the ball himself if she went to see him. The laws of society, inexorable in their formulation, often pass a verdict of guilt on an apparent criminal who deserves to be acquitted in view of the countless mitigating factors produced within families by differences of character, or diversity of interests and situations. Eugène wanted to deceive himself, he was quite ready to sacrifice his conscience for his mistress. In the past two days his whole life had changed. A woman had turned everything upside down, overshadowed his family, appropriated all he had for her own benefit. Rastignac and Delphine had met in ideal conditions for giving each other the most intense pleasure. Their long-nurtured passion had thrived on what is finally death to passion, pleasure. Possession of this woman made Eugène realize that up till then he had only felt desire for her, love came only in the aftermath of happiness; perhaps love is only gratitude for pleasure. Infamous or sublime, he adored this woman for the sensual delights he had brought her as a dowry, and for all those which he had received from her. Similarly, Delphine loved Rastignac as much as Tantalus would have loved the angel come to satisfy his hunger, or assuage the thirst of his parched throat.

'Well! How is my father?' Madame de Nucingen asked when he returned, dressed for the ball.

'Extremely ill,' he answered. 'If you want to give me proof of your affection, we'll dash off and see him.'

'All right, we'll do that,' she said, 'but after the ball. Dear Eugène, be nice and don't give me moral lectures, come along.'

They set off. Eugène stayed silent for part of the journey.

'What's the matter with you?' she asked.

'I can hear your father's dying gasps,' he replied, somewhat coolly, and began to describe with the fervent eloquence of youth the inhuman action to which vanity had driven Madame de Restaud, the fatal turn brought on by her father's ultimate act of devotion, and the final cost of Anastasie's ball-gown. Delphine wept.

'I am going to look hideous,' she thought, and her tears dried up. 'I'll go and look after my father, I won't leave his bedside,' she went on.

'Ah! that's how I wanted you to be,' exclaimed Rastignac.

The lamps from five hundred carriages lit up the approaches to the Hôtel de Beauséant. On each side of the brightly lit entrance stood a swaggering gendarme. High society had thronged there in such numbers, with everyone eager to see this great lady at the moment of her downfall, that the ground-floor apartments were already full when Madame de Nucingen and Rastignac arrived. Never since the time the whole Court rushed to the Grande Mademoiselle,* whose lover Louis XIV had wrenched from her, had any love affair ended with a more spectacular disaster than that of Madame de Beauséant. In such a situation the last daughter of the virtually royal house of Burgundy* proved herself able to rise above her misfortune, and until her final moments dominated the world whose vanities she had only accepted in order to exploit them for the triumph of her passion. The most beautiful women in Paris enlivened the reception with their dazzling dresses and smiles. The most distinguished courtiers, ambassadors, ministers, illustrious men of every kind, glittering with crosses, insignia, multi-coloured sashes, pressed round the vicomtesse. Strains of music from the orchestra echoed and re-echoed from the gilded panelling of this palace that seemed to its queen a desert waste. Madame de Beauséant stood at the entrance to the first room to receive her supposed friends. Dressed in white, her hair in simple braids without ornament, she looked calm and displayed neither grief nor arrogance nor simulated gaiety. No one could read her inner heart. She might have been a marble statue of Niobe. To her close friends there was sometimes a hint of mockery in her smile, but she appeared to everyone like her usual self, and looked so exactly as she had looked when happiness filled her with radiance, that even the least sensitive admired her, just as young Roman women applauded the gladiator who managed to die smiling. Society seemed to have put on all its finery in farewell tribute to one of its sovereigns.

'I was afraid you would not come,' she said to Rastignac.

'Madame,' he replied, his voice betraying his emotion, for

he took her words as a rebuke, 'I came so that I could be the last to leave.'

'Good,' she said, taking him by the hand, 'You are perhaps the only person here I can trust. My friend, make sure you love a woman whom you can love always. Never forsake a woman.'

Taking Rastignac's arm, she led him to a sofa in the room where people were gambling.

'Go and call on the marquis,' she told him, 'Jacques, my footman, will take you there, and give you a letter for him. I am asking him to return my letters. He'll hand them all back to you, I like to think. If you have my letters when you come back, go up to my room. Someone will let me know.'

She rose to meet the Duchesse de Langeais, her best friend, who was coming over to join them. Rastignac left, asked for the Marquis d'Ajuda at the Hôtel de Rochefide, where he was most likely spending the evening, and indeed found him there. The marquis invited him round to his own house, and, handing a box to the student, said, 'They are all in there.' He looked as though he would have liked to talk to Eugène, either to ask him how the ball was going and about the vicomtesse, or to admit that he was already filled with despair about his marriage, as was later to be the case, but there was a glint of pride in his eyes, and regrettably he had the courage to keep his noblest feelings to himself. 'Don't say anything to her about me, my dear Eugène.' He pressed Rastignac's hand sadly and with affection, and dismissed him with a gesture. Eugène returned to the Hôtel de Beauséant, and was shown into the vicomtesse's room, where he saw preparations for departure. He sat down by the fire, looked at the cedar-wood casket, and fell into a deeply melancholy reverie. For him Madame de Beauséant had the stature of the goddesses in the *Iliad*.

'Ah! my friend,' said the vicomtesse as she came in and laid a hand on Rastignac's shoulder.

He saw his cousin in tears, eyes uplifted, one hand

trembling, the other raised. She took the box suddenly, put it on the fire and watched it burn.

'They are dancing! They all came punctually, but death will be late coming. Hush! my friend,' she said, putting a finger on Rastignac's lips as he was about to speak. 'I shall never again see Paris or this society world. Tomorrow morning at five o'clock I am leaving to bury myself in the depths of Normandy. Ever since three o'clock this afternoon I have been obliged to make my preparations, sign documents, attend to business matters. I couldn't send anyone to ...' she paused. 'He was certain to be with ...' she paused again, overcome by grief. At such times everything is painful, and certain words cannot be uttered. 'In short,' she went on, 'I was counting on you this evening for this last service. I would like to give you some token of my friendship. I shall often think of you, looking so kind and noble, young and sincere in such a world as this where such qualities are so rare. Here,' she said, looking round, 'here is my glove-box. Every time I took gloves from it before a ball or a theatre I was sure I looked beautiful, because I was happy, and I never touched it without leaving in it some kindly thought. There is a lot of me in there, a whole Madame de Beauséant who has ceased to exist. Please take it. I'll see that it is delivered to your apartment in the rue d'Artois. Madame de Nucingen is looking in very good form this evening; you must love her truly. If we never see each other again, my friend, rest assured of my warmest good wishes for you, you have been so kind to me. Let's go down, I don't want people to think I have been crying. I have an eternity before me in which to be alone, with no one to call me to account for my tears. One more look round this room.' She paused, then hiding her eyes behind her hand for a moment, she wiped them, bathed them in cold water and took the student's arm. 'Let's go down!' she said.

Rastignac had never before known any emotion as powerful as this contact with a grief so nobly contained. Returning to the ball, Rastignac escorted Madame de Beauséant as she circulated among the guests, a last delicate mark of favour from this gracious lady. He soon caught sight of the two sisters, Madame de Restaud and Madame de Nucingen. The comtesse looked magnificent with all her diamonds splendidly displayed, though she must have felt them as hot coals, since she was wearing them for the last time. Powerful as her pride and love might be, she flinched before her husband's gaze. Such a sight did nothing to lighten Rastignac's gloomy thoughts. Behind the diamonds of the two sisters he saw once more Père Goriot lying on his wretched pallet. The vicomtesse misconstrued his melancholy expression and withdrew her arm.

'Go on. I don't want to deprive you of a pleasure,' she said.

Eugène was soon claimed by Delphine, pleased with the impression she was making and eager to lay at the student's feet the tributes she was collecting in this society where she was hoping to win acceptance.

'What do you think of Nasie?' she asked him.

'She sees even her father's death in terms of percentage profit,' said Rastignac.

At about four in the morning the crowd in the reception-rooms began to thin out. Soon the music stopped. The Duchesse de Langeais and Rastignac found themselves alone in the main room. The vicomtesse, expecting to find only the student there, came in after taking leave of Monsieur de Beauséant, who kept saying as he went off to bed:

'You are wrong, my dear, to go and shut yourself up at your age! Do stay with us.'

At the sight of the duchesse Madame de Beauséant could not suppress an exclamation of surprise.

'I guessed what you were about, Clara,' said Madame de Langeais. 'You are leaving, never to return, but before you go you must hear me out and we must understand each other.'

She took her friend by the arm, led her into the next room and there, looking at her with tears in her eyes, she hugged her and kissed her on both cheeks. 'I don't want to part from you coldly, my dear, that would lie too heavily on my conscience. You can trust me as you would yourself. You displayed real greatness this evening, I felt worthy of you and want to prove it. I have sometimes wronged you, I have not always behaved very well. Forgive me, my dear. I withdraw anything that may have hurt you, I wish I could take back my words. The same grief unites our two hearts, and I don't know which of us is going to be the more unhappy. Monsieur de Montriveau was not here this evening, you understand? No one who saw you at this ball, Clara, will ever forget you. For my part, I am going to make one last effort. If I fail, I shall go into a convent. And where are you going?'

'To Normandy, to Courcelles, to go on loving, praying, until the day God delivers me from this world.'

'Come, Monsieur de Rastignac,' said the vicomtesse in a voice unsteady with emotion, thinking the young man was waiting. The student bent his knee, took his cousin's hand and kissed it.

'Farewell, Antoinette!' went on Madame de Beauséant. 'I wish you happiness. As for you, you are happy, you are young, you can still believe in something,' she said to the student. 'As I leave this world, I am surrounded, like a privileged few on their death-beds, by people with sincere and faithful feelings!'

Rastignac left at about five o'clock, after seeing Madame de Beauséant into her travelling-coach and receiving her tearful farewell, proof that persons of the highest degree are not exempt from the laws of the heart and do not live untouched by sorrow, as some who court these people would have them believe. It was cold and damp as Eugène walked back to the Maison Vauquer. His education was almost complete.

'We shan't be able to save poor Père Goriot,' Bianchon said to him as Rastignac came into his neighbour's room.

'My friend,' said Eugène, after a look at the sleeping old man, 'stay on the path that leads to the modest goal you have been content to set yourself. As for me, I am in hell, and must stay there. No matter what ugly things you may hear about the world, you must believe them. A Juvenal could not depict the horrors masked by its gold and glittering jewels.'

Next day Rastignac was roused at about two in the afternoon by Bianchon, who had to go out, and asked him to look after Père Goriot, whose condition had grown seriously worse during the morning.

'The old fellow has less than two days, maybe less than six hours to live,' said the medical student, 'and yet we can't give up the fight against his sickness. He is going to need expensive treatment. We two will nurse him, of course, but I don't have a penny to my name. I've turned out his pockets, searched his cupboards: nil result. I questioned him during one of his lucid moments, and he said that he hadn't a brass farthing. What have you got?'

'I have twenty francs left,' said Rastignac, 'but I'll go gambling with it and win more.'

'And if you lose?'

'I will ask his sons-in-law and daughters for money.'

'And if they won't give you any?' went on Bianchon. 'The most urgent thing at the moment isn't finding money; we must wrap the old man up in a boiling mustard plaster from his feet to half-way up his thighs. If he cries out, there's still some hope. You know how to apply it. In any case Christophe will help. I'll go along to the apothecary to have them put on my account all the medicine we get there. It's a pity the poor man couldn't be moved to our hospital, he would have been better off there. Come on, let me see you settled in. Don't leave him before I come back.'

The two young men went into the room where the old man lay. Eugène was horrified at the change in the distorted face, drained of all colour and vitality.

'Well, Papa?' he said, leaning over the wretched bed.

Goriot raised dull eyes and stared hard at Eugène without recognizing him. The student found the sight too much for him; tears welled up in his eyes.

'Bianchon, shouldn't there be curtains at the windows?'

'No, atmospheric conditions don't affect him any more. I only wish he could feel heat or cold, but that's too much to hope for. All the same we shall need a fire for making him hot drinks and for preparing various things. I'll send up some bundles of sticks which will do until we can get some proper firewood. Yesterday and last night I burned what you had and all the poor man's peat. It was so damp in here the water was dripping from the walls. I was scarcely able to get the room dried out. Christophe took a broom to it, it's really as bad as a stable. I burned some juniper, the smell was so awful.'

'Good Lord!' said Rastignac, 'but what about his daughters?'

'Look, if he asks for a drink, give him some of this,' said the houseman, showing Rastignac a big white jug. 'If you hear him groan and his belly feels hot and hard, get Christophe to help you give him—you know. If by any chance he gets very excited, talks a lot, becomes a bit delirious, let him be. It won't be a bad sign. But send Christophe to Cochin; our doctor, my colleague or I will come and apply moxas.* This morning, while you were asleep, we had a major consultation with a pupil of Dr Gall, a senior doctor at the Hôtel-Dieu and our own man. These gentlemen thought they recognized some odd symptoms, and we are going to follow the progress of the illness to throw some light on a number of scientific points of some importance. One of them maintained that the pressure of the exudate on one part of the brain rather than another might produce specific effects. So listen to him carefully if he starts talking, so as to establish the class of ideas to which his words belong: whether they derive from memory, analysis or judgement; whether he is concerned with material things or emotions; whether he is making plans or going back into the past; in a word make sure you can give us an exact report. It is possible that the oedema may become generalized, in which case he'll die an imbecile as he is at the moment. In this kind of illness everything is most peculiar! If the balloon bursts here,' said Bianchon, indicating the occiput, 'there are examples of some very odd phenomena; the brain recovers some of its faculties, and death comes more slowly. The exudate may be drawn from the brain, and follow a course only detectable by an autopsy. At the Incurables hospital there is an old man reduced to total idiocy; in his case the oedema followed the spinal column. He is in terrible pain, but he is alive.'

'Did they have a good time?' asked Père Goriot, recognizing Eugène.

'Oh! all he thinks about is his daughters,' said Bianchon. He kept saying to me time after time last night, "They are dancing! She has her ball-gown." He called them by their names. He made me weep, devil take it! the way he said, "Delphine! my little Delphine! Nasie!" Upon my word,' said the medical student, 'it was enough to bring anyone to tears.'

'Delphine,' said the old man, 'she is there, isn't she? I knew she was.' And his eyes began feverishly scanning the walls and the door.

'I'll go down and tell Sylvie to prepare the mustard plasters,' cried Bianchon, 'This is a good moment for them.'

Rastignac stayed alone with the old man, sitting at the foot of the bed, gazing at the dreadful, heart-rending face.

'Madame de Beauséant has fled, the old man is dying,' he said, 'Noble souls cannot stay long in this world. Indeed, how could deep feelings keep company with such a mean, petty, superficial society?'

His memory brought back images of the party he had attended, contrasting with the death-bed scene before his eyes. Bianchon suddenly reappeared.

'Look, Eugène, I have just seen our senior doctor, and I've run all the way here. If he shows any signs of being rational, if he speaks, lay him on top of a long mustard poultice, so that he is wrapped in mustard from his neck to the base of his spine, and send for us.'

'Dear Bianchon,' said Eugène.

'Oh! it's a case of some scientific significance,' the medical student went on, with all the enthusiasm of a neophyte.

'Now, now,' said Eugène, 'so I'm the only one looking

after this poor old man out of affection.'

'If you had seen me this morning you wouldn't say that,' Bianchon replied, without taking offence at the remark. 'Doctors who have been in practice only see the illness, I can still see the patient, my dear fellow.'

He went off, leaving Eugène alone with the old man, and apprehensive of a crisis which was not long coming.

'Ah! it's you, my dear boy,' said Père Goriot, recognizing Eugène.

'Do you feel better?' asked the student, taking his hand.

'Yes, I do. My head felt as if it were being gripped in a vice, but it's clearing now. Did you see my daughters? They'll soon be coming to see me. They'll hurry here as soon as they hear I'm ill. They looked after me so well in the rue de la Jussienne! Goodness me! I wish my room were fit to receive them. There's some young fellow who burned up all my peat.'

'I hear Christophe,' Eugène told him, 'he's bringing up some firewood that young fellow has sent.'

'Good! But how am I going to pay for the wood? I haven't a penny, my boy. I have given away everything, everything! I'll have to live on charity. Was the gold lamé dress really beautiful though? (Oh! I'm in such pain!) Thank you, Christophe. God will reward you, my lad; I have nothing left myself.'

'I'll pay you well, you and Sylvie,' Eugène whispered to the lad.

'My daughters did tell you they would come, didn't they, Christophe? Go to them again. I'll give you five francs. Tell them I don't feel well, and I'd like to embrace them and see them once more before I die. Tell them that, but don't frighten them unduly.'

At a sign from Rastignac Christophe went out.

'They'll come,' went on the old man, 'I know them. Dear good Delphine, how I'll upset her if I die! Nasie too. I'd rather not die, to spare their tears. Dying, my good Eugène, means not seeing them again. I'll find the place I'm going to very dull. For a father, hell is being without his children, and I've already served my apprenticeship at that since they were married. My heaven was the rue de la Jussienne. You know what, if I go to heaven I'll be able to come back to earth as a spirit and be beside them. I have heard tell of that sort of thing. Is it true? Just at this moment I can picture them as they were at the rue de la Jussienne. They would come down in the morning "Good morning, Papa," they would say. I used to take them on my knee, play all kinds of teasing games and tricks on them. They would kiss me so sweetly. Every morning we had breakfast together, we had dinner together, I really was a father. I delighted in my children. When they lived in the rue de la Jussienne they didn't argue, they didn't know anything about the world, they truly loved me. Goodness! Why couldn't they always have stayed children? (Oh! I'm in such pain! My head is killing me.) Ah! ah! I'm sorry, children! The pain is so terrible, and it must be real agony, because you have hardened me to mere hurt. Goodness! If only I could hold their hands I wouldn't feel the pain. Do you think they are coming? Christophe is so stupid, I should have gone myself. He'll be able to see them. But you were at the ball yesterday, tell me how they were? They didn't know anything about my illness, did they? They wouldn't have gone dancing, poor girls! Oh! I don't want to go on being ill. They still need me too much. Their fortunes are in jeopardy. And look at the husbands at whose mercy they are! Cure me, cure me! (Oh! the pain! ah! ah! ah!) You see, I must be cured, because they need money, and I know where to earn it. I'll go to Odessa and make starch crystals. I'm a crafty fellow, I'll make millions. (Oh! the pain is too much!)'

Goriot stayed silent for a moment, apparently striving with all his might to summon up enough strength to bear the pain.

'If they were here I shouldn't be moaning,' he said, 'so why moan now?'

He fell into a light doze which lasted a long time. Christophe came back. Thinking Père Goriot was asleep, Rastignac let the servant report on his mission without lowering his voice.

'Monsieur,' he said, 'first I went to Madame la comtesse, but I was not able to speak to her, she had important matters to discuss with her husband. When I persisted, Monsieur de Restaud himself came, and said to me just like that, "Monsieur Goriot is dying, is he? Well that's the best thing he could do. I need to finish off some important business with Madame de Restaud. She'll come as soon as it is all settled ..." He looked very angry, the gentleman did. I was just going out, when Madame came into the anteroom through a door I hadn't noticed, and said, "Christophe, tell my father I am having a discussion with my husband, and I can't leave him; it's a matter of life and death for my children; but as soon as it's all settled, I'll come." As for Madame la baronne, that's another story! I didn't see her, and was not able to speak to her. "Ah!" her maid told me, "Madame came home from the ball at a quarter-past five and she's asleep. If I wake her up before noon she'll scold me. I'll tell her that her father is worse when she rings for me. When it comes to giving her bad news, any time is soon enough." It was no good begging her! That's a fact! I asked to speak to Monsieur le baron, but he was out.'

'Neither of his daughters is coming!' exclaimed Rastignac, 'I'll write to both of them.'

'Neither one,' answered the old man, sitting up in bed. 'They are busy, they are sleeping, they won't come. I knew it. You have to be dying to learn what children are. Ah! my friend, don't get married, don't have children! You give them life, they give you death. You bring them into the world, they drive you out of it. No, they won't come! For ten years I have known how it would be. I sometimes said so to myself, but I didn't dare to believe it.'

Tears welled up in his red-rimmed eyes, but did not fall.

'Ah! if I were rich, if I had kept my fortune, if I had not given it away to them, they would be here, smothering my face with their kisses! I should be living in a mansion, I should have fine rooms, servants, my own fire; and they would be there, bathed in tears, with their husbands and children. I would have all of that. But now I have nothing. Money buys anything, even daughters. Oh! where is my money? If I still had wealth to leave, they would be tending me, looking after me; I should hear them, see them. Ah! my dear boy, my only child, I'd rather be abandoned and wretched as I am! At least when a poor wretch is loved he can be sure of that love. No, I'd rather be rich, I could see them then. My word, who knows? They both have hearts of stone. I gave them too much love for them to have any for me. A father should always be rich, he should keep his children on a rein as he would a restive horse. And I went down on my knees to them. What wretches! This is a fitting climax to the treatment I've had from them over the past ten years. If you knew how attentive they were to me when they were first married! (Oh! this pain is sheer torture!) I had just given each of them nearly eight hundred thousand francs, and neither they nor their husbands could very well be rude to me. They welcomed me with "Father" here, "my dear Father" there. My place at their tables was always laid. In fact I dined with their husbands, who treated me with every consideration. It looked as though I might still have something left. Why? I never said anything about my affairs. A man who can give eight hundred thousand francs to both his daughters is a man to be handled with care. So they were most attentive, but it was all for my money. High society is not all that fine, I saw that for myself! They would drive me to the theatre in a carriage, and I stayed as long as I liked at their parties. In a word they called themselves my daughters, and acknowledged me as their father. I am still pretty shrewd, though, and not much escaped me. It was all done with an aim in view, and that was like a stab in the heart. I saw very well that it was all a charade, but there was no way to put things right. I didn't feel as much at ease in their houses as at the table downstairs here. I never knew what to say. So when some of these society people whispered in my son-in-law's ear, "Whoever is that gentleman?"—"He's daddy moneybags, he is a rich man"—"The devil he is!" they would say, and look at me with all the respect due to moneybags. But if I sometimes caused them a bit of embarrassment, I more than redeemed my failings! Besides, is anyone perfect? (My head's like an open wound!) At the moment, dear Monsieur Eugène, I am suffering as one has to suffer when one is dying; well! this is nothing compared to the pain I felt the first time Anastasie gave me a look that made me realize I had just said something stupid which humiliated her; her look cut right through me. I would like to have been knowledgeable, but one thing I knew for sure was that I was in the way here on earth. Next day I went round to Delphine for consolation, and there I committed some stupid blunder that made her angry with me too. I felt as if I were going mad. For a week I didn't know which way to turn. I didn't dare go and see them, for fear of their rebukes. So there I was, shown the door by my own daughters. Oh, God, since you know the misery and suffering I have endured; since you know how often I have been stabbed in the back throughout this time that has aged me, broken me, changed me, turned my hair white, why do you make me go on suffering today? I have fully expiated my sin of loving them too dearly. They have exacted revenge in full for my affection, they have tortured me like executioners. Yes, indeed, fathers are so stupid! I loved them so dearly that I went back to them like a gambler to the gaming table. My vice was my daughters; for me they were mistresses, everything. They were both always needing some finery or other. Their maids would tell me, and I would give it to them to earn a welcome! But all the same they gave me a few little lessons on social behaviour. Oh! Their patience soon ran out. They were beginning to be ashamed of me. That's what comes of giving one's children a good education. But at my age I couldn't go back to school. (God, this pain is terrible! Doctors! doctors! if they could open my head up it wouldn't hurt so much!) My daughters, my daughters, Anastasie, Delphine! I want to see them! Send the police after them, force them to come! Justice is on my side, everything is on my side, nature, civil law. I protest. The country will perish if fathers are trampled down. That's obvious. Society, the world, turns on fatherhood, everything breaks up if children don't love their fathers. Oh! if I could see them, hear them, whatever they might say, so long as I could hear their voices, that would ease the pain, particularly Delphine. But tell them, when they come, not to give me the chilly looks they usually do. Ah! my good friend, Monsieur Eugène, you don't know what it means to find a look of pure gold suddenly change into leaden blankness. Ever since their eyes stopped shining on me it has been winter all the time, bitterness has been my only portion, and I have drained the cup to the dregs. My life has been all humiliation and insults. I love them so much that I swallowed all the indignities they set as their price for allowing me a few pathetic little moments of guilty pleasure. A father hiding himself to see his daughters! I have given them my whole life, and they won't give me just one hour today! I thirst, I hunger, my heart burns within me, and they won't come to lighten my last moments, for I am dying, I can feel it. But don't they know then what it means to tread on your father's corpse! There is a God in heaven to avenge us fathers, though we may not ask for revenge. Oh! They will come! Come my darlings, come and give me a kiss, one last time, a viaticum for your father, who will pray to God for you, say that you have been good daughters, plead for you! After all, you are innocent. They are innocent, my friend! Make sure you tell everyone, so that they are not harried on my account. It's all my fault, I let them grow used to trampling me underfoot. I liked it, in fact. It is no concern of anyone else, not of human or divine justice. God would be unjust if he condemned them because of me. I didn't know how to behave, I was stupid enough to renounce my rights. I would have stooped to anything for their sakes! What do you expect? The noblest nature, the best of souls would have given way before the corruption of such paternal indulgence. I am a wretch, justly punished.

I am the sole cause of my daughters' misconduct, I spoiled them. Today it's pleasure they want, as they once used to want sweets. I always let them gratify their childish whims, they had their own carriage at fifteen! They always got their own way. I alone am guilty, but guilty out of love. Their voice would tug at my heartstrings. I can hear them, they are coming. Oh! yes, they'll come. It is the law that one must come and see one's father die, the law is on my side. In any case it will only cost them a cab-ride, and I'll pay for that. Write and tell them I have millions to leave them! Word of honour. I'll go to Odessa and make Italian pasta. I know how. There are millions to be made from this scheme of mine. No one has ever thought of it before. That won't spoil in transit like wheat or flour. Eh, eh and starch? There's millions in that! You won't be telling them a lie, say millions, and even if they only come out of greed, I'd rather be deceived, at least I'll see them. I want my daughters! I made them! they are mine!' he said, sitting up in bed, head turned towards Eugène with every scanty white hair bristling and menace written in every line of his face.

'Come now,' Eugène said to him, 'lie down again, good Père Goriot. I'll write to them. As soon as Bianchon returns I'll go for them if they don't come.'

'If they don't come?' the old man repeated, sobbing. 'But I shall be dead, dead in a fit of rage, rage, rage! Rage is overcoming me! At this moment I can see my whole life. I have been their dupe! They don't love me, they have never loved me! That is quite clear. If they haven't come, they won't come now. The more they delay, the less likely they are to make up their minds to give me that joy. I know them. They have never had the slightest inkling of my troubles, my sufferings, my needs. They won't have any better idea of my death; they don't even share the secret of my affection. Yes, I can see that my habit of giving with heart and soul has cheapened everything I did for them. If they had asked to gouge out my eyes, I would have told them, "Gouge them out." I have been so stupid. They think all fathers are like theirs. One must always insist on proper respect. Their children will avenge me. But it is in their own interest to come. Warn them then that they are putting their own last hours at risk. They are committing every crime with this one. Go then, tell them that failure to come amounts to parricide! They have committed enough crimes without adding that one. Cry out as I am doing, "Hey, Nasie! Hey, Delphine! Come to your father who has been so good to you and is in pain!" Nothing, no one. Am I then to die like a dog? That's my reward, to be deserted. They are infamous, wicked. I abominate, I curse them. At night I shall rise from my coffin to curse them anew, for really, friends, is it wrong of me? They are behaving so badly! Eh! what am I saying? Didn't you tell me Delphine was here? She's the kinder of the two. You are my son, Eugène, you! Love her, be a father to her. Her sister is very unhappy. And their fortunes! Ah, God! I am at my last gasp, the pain is a bit too much for me! Cut off my head, just leave my heart.'

'Christophe, go and get Bianchon,' cried Eugène, frightened at the way the old man was now groaning and crying, 'and fetch a cab for me.'

'I'm going to fetch your daughters, my good Père Goriot, and bring them back here.'

'Use force, force! Demand the guards, soldiers of the line, everyone! everyone!' he said, looking at Eugène with a last flicker of sanity. 'Tell the government, the Attorney-General, to have them brought to me. That's what I want!'

'But you cursed them.'

'Whoever said so?' the old man replied in astonishment. 'You know very well that I love them, I adore them! I'd be cured if I could see them ... Go, my good neighbour, my dear boy, go. You are a kind man. I would like to show my thanks, but all I have to give you is a dying man's blessing. Ah! I would like to see Delphine at least to tell her to pay off my debt to you. If her sister can't come, bring Delphine. Tell her that you won't go on loving her if she refuses to come. She loves you so much that she will come. Give me a drink, my insides are on fire! Put something on my head. My daughters' hand would save me, I feel sure ... Goodness! who will build up their fortunes again if I go? I want to go to Odessa for them, to Odessa, to manufacture pasta.'

'Drink this,' said Eugène, raising the dying man with his left arm while the other held a cup of tisane.

'You must love your father and mother!' said the old man, clasping Eugène's hand feebly in his own. 'Do you realize that I am going to die without seeing my daughters? Always thirsty, and with never a drop to drink, that's how I have lived for the past ten years ... two sons-in-law have killed my daughters. Yes, I have had no daughters since their marriage. Fathers, tell the Chambers to introduce a bill on marriage! In fact don't let your daughters marry if you love them. A son-in-law is a rogue who spoils and soils everything in a daughter. No more marriages! That's what takes our daughters away from us, and we don't have them any more when we are dying. Bring in a bill on dying fathers. It's appalling, this is! Revenge! It is my sons-in-law who are preventing them from coming. Kill them! Death to Restaud, death to the Alsatian, they are my murderers! Death or my daughters! Ah! it is finished, I'm dying without them. Nasie, Fifine, come on, do come! Your papa is leaving ...'

'My good Père Goriot, calm down, now, now, stay quiet, don't upset yourself, don't think about it.'

'Not seeing them, that's the real agony!'

'You are going to see them.'

'Truly!' cried the confused old man. 'Oh! to see them, to hear their voices! I'll die happy. Yes, indeed, I don't ask to go on living, I had lost interest in that, the sorrows kept getting worse. But to see them, touch their dresses, ah! just their dresses, that's little enough. Let me just feel something of theirs! Let me touch their hair ... haaair.'

His head fell back on the pillow as though he had been clubbed. His hands fluttered on the blanket as if searching for his daughters' hair.

'They have my blessing,' he said with an effort, 'my

blessing.'

He suddenly collapsed. At that moment Bianchon came in.

'I ran into Christophe,' he said, 'he is going to get you a cab.' Then he looked at the sick man, and pulled back his eyelids; the two students saw the eyes, now cold and lifeless.

'He won't recover now,' said Bianchon, 'I don't think so.' He felt for a pulse, put his hand on the old man's heart.

'The machine is still running, but in his condition that's a great pity. It would be better for him to die.'

'My word, it would,' said Rastignac.

'What's the matter with you? You have gone deathly pale.'

'My friend, I have been listening to him crying and moaning. There is a God! Oh! yes, there is a God, and he must have made a better world for us, or life on earth makes no sense. If it had not been so tragic I should burst into tears, but I am gripped by a terrible feeling of anguish.'

'Look, we are going to need lots of things; where are we going to get some money?'

Rastignac pulled out his watch.

'Here, quick, go and pawn this. I don't want to stop on the way, for I'm afraid of losing a minute and I'm only waiting for Christophe. I haven't a brass farthing, and I'll have to pay my cabby when I come back.'

Rastignac hurtled down the stairs, and left for Madame de Restaud's house in the rue du Helder. On the way the appalling scene he had witnessed affected him so deeply that recalling it fuelled his anger. When he arrived in the anteroom and asked for Madame de Restaud, he was informed that she was not seeing anyone.

'But', he said to the footman, 'I am here on behalf of her dying father.'

'Monsieur, Monsieur le comte has given us the strictest orders.'

'If Monsieur de Restaud is there, inform him of his father-in-law's condition and tell him that I must speak to him immediately.'

Eugène waited a long time.

'Perhaps he is passing away at this very moment,' he thought.

The footman showed him into the first drawing-room, where Monsieur de Restaud received him standing, without offering him a seat, in front of an empty fireplace.

'Monsieur le comte,' Rastignac said to him, 'Monsieur Goriot your father-in-law is at this moment breathing his last in a squalid hovel, without a farthing to buy wood for a fire. He is about to die and is asking to see his daughter ...'

'Monsieur,' the Comte de Restaud replied coldly, 'you may have observed that I feel very little affection for Monsieur Goriot. He has discredited himself with Madame de Restaud, he has caused me great misfortunes. I regard him as a trouble-maker. Whether he dies or lives is a matter of absolute indiffer-ence to me. That is how I feel about him. People may blame me; I despise public opinion. I have more important things in hand just now than concerning myself with what fools or people of no account may think of me. As for Madame de Restaud, she is in no state to go out. Besides, I do not wish her to leave the house. Tell her father that as soon as she has done her duty by me and my son she will come to see him. If she really loves her father she could be free in a few minutes ...'

'Monsieur le comte, it is not for me to judge your conduct, you have authority over your wife, but can I rely on your word? Well, then, simply promise to tell her that her father will not live another day, and has already cursed her for not being at his bedside.'

'Tell her yourself,' replied Monsieur de Restaud, impressed by the indignation evident in Eugène's tones.

Rastignac followed the comte into the room where the com-tesse was usually to be found. He saw her drenched in tears, huddled in the depths of an armchair, like a woman who longed to die. He felt sorry for her. Before looking at Rastig-nac, she cast timid glances at her husband, showing how utterly his physical and moral tyranny had crushed her into helpless submission. The comte nodded, and she took this as permission to speak.

'Monsieur, I heard everything. Tell my father that if he knew my present predicament he would forgive me. I was not expecting such torture, it is more than I can stand, Monsieur, but I shall resist to the end,' she said to her husband. 'I am a mother. Tell my father that I am blameless where he is concerned, despite all appearances,' she cried in despair to the student.

Eugène took his leave of the couple, guessing the wife's dreadful situation, and withdrew, stunned with shock. Monsieur de Restaud's tone had shown him how useless his initiative had been, and he realized that Anastasie was no longer free. He hurried to Madame de Nucingen's house, and found her in bed.

'I am not well, my poor friend,' she told him, 'I caught a chill coming away from the ball. I'm afraid of catching pneumonia. I'm expecting the doctor ...'

'Even if you are at death's door,' said Eugène, interrupting her, 'you must drag yourself to your father's side. He is calling for you. If you could hear his least cry you would stop feeling ill yourself.'

'Eugène, perhaps my father is not as ill as you say; but I should be desperately sorry to appear the least bit blameworthy in your eyes, and I shall behave just as you wish. Father, I know, would die of grief if my illness proved fatal as a result of my going out now. Very well! I'll come as soon as the doctor has been. Ah! Why aren't you wearing your watch any more?' she asked, noticing that the chain was missing. Eugène went red. 'Eugène, Eugène, if you have already sold it, or lost it ... oh! that would be very wicked of you!'

The student bent over Delphine's bed and whispered in her ear, 'You really want to know? All right! I'll tell you! Your father has no money to buy the shroud he'll be wrapped in this evening. I have pawned your watch, it was all I had left.'

Delphine suddenly jumped out of bed, ran to her desk, took out her purse and handed it to Rastignac. She rang and cried, 'I'll come, I'll come, Eugène. Let me get dressed; but I should be a monster if I didn't! Go on, I'll be there before you! Thérèse,' she called to her maid, 'ask Monsieur de Nucingen to come up for a word with me right away.'

Eugène, glad to be able to tell the dying man that one of his daughters was coming, was almost cheerful when he reached the rue Neuve-Sainte-Geneviève. He rummaged in the purse for money to pay the cabby without delay. The purse of this rich and elegant young woman contained just seventy francs. Hurrying up the stairs, he found Père Goriot supported by Bianchon, while the surgeon from the hospital worked on him under the doctor's supervision. They were burning his back with moxas, the ultimate remedy available to medical science, but a remedy with no effect.

'Can you feel them?' the doctor asked.

Père Goriot, catching sight of the student, answered:

'They are coming, aren't they?'

'He may come out of it yet,' said the surgeon, 'he can still speak.'

'Yes,' answered Eugène, 'Delphine is on her way.'

'Come now,' said Bianchon, 'he was talking about his daughters. He's calling out for them as a man impaled on a stake cries for water, so they say.'

'Stop now,' the doctor told the surgeon, 'there's nothing more to be done, we shan't save him.'

Bianchon and the surgeon laid the dying man down flat on his filthy pallet.

'The linen ought to be changed, though,' said the doctor. 'Although there's no hope now, the human being in him deserves respect. I'll come back, Bianchon,' he said to the student. 'If he complains again, apply opium to his diaphragm.'

Surgeon and doctor left.

'Come, Eugène, cheer up my son!' said Bianchon to Rastignac when they were alone. 'We'll put a clean shirt on him and change his bedding. Go and tell Sylvie to bring up some sheets and give us a hand.'

Eugène went down and found Madame Vauquer laying the table with Sylvie. As soon as Rastignac began to speak to her, she came up to him, with the sweet and sour look of a suspicious shopkeeper equally unwilling to lose money or offend the customer.

'My dear Monsieur Eugène,' she said, 'you know as well as I do that Père Goriot hasn't a penny left. Giving sheets to a man who's about to croak is a pure waste, especially as one sheet will have to be written off for the shroud. So, you already owe me a hundred and forty four francs; let's say forty for sheets and a few other sundries, the candle that Sylvie will give you; that all comes to at least two hundred francs, which a poor widow like me can't afford to lose. Why, be fair, Monsieur Eugène, I've lost quite enough these last five days with all the bad luck that's come on my house. I would have given thirty francs to have got the old fellow away these last few days, as you said he would be. It's affecting my boarders. For two pins I would have him taken to the poorhouse. My boarding house comes first, it's my whole life after all.'

Eugène hurried back to Père Goriot's room.

'Bianchon, where's the money from the watch?'

'Over there on the table. There's three sixty and some odd francs left. I've paid off all we owed out of what I got for it. The ticket is under the money.'

Rastignac rushed down the stairs filled with dread, and said, 'Here you are, Madame, settle our accounts with this. Monsieur Goriot won't be staying with you for long, and I ...'

'Yes, he'll go out feet first, poor old fellow,' she said, counting out two hundred francs, her face registering delight and sadness in equal measure.

'Let's have done,' said Rastignac.

'Sylvie, give him the sheets, and go up and help the gentlemen.'

'You won't forget Sylvie,' Madame Vauquer whispered in Eugène's ear, 'she's been up the past two nights.'

As soon as Eugène's back was turned the old woman rushed to her cook, 'Take those remade sheets from number seven. 'Pon my soul, that's quite good enough for a dead man,' she said in a low voice.

Eugène, who had already started up the stairs, did not hear their old hostess's words.

'Come now,' Bianchon said to him, 'let's put on his shirt. Hold him up straight.'

Eugène went to the head of the bed and supported the dying man, while Bianchon removed his shirt. The old man made a movement as if to keep something he had on his chest, and uttered inarticulate, doleful cries like an animal in great pain.

'Oh! oh!' said Bianchon, 'he wants a little chain of woven hair with a little locket that we took off him earlier so that we could apply the moxas. Poor man! We must give it back to him. It's on the mantelpiece.'

Eugène went over to fetch a chain woven from ash-blonde hair, no doubt Madame Goriot's. On one side of the locket he read *Anastasie*, and on the other *Delphine*. A symbol of his inmost heart which he always wore over his heart. The locks of hair it contained were so fine that they must have been cut when his daughters were very small. When the locket touched his chest, the old man gave a long sigh of content; it was an awesome sight, a last ripple of a consciousness which seemed to be withdrawing into that secret core which both transmits and receives our reactions to the world outside. His distorted features took on an expression of unnatural joy. The two students, impressed by this frightening outburst of emotion, powerful enough to survive the faculty of thought, both wept tears over the dying man, who gave a shrill cry of pleasure:

'Nasie! Fifine!' he cried.

'He's still alive,' said Bianchon.

'What's the point?' said Sylvie.

'To go on suffering,' answered Rastignac.

Bianchon, making a sign to his companion to follow his lead, knelt down to slip his arms under the patient's knees, while Rastignac did likewise on the other side of the bed to get his hands under the patient's back. Sylvie stood ready to pull off the sheets once the dying man was lifted clear, and then replace them by those she had brought. No doubt misled by feeling the students' tears, Goriot stretched out his hands with a supreme effort, felt their heads on either side of the bed, grasped them convulsively by the hair and could just be heard feebly muttering: 'Ah! my angels!' Two words, two whispers, emphasized by the soul passing away as they were spoken.

'Poor dear man,' said Sylvie, touched by this exclamation, expressive of a supreme emotion which the most gruesome, most involuntary deception had excited for the last time.

The father's last sigh was to be a sigh of joy. That sigh summed up his whole life; he deceived himself to the end. Père Goriot was laid down again reverently on his bed. From that moment his features bore the painful imprint of the life-and-death struggle being waged in a machine now deprived of the mental awareness which allows the human being to feel pleasure and pain. Destruction was now only a question of time.

'He'll stay like that for some hours yet, and die without anyone noticing. There won't even be a death-rattle. The oedema must have spread over his whole brain.'

Just at that moment they heard a young woman panting up the stairs.

'She has come too late,' said Rastignac.

It was not Delphine, but her maid, Thérèse.

'Monsieur Eugène,' she said, 'Monsieur and Madame have had a violent argument over the money that my poor mistress wanted for her father. She fainted, the doctor came. She had to be bled, and she kept crying, "My father is dying, I want to see papa." Truly heart-rending cries.'

'That will do, Thérèse. Even if she came there would be

no point now. Monsieur Goriot is no longer conscious.'

'Poor dear gentleman, is he as bad as that!' said Thérèse.

'You don't need me any more, I must go and see to my dinner, it's half-past four,' said Sylvie, almost colliding with Madame de Restaud at the head of the stairs.

The appearance of the comtesse was solemn and terrible. She looked at the death-bed, lit dimly by a single candle, and shed tears as she took in her father's dying mask, still twitching with the last flickers of life. Bianchon withdrew discreetly.

'I couldn't get away soon enough,' the comtesse said to Rastignac.

The student sadly nodded assent. Madame de Restaud took her father's hand and kissed it.

'Forgive me, Father! You used to say that my voice would bring you back from the grave; very well, come back to life for a moment to bless your penitent daughter. You must hear me. This is appalling! Now the only blessing I can ever receive on earth is from you. Everyone else hates me, you are the only one who loves me. Even my children hate me. Take me with you, I'll love you, look after you. He can't hear any more, I'm going out of my mind.' She fell to her knees and gazed at the wreck of a body as though delirious.

'My misery is complete,' she said, looking at Eugène, 'Monsieur de Trailles has gone, leaving behind huge debts, and I have learned that he was deceiving me. My husband will never forgive me, and I have handed over control of my fortune to him. I have lost all my illusions. Alas! For whose sake did I betray the only heart (pointing to her father) which adored me? I ignored him, rejected him, hurt him time after time, shameful wretch that I am!'

'He knew it,' said Rastignac.

Just then Père Goriot opened his eyes, but it was only the effect of a spasm. The comtesse's eager start of renewed hope was in its way as dreadful a sight as the eyes of the dying man.

'Can he hear me?' cried the comtesse. 'No,' she answered

herself, as she sat down beside him.

As Madame de Restaud had expressed the wish to watch over her father, Eugène went down for a bite to eat. The boarders were already gathered round the table.

'Well,' the artist said to him, 'apparently we are going to have a little *deathorama* upstairs?'

'Charles,' said Eugène, 'it seems to me that you ought to find a less mournful subject for your jests.'

'So we can't have a laugh here any more?' retorted the artist. 'What does it matter, since Bianchon says the old man is quite unconscious?'

'Well,' the Museum attendant put in, 'then he will die as he lived.'

'My father is dead!' cried the comtesse.

At this terrible cry, Sylvie, Rastignac and Bianchon ran upstairs and found Madame de Restaud in a faint. When they had brought her round, they helped her down the stairs into the waiting cab. Eugène handed her into Thérèse's care, with orders to drive her to Madame de Nucingen.

'Oh, he is dead right enough,' said Bianchon as he came down.

'Come now, gentlemen, sit down to your dinner,' said Madame Vauquer, 'the soup will get cold.'

The two students sat next to one another.

'What is there to be done now?' Eugène asked Bianchon.

'Well, I've closed his eyes and arranged him decently. When we've reported his death at the town hall and had it certified by the doctor there, he'll be sewn up into a shroud and buried. What do you expect us to do with him?'

'He won't be sniffing his bread like this any more,' said one of the boarders, wrinkling his nose in imitation of the old man.

'Hang it all, gentlemen,' said the tutor, 'can't you give Père Goriot a rest and stop ramming him down our throats? For the past hour we've had him served up this way and that. One of the privileges of this good city of Paris is that you can be born there, live and die there, without anyone taking

any notice. So let's avail ourselves of the benefits of civilization. There'll be sixty deaths today, do you want to make
us weep over the massive heaps of Parisian dead? If Père Goriot
has croaked, so much the better for him! If you adore him
so much, go and watch over him and let the rest of us eat
in peace.'

'Oh! yes,' said the widow, 'so much the better for him
if he is dead! It seems that the poor man had to put up with
a load of trouble all his life long.'

This was the only funeral tribute to a person who, for
Eugène, represented Fatherhood. The fifteen boarders began
to chat as they usually did. When Eugène and Bianchon had
finished eating, the clink of forks and spoons, the talk and
laughter, the various expressions on these greedy, indifferent
faces, their total unconcern, the whole atmosphere chilled
them with horror. They went out to find a priest to watch
and pray beside the body during the night. They had to gauge
the last respects due to the old man by the limited sum of
money they had available. At about nine in the evening the
body was placed on the bed frame, with a candle to either
side, in that bare room, and a priest came to sit by it. Before
going to bed Rastignac had made enquiries of the cleric as
to the cost of the funeral service and arrangements, and wrote
a note to the Baron de Nucingen and the Comte de Restaud,
requesting them to send their representatives with money
to cover the funeral expenses. He sent Christophe to deliver
the notes, then went to bed and fell asleep overcome with
weariness. Next morning Bianchon and Rastignac were
obliged to go and report the death themselves, and the certificate was issued at about midday. Two hours later neither
of the sons-in-law had sent any money, no one had appeared
in their name, and Rastignac had already had to pay the priest's
fee. When Sylvie asked for ten francs to lay out the old man
and sew him in a shroud, Eugène and Bianchon worked out
that if the dead man's family refused to be involved, they
would scarcely have enough to meet their expenses. The medical student therefore undertook to lay out the body himself

in a pauper's coffin, and had one sent round from his hospital, where he could get it on more favourable terms.

'Play a trick on these rascals,' he said to Eugène. 'Go and buy a plot for five years at the Père Lachaise, and order a third-class service from the church and the undertakers. If the sons-in-law and daughters won't reimburse you, have this inscription carved on the gravestone: "Here lies Monsieur Goriot, father of the Comtesse de Restaud and the Baronne de Nucingen, buried at the expense of two students."'

Eugène only followed his friend's advice after paying fruitless calls on Monsieur and Madame de Nucingen and Monsieur and Madame de Restaud. He got no further than the door. The porters in each case had strict orders.

'Monsieur and Madame', they said, 'are receiving no one. Their father has died and they are in deepest mourning.'

Eugène had enough experience of Paris society to know that he must not press this point. His heart felt strangely constricted when he realized he had no way of reaching Delphine.

'Sell some jewellery,' he wrote to her from the porter's lodge, 'so that your father can be brought decently to his last abode.'

He sealed the note, and asked the baron's porter to give it to Thérèse for her mistress, but the porter gave it direct to the baron, who threw it into the fire. After making all these arrangements, Eugène returned to the boarding house at about three o'clock, and could not hold back his tears when he saw the coffin, barely covered by a black cloth, resting on two chairs before the wicket-gate in the deserted street. A shabby sprinkler, so far unused, lay in a silver-plated brass bowl filled with holy water. There were not even black hangings at the door. It was a pauper's death, without ceremony, mourners, friends or family. Bianchon, who had to be at his hospital, had left a note for Rastignac reporting the arrangements he had made with the church. The houseman advised him that a Mass was beyond their means, that they would have to make do with the less expensive service of Vespers, and that he had sent Christophe with a note to the undertaker. Just as Eugène finished reading Bianchon's scrawl, he saw Madame Vauquer handling the gold locket containing the two daughters' hair.

'How could you dare to take that?' he asked.

'Goodness! was it meant to be buried along with him?' Sylvie replied, 'it's gold.'

'Certainly!' Eugène retorted indignantly, 'let him at least take with him the only thing that can represent his daughters.'

When the hearse arrived, Eugène had the coffin put in, opened it up and reverently placed on the old man's chest an image from the time when Delphine and Anastasie were young, unspoiled and pure, and 'did not argue', as he had cried in his dying moments. Rastignac and Christophe, with two undertaker's men, were the only ones to accompany the cart which took the poor man to the church of Saint-Étienne-du-Mont, quite close to the rue Neuve-Sainte-Geneviève. When they arrived there, the body was borne into a dark, low-roofed little chapel, where the student looked round in vain for Père Goriot's two daughters or their husbands. He was alone there with Christophe, who felt obliged to pay his last respects to a man who had put him in the way of some handsome tips. As they waited for the two priests, the server and the verger, Rastignac clasped Christophe's hand, unable to utter a word.

'Yes, Monsieur Eugène,' said Christophe, 'he was a decent, good man, who never raised his voice, never hurt anybody and never did any harm.'

The two priests, the server and the verger came in and gave their seventy francs' worth, this at a time when the church is not rich enough to offer prayers without payment. The clergy chanted a psalm, the *Libera* and *De Profundis*.* The service lasted twenty minutes. There was only one funeral carriage for a priest and server, and they agreed to let Eugène and Christophe share it with them.

'There's no one following,' said the priest. 'We can go there quite fast, so that we don't lose time; it is half-past five already.'

However, just as the body was put into the hearse, two carriages bearing coats-of-arms, one that of the Comte de Restaud, the other of the Baron de Nucingen, but empty, appeared and followed the hearse to the Père Lachaise. At six o'clock Père Goriot's body was lowered into the grave, round which stood his daughters' servants, who disappeared with the clergy as soon as they had finished saying the brief prayer due to the old man which the student's money had secured. When the two grave-diggers had thrown a few spadefuls of earth on the coffin to cover it, they straightened up, and one of them turned to ask Rastignac for their tip. Eugène turned out his pockets, but found them empty, and was obliged to borrow five francs from Christophe. This detail, trivial enough in itself, filled Rastignac with a wave of dreadful depression. Darkness was falling, the damp half-light set his nerves on edge, he looked at the grave and buried in it the last tears of his youth. Tears wrenched from him by the sacred emotions of a pure heart, such tears as fall on earth only to rebound up to heaven. He crossed his arms, gazed at the clouds and when Christophe saw him standing like that, he left him there.

Rastignac, now all alone, walked a few paces to the higher part of the cemetery, and saw Paris spread out along the winding banks of the Seine, where the lights were beginning to shine. His eyes fastened almost hungrily on the area between the column in the place Vendôme* and the dome of the Invalides, home to that fashionable society to which he had sought to gain admission. He gave this murmuring hive a look which seemed already to savour the sweetness to be sucked from it, and pronounced the epic challenge: 'It's between the two of us now!'

And as the first shot in the war he had thus declared on Society, Rastignac went to dine with Madame de Nucingen.

1 RUE DU HELDER	8 BANQUE DE FRANCE
2 RUE D'ARTOIS	9 PALAIS ROYAL
3 MADELEINE	10 RUE DE LA JUSSIENNE
4 BOULEVARD DES ITALIENS	11 HALLE AUX BLES
5 THEATRE DES ITALIENS	12 PLACE DE LA CONCORDE
6 PASSAGE DES PANORAMAS	13 LOUVRE
7 OPERA	14 PLACE DE GREVE

BOULEVARD ST-MARTIN

BOULEVARD DU TEMPLE

15

14

SEINE

25

OBOURG
T-MARCEL

15 PERE LACHAISE CEMETERY	22 ST-ETIENNE-DU-MONT
16 POLICE HQ	23 RUE DE L'ESTRAPADE
17 NOTRE-DAME	24 RUE NEUVE-STE-GENEVIEVE
18 INVALIDES	25 JARDIN DES PLANTES
19 SORBONNE	26 VAL DE GRACE
20 JARDIN DU LUXEMBOURG	27 RUE DE LA BOURBE
21 PANTHEON	28 COCHIN HOSPITAL

NOTE ON THE MAP

The map represents Paris as it was in about 1819, when the main events of the novel take place. The names of some streets and the location of some institutions (e.g. the Opéra) had already changed by the time Balzac wrote. The dotted lines are meant to show the centre rather than the circumference of the districts indicated. The boulevards (= ramparts, bulwarks) were originally created from the end of the 17th century onward when the medieval fortifications were razed, and constitute one of the rare features already existing of the street plan of modern Paris, with its spacious avenues constructed by Haussmann and his successors under the Second Empire. Modern thoroughfares conspicuously absent from the city of 1819 include the boulevards Saint-Germain and Saint-Michel on the Left Bank and the avenue de l'Opéra, rue de Rivoli and the system of avenues radiating from the Etoile on the Right Bank.

EXPLANATORY NOTES

1   *rue Neuve-Sainte-Geneviève*: now the rue Tournefort.

2   *All is true*: the subtitle to *Henry VIII* (1613), attributed to
    Shakespeare; in English, for emphasis, in the original.

3   *treatment*: the Hospital for Venereal Diseases was in the
    rue Saint-Jacques nearby.

    Voltaire: Voltaire left Paris in 1750, for Potsdam and then
    Ferney, near Geneva, returning to a triumphal welcome
    only a few months before his death in May 1778. He com-
    posed the distich quoted for his friend des Maisons.

4   *Télémaque*: a didactic novel (published 1699) by François
    de Salignac de la Mothe-Fénélon, written for Louis XIV's
    grandson, whose tutor he was, and recounting the adven-
    tures of Telemachus, Ulysses' son. The nymph Calypso also
    figures in the *Odyssey*.

7   *Georges or Pichegru*: Georges, alias Cadoudal, a royalist
    leader, and Pichegru, a former revolutionary general, joined
    in conspiracy against Napoleon, and were finally betrayed,
    arrested, and executed in 1804. The implication here is that
    political, or other principles, always came second to money
    for Madame Vauquer.

    Père Goriot: see Introduction, p. xiv.

9   *Bourbe*: rue de la Bourbe, now part of the boulevard de
    Port-Royal.

10 *sons of Japhet*: Japhet was Noah's son, progenitor of what
    are now called (at least in America) Caucasians.

    as in the Fable: 'The Monkey and the Cat' by La Fontaine
    (1621–95), *Fables*, ix. 16.

15 *louis*: at the time the gold louis was worth 20 francs (or
    livres).

17   *macouba*: snuff from Martinique of high quality.

       Choisy, Soisy, Gentilly: rural villages on the Marne, the Seine and in the forest respectively, just outside Paris and favoured sites for weekend excursions.

19   *La Petite Jeannette*: a well-known shop near the Palais-Royal.

       Bœuf à la mode: a restaurant near the Palais-Royal. The sign portrayed an ox dressed fashionably in hat and shawl as a pun on the popular dish from which the establishment took its name.

23   *prunella*: woollen stuff, usually black, used for women's boots.

25   *sous*: there were 20 sous to the franc.

26   *Capifers*: a facetious coinage for cap-wearers.

29   *Prado ... Odéon*: theatres in which balls were held from time to time.

30   *Ossianic*: from about 1760, poems that purported to be translations from the original Gaelic of the third-century poet Ossian, son of Fingal, enjoyed immense success with a public eager for romantic literature, in France and Germany as well as Britain. The real author, James Macpherson, had succeeded in striking the right romantic note, with some support from traditional Gaelic originals, and cannot be written off merely as an ingenious fraud.

       Bouffons: another name for the Théâtre des Italiens, or Opéra-Comique.

       Maulincourt ... Montriveau: this list of titled men and women refers to the fictional world created by Balzac in the *Comédie humaine*.

31   *St Joseph*: patron saint of carpenters, popularly described as accompanying their labours with grunts.

32   *Augustus of Poland*: Augustus II (1670–1733, king from 1697). His legendary reputation for physical strength seems principally to derive from the total of 300 children whom he is alleged to have fathered.

37   *rue des Grès*: now rue Cujas.

38   *O innocent ... women*: title of a recent parody of a popular melodrama.

45   *usque ad talones*: students' dog-Latin for 'down to my heels'.

46   '*A rose ... one brief morning*': from the ode 'Consolation à M. du Périer' by Malherbe (1555–1628).

49   *Talleyrand*: Charles-Maurice de Talleyrand-Périgord (1754–1838); he is credited with the advice to a young diplomat 'never be too zealous' ('surtout pas trop de zèle').

60   *the Opera*: at that time opposite the Bibliothèque Royale (now Nationale) in the rue de Richelieu, not far from the Opéra-Comique in the boulevard des Italiens.

68   *ejusdem farinae*: literally 'of the same flour', or 'from the same stable'.

70   *the old revolutionary of '93*: supporter of the revolutionary Terror of that year.

72   *rue Saint-Lazare ... rue de Grenelle*: that is, from the financial quarter of the Chaussée-d'Antin to the aristocratic Faubourg Saint-Germain across the river.

74   *ultima ratio mundi*: 'the world's ultimate argument'.

79   *presidency of his section*: chairman of the local branch of the revolutionary movement.

80   *Doliban*: a ridiculous character in a comedy by Desforges (1790).

88   *rue Saint-Jacques ... rue des Saints-Pères*: the university quarter.

90   *Murat*: Joachim Murat (1767–1815), an impetuous cavalry commander and one of Napoleon's marshals, came from the SW of France. He became King of Naples, but lost his kingdom at Napoleon's fall and died in an attempt to win it back.

     the King of Sweden: Charles-Jean Bernadotte (1764–1844), a native of Pau and another of Napoleon's marshals, was elected in 1810 as eventual successor to the crown of Sweden, joined in the war against Napoleon and became king (Charles XIV) in 1818. He founded the present Swedish royal dynasty.

93   *Benvenuto Cellini*: an outstanding goldsmith and adventurer

(1500–71). His *Memoirs* were first published in 1728, and reveal enormous self-confidence, resourcefulness and courage, just the qualities to appeal to Vautrin.

94   *the nets at Saint-Cloud*: the bodies of those drowned in the river were collected in nets cast downstream from Paris at Saint-Cloud.

95   *TF*: for Travaux Forcés, or hard labour.

Villèle … Manuel: contemporary political rivals.

97   *Longchamp*: a fashionable venue in the Bois de Boulogne, a racecourse since the mid-nineteenth century.

98   *Aubry*: François Aubry (1747–98) as Minister of War opposed Napoleon in his early command, but was himself disgraced and deported to Cayenne.

100   *Cadran Bleu … Ambigu-Comique*: a popular restaurant on the boulevard du Temple and a theatre conveniently close on the boulevard Saint-Martin.

101   *subscribers*: a reference to newspaper owners who sold their paper to the highest bidder complete with a captive readership.

102   *La Fayette … the prince*: Marie-Joseph, Marquis de La Fayette (1757–1834) was a fervent defender of liberty, in America, in the early stages of the French Revolution and then, after exile, at the Restoration. In 1830, after the events of this book but before it was written, he helped the July Revolution to expel Charles X. Balzac disliked him intensely, and against all popular opinion preferred 'the prince', that is Talleyrand (created Prince de Benevento in 1806 by Napoleon), whose wit and realism (cynicism?) did indeed serve France well at the Congress of Vienna (1815), but changed allegiance with every new regime.

109   *Duc d'Escars*: Louis XVIII's companion in exile, a noted gourmet, who is said to have died (1822) of overeating.

111   *Variétés*: the Théâtre des Variétés on the boulevard Montmartre, specialized in light comedies.

112   *Duchesse de Berry*: married to the son of the future Charles X. Her husband was assassinated in 1820.

116   *Cherubino*: the ingenuous page in Beaumarchais's (and thence Mozart's) *Marriage of Figaro*.

118   *Alceste*: eponymous hero of Molière's *Misanthrope* (1666).

       Jeanie Deans: she, her father, and her sister appear in *The Heart of Midlothian* (1818).

124   *Rousseau*: the passage in question comes in fact from Chateaubriand, not Rousseau.

125   *Cuvier*: Georges Cuvier (1769–1832), geologist and palaeontologist, professor at the Natural History Museum, of which the Jardin des Plantes (or Jardin du Roi) formed part.

       la Fodor ... Pellegrini: celebrated Italian opera-singers.

126   *ladies of the Petit-Château*: the Court circle closest to the King.

132   *Napoleon's former prefects*: this is in 1819, only four years after Waterloo. A prefect was a person of some distinction, a very high official under the Empire.

141   *Mirabeau*: Honoré-Gabriel de Riqueti, Comte de Mirabeau (1749–91), one of the leading orators of the Revolution, renowned for dissolute living and huge debts.

142   *La Bruyère*: the *Caractères* of Jean de La Bruyère (definitive edition 1696) include a long set of anecdotes about an Absent-minded man ('le Distrait'), but the trait mentioned by Balzac is not among them.

144   *St Hubert*: patron saint of hunting; his feast day, 3 November, marked the start of the season.

147   *Turenne*: Henri de la Tour d'Auvergne, Maréchal de Turenne (1611–75), one of the most admired figures of French military history. The brigands referred to here may be the rebels of the Fronde, with whom he initially threw in his lot, before changing sides in 1652 and defeating Condé, their leader.

       interest rate: 500 francs annual interest on a loan of 3,000 represents some 16.6 per cent, in 1819 an exorbitant rate.

148   *Pierre and Jaffeir*: characters in Thomas Otway's *Venice Preserv'd* (1682), which enjoyed considerable success on the Continent as well as in Britain. Jaffeir, a noble youth, is

befriended by Pierre, a foreign soldier, and conspires with him against the State. Condemned to death, Jaffeir kills first Pierre, then himself, on the scaffold to avoid the ignominy of execution. Vautrin, whose homosexual preferences are discreetly mentioned in the novel, is giving a highly subjective interpretation of Otway's drama, but thereby reveals his character and aspirations.

150   *rue de Jérusalem*: at that time the Parisian equivalent of Scotland Yard; the street was cleared away in the later reconstruction of the area round the Palais de Justice.

     plumigerous: feather- or quill-bearing; minor bureaucrats.

151   *Il Bondo Cani*: the eponymous hero of Boïeldieu's opera *The Caliph of Baghdad* (1800) uses this pseudonym to roam the streets of his capital incognito.

154   *Cogniard affair*: an escaped convict, Pierre Coignard (*sic*), using the pseudonym Comte de Sainte-Hélène, had joined the army and risen to the rank of lieutenant-colonel when finally arrested and sent back to gaol in 1819. It is known that Balzac used him as a model for Vautrin.

155   *he doesn't like women*: this remark, coming so soon after mention of the young Italian whose crime Vautrin took on himself, discreetly confirms his sexual orientation.

156   *petite rue Sainte-Anne*: near the rue de Jérusalem, and cleared away in the same reconstruction.

157   *Ragoulleau ... Morin*: a genuine trial, which took place in 1812. Morin was accused, and convicted, of attempting to murder Ragoulleau for his money.

159   *redoubt at Clignancourt*: duels were often fought, as here, in the outer fortifications of Paris, which had not yet been built over.

     Papa d'Oliban: see earlier note to p. 80 on Doliban.

160   *rue d'Artois*: now the rue Laffitte, very near rue Saint-Lazare, not the present rue d'Artois, off the Champs-Élysées.

161   *passage des Panoramas*: a shopping arcade, still to be seen, off the boulevard Montmartre.

163   *O Richard ...*: a well-known aria from Grétry's opera *Richard Cœur de Lion* (1784).

164   *Lafitte*: spelt with one 'f', one *or* two 't's, was, and is, a Bordeaux of the highest quality; Laffitte (two 'f's, two 't's) was the name of a banker and politician (d. 1844).

167   *Mont Sauvage ... le Solitaire ... Chateaubriand*: Le Mont-Sauvage was a melodrama by Pixérécourt from the novel by Arlincourt (1821). The heroine is called Élodie. Madame Vauquer confuses the novel *Atala* by René de Cheateaubriand (1801), at which she may well have cried, with the author's name. There is no connection, apart from the tears, between the two works, and no Élodie in Chateaubriand.

       Sleep, my dearest loves ...: a song from Scribe's vaudeville *La Somnambule* (1819).

168   *Sun, sun ...*: a popular song of 1819. It will be noted that Vautrin's repertory of tunes is always up to date.

170   *Bernardin de Saint-Pierre*: the immensely popular novel *Paul et Virginie* (1787) is the tale of two tragic, and genuinely innocent young lovers.

177   *col tempo*: 'with time.'

185   *Ninon ... Pompadour*: Ninon de Lenclos, a highly cultivated woman who had a succession of noble lovers (d. 1705), and Madame de Pompadour, Louis XV's mistress (d. 1764), are models of women who used their charms to win success; the Venus of the Père Lachaise represents sordid carnality.

       quai des Orfèvres: still current periphrasis for the Paris CID from its location on the river near the Palais de Justice.

186   *Jean-Jacques*: Rousseau (1712–78).

188   *Flicoteaux's*: a restaurant popular with students.

192   *Café des Anglais*: a noted restaurant on the boulevard des Italiens.

203   *Mademoiselle de La Vallière*: Louis XIV's mistress from 1661 until she became a Carmelite nun in 1674. Louis, Comte (not Duc) de Vermandois (1667–83), was one of four children she bore the King, and was subsequently legitimized. The anecdote is of dubious authenticity.

217   *Sainte-Pélagie*: the debtors' prison.

224   *cerebral oedema*: Balzac uses medical terms whose literal

translation would confuse the modern reader (e.g. here 'congestion séreuse' or 'serous congestion'), and with advice from a distinguished medical colleague, Professor Henry Harris, who is also an expert linguist, I have rendered the course of this illness by terms which should be intelligible today without being seriously anachronistic.

224 *extremities*: by analogy with blood-letting, to reduce blood pressure, it was wrongly believed that the watery fluid could be drawn off from the brain by raising blisters and weals lower down, whence the use of mustard plasters and moxas (see below).

230 *Moses' prayer*: from Rossini's *Moses in Egypt*, not in fact produced in Paris until 1822.

234 *Grande Mademoiselle*: Mademoiselle de Montpensier, first cousin to Louis XIV and reputedly the richest heiress in Europe, had secured the King's reluctant permission to marry her lover, Lauzun, when Louis suddenly changed his mind and put Lauzun in prison for ten years (1670). It is generally believed that on his release they were morganatically married.

Burgundy: though the Duke of Burgundy ruled over lands at one period more extensive than the Kingdom of France, the duchy never became a kingdom.

240 *moxas*: rolls of cotton applied burning to the patient's skin to raise blisters. The details that follow represent standard medical theories of the time, dangerously false as they were.

262 *Libera ... Profundis*: *De Profundis* is Psalm 129 in the Vulgate, and part of funeral Vespers; the office concludes with the verses and responses beginning *Libera me, Domine*.

263 *place Vendôme ... Invalides*: behind the place Vendôme, from Rastignac's standpoint east of the city, lies the Chaussée-d'Antin, where the two sisters live on the right bank, while on the left bank, round the Invalides, is the Faubourg Saint-Germain.

THE WORLD'S CLASSICS

A Select List

HANS ANDERSEN: Fairy Tales
Translated by L. W. Kingsland
Introduction by Naomi Lewis
Illustrated by Vilhelm Pedersen and Lorenz Frølich

JANE AUSTEN: Emma
Edited by James Kinsley and David Lodge

Mansfield Park
Edited by James Kinsley and John Lucas

J. M. BARRIE: Peter Pan in Kensington Gardens & Peter and Wendy
Edited by Peter Hollindale

WILLIAM BECKFORD: Vathek
Edited by Roger Lonsdale

CHARLOTTE BRONTË: Jane Eyre
Edited by Margaret Smith

THOMAS CARLYLE: The French Revolution
Edited by K. J. Fielding and David Sorensen

LEWIS CARROLL: Alice's Adventures in Wonderland
and Through the Looking Glass
Edited by Roger Lancelyn Green
Illustrated by John Tenniel

MIGUEL DE CERVANTES: Don Quixote
Translated by Charles Jarvis
Edited by E. C. Riley

GEOFFREY CHAUCER: The Canterbury Tales
Translated by David Wright

ANTON CHEKHOV: The Russian Master and Other Stories
Translated by Ronald Hingley

JOSEPH CONRAD: Victory
Edited by John Batchelor
Introduction by Tony Tanner

DANTE ALIGHIERI: The Divine Comedy
Translated by C. H. Sisson
Edited by David Higgins

VIRGIL: The Aeneid
Translated by C. Day Lewis
Edited by Jasper Griffin

HORACE WALPOLE : The Castle of Otranto
Edited by W. S. Lewis

IZAAK WALTON and CHARLES COTTON:
The Compleat Angler
Edited by John Buxton
Introduction by John Buchan

OSCAR WILDE: Complete Shorter Fiction
Edited by Isobel Murray

The Picture of Dorian Gray
Edited by Isobel Murray

VIRGINIA WOOLF: Orlando
Edited by Rachel Bowlby

ÉMILE ZOLA:
The Attack on the Mill and other stories
Translated by Douglas Parmée

A complete list of Oxford Paperbacks, including The World's Classics, OPUS, Past Masters, Oxford Authors, Oxford Shakespeare, and Oxford Paperback Reference, is available in the UK from the Arts and Reference Publicity Department (BH), Oxford University Press, Walton Street, Oxford OX2 6DP.

In the USA, complete lists are available from the Paperbacks Marketing Manager, Oxford University Press, 200 Madison Avenue, New York, NY 10016.

Oxford Paperbacks are available from all good bookshops. In case of difficulty, customers in the UK can order direct from Oxford University Press Bookshop, Freepost, 116 High Street, Oxford, OX1 4BR, enclosing full payment. Please add 10 per cent of published price for postage and packing.